Bernard Shaw

Series Editors
Nelson O'Ceallaigh Ritschel
Massachusetts Maritime Academy
Pocasset, MA, USA

Peter Gahan
Independent Scholar
Los Angeles, CA, USA

The series *Bernard Shaw and His Contemporaries* presents the best and most up-to-date research on Shaw and his contemporaries in a diverse range of cultural contexts. Volumes in the series will further the academic understanding of Bernard Shaw and those who worked with him, or in reaction against him, during his long career from the 1880s to 1950 as a leading writer in Britain and Ireland, and with a wide European and American following.

Shaw defined the modern literary theatre in the wake of Ibsen as a vehicle for social change, while authoring a dramatic canon to rival Shakespeare's. His careers as critic, essayist, playwright, journalist, lecturer, socialist, feminist, and pamphleteer, both helped to shape the modern world as well as pointed the way towards modernism. No one engaged with his contemporaries more than Shaw, whether as controversialist, or in his support of other, often younger writers. In many respects, therefore, the series as it develops will offer a survey of the rise of the modern at the beginning of the twentieth century and the subsequent varied cultural movements covered by the term modernism that arose in the wake of World War 1.

More information about this series at
http://www.palgrave.com/gp/series/14785

Mary Christian

Marriage and Late-Victorian Dramatists

palgrave
macmillan

Mary Christian
Warner Robins, GA, USA

Bernard Shaw and His Contemporaries
ISBN 978-3-030-40641-7   ISBN 978-3-030-40639-4 (eBook)
https://doi.org/10.1007/978-3-030-40639-4

© The Editor(s) (if applicable) and The Author(s) 2020
This work is subject to copyright. All rights are solely and exclusively licensed by the Publisher, whether the whole or part of the material is concerned, specifically the rights of translation, reprinting, reuse of illustrations, recitation, broadcasting, reproduction on microfilms or in any other physical way, and transmission or information storage and retrieval, electronic adaptation, computer software, or by similar or dissimilar methodology now known or hereafter developed.
The use of general descriptive names, registered names, trademarks, service marks, etc. in this publication does not imply, even in the absence of a specific statement, that such names are exempt from the relevant protective laws and regulations and therefore free for general use.
The publisher, the authors and the editors are safe to assume that the advice and information in this book are believed to be true and accurate at the date of publication. Neither the publisher nor the authors or the editors give a warranty, expressed or implied, with respect to the material contained herein or for any errors or omissions that may have been made. The publisher remains neutral with regard to jurisdictional claims in published maps and institutional affiliations.

This Palgrave Macmillan imprint is published by the registered company Springer Nature Switzerland AG.
The registered company address is: Gewerbestrasse 11, 6330 Cham, Switzerland

Acknowledgments

My first thanks go to "Bernard Shaw and His Contemporaries" series editors Nelson Ritschel and Peter Gahan, and Eileen Srebernik and Jack Heeney at Palgrave Macmillan, for their valuable editing advice and support throughout the publication process.

I am also grateful to Stephen Watt, Ivan Kreilkamp, Lara Kriegel, Ellen MacKay, and Andrew Miller for guidance in the early stages of this project and feedback on numerous drafts.

I also thank fellow scholars at Middle Georgia State University and Indiana University who offered comradeship and accountability at all stages of the project, as well as useful suggestions on various sections: Chip Rogers, Amy Berke, Chris Cairney, Lorraine Dubuisson, Mahasweta Baxipatra, Natalie Bainter, Beth Bevis, Molly Boggs, Jeff Kessler, Mallory Cohn, Lindsay Munnelly, Brian Eschrich, and Carina Saxon.

I thank my colleagues of the International Shaw Society, especially Richard Dietrich, Jean Reynolds, Sally Peters, Ellen Dolgin, and Michael O'Hara, for their generous mentoring and frequent queries of "Have you submitted the book proposal yet?"

Thanks also go to Emily King and the staff at Fales Library for assistance in accessing the Elizabeth Robins papers.

Portions of Chaps. 2 and 6 were previously published as journal articles that have since been expanded and revised. I am indebted to the anonymous reviewers for their constructive revision advice on these sections, as well as to editors Harvey Young and Michel Pharand. Permission to include this material has been granted by the following presses:

By permission of Cambridge University Press: "Performing Marriage: *A Doll's House* and Its Reconstructions in Fin-de-Siècle London," *Theatre Survey* 57, no. 1 (2016), 43–62.

By permission of The Pennsylvania State University Press: "'Not a Play': Redefining Theater and Reforming Marriage in *Candida*," *SHAW: The Journal of Bernard Shaw Studies* 35, no. 2 (2015), 238–53.

Finally, I am deeply grateful to the many family members and friends, too many to name, whose encouragement has kept me going, especially my parents, Ed Christian and Margaret Ernst, my first and best models of the scholarly life.

Praise for *Marriage and Late-Victorian Dramatists*

"At last and all in a single volume, Mary Christian has deftly laid out the evolving architecture of marriage upon the stage, from Henrik Ibsen's *A Doll's House* (1879) to Elizabeth Robins's *Votes for Women* (1907). In a style as provocative as it is persuasive, this volume leads the reader adroitly through the metatheatrical mirrors and disguises that form the public face of the institution into its more poignant, private, and sequestered heart. Set against the backdrop of the suffragette movement, Christian portrays the battle for the soul of the theatre as it wrestles to determine the substance and significance of women both in marriage and beyond."

—Bob A. Gaines, *President of the International Shaw Society*

Contents

1 Introduction: Marriage, Theater, and Theatrical Marriage   1

2 Doll and Director: Ibsen's Old and New Drama   21

3 Wilde's Personal Drama   45

4 Pinero's Old-Fashioned Playgoer   81

5 Henry Arthur Jones and the Business of Morality   103

6 Shaw's Marriage Sermons   131

7 A Woman's Play: Elizabeth Robins and Suffrage Drama   161

Index   199

Abbreviations

The abbreviations listed below refer to works frequently cited. Those abbreviations followed by a number in the text indicate from which volume of an edition a quotation or other material is taken.

AW Elizabeth Robins and Florence Bell. *Alan's Wife: A Dramatic Study in Three Scenes.* Edited by J. T. Grein. London: Henry, 1893.

AWP Arthur Wing Pinero. *The Social Plays of Arthur Wing Pinero.* Edited by Clayton Hamilton. 4 vols. New York: Dutton, 1917.

BH Bernard Shaw. *The Bodley Head Bernard Shaw: Collected Plays with Their Prefaces.* Edited by Dan H. Laurence. 7 vols. London: The Bodley Head, 1970.

CLS Bernard Shaw. *Bernard Shaw: Collected Letters.* Edited by Dan H. Laurence. 4 vols. New York: Viking, 1965.

DH Henrik Ibsen. *A Doll's House.* 1879. Translated by William Archer. London: T. Fisher Unwin, 1889.

HAJ Henry Arthur Jones. *Representative Plays by Henry Arthur Jones.* Edited by Clayton Hamilton. 4 vols. Boston: Little, Brown, & Co., 1925.

MAS Henry Arthur Jones. *The Masqueraders.* London: Macmillan, 1899.

OW Oscar Wilde. *The Complete Works of Oscar Wilde.* 12 vols. Edited by Edgar Saltus, A. B. Walkley, et al. New York: Doubleday, 1923.

QI Bernard Shaw. *The Quintessence of Ibsenism.* 1891, 1913. *Shaw and Ibsen: Bernard Shaw's The Quintessence of Ibsenism and Related Writings.* Edited by J. L. Wisenthal, 97–237. Toronto: University of Toronto Press, 1958.

TN Bernard Shaw. *Our Theatres in the Nineties.* 3 vols. London: Constable, 1932.

VW   Elizabeth Robins. *Votes for Women!: A Dramatic Tract in Three Acts*. 1907. *Votes for Women and Other Plays.* Edited by Susan Croft, 21–106. Twickenham, UK: Aurora Metro, 2009.

WAI William Archer. *William Archer on Ibsen: The Major Essays, 1889–1919.* Edited by Thomas Postlewait. Westport, CT: Greenwood, 1984.

CHAPTER 1

Introduction: Marriage, Theater, and Theatrical Marriage

Nora Helmer, the young wife in Henrik Ibsen's *Doll's House*, prides herself on her ability to charm her husband by "dressing up and acting," taking up the roles of Italian tarantella dancer, moonlit elf, and the incompetent child that Torvald supposes to be her real identity (*DH*, 21). At the end of the play, the disillusioned Nora sums up her married life: "I lived by performing tricks for you…. That has been our marriage, Torvald" (*DH*, 114–115).

The metatheatrical outlook in *A Doll's House*—Nora as actress, marriage as play—evidently made an impression on Bernard Shaw. In *The Quintessence of Ibsenism*, two years after the play's first professional London production, he repeatedly underscored Ibsen's stage metaphors, describing the Helmers' supposedly idyllic marriage as a theatrical performance, two actors "playing at ideal husband and father, wife and mother" (*QI*, 152). More than twenty years later, in his 1913 edition of the essay, Shaw took Nora's theatrical marriage, and her ultimate repudiation of it, as the foundational challenge both to traditional marriage and to traditional theater:

> Up to a certain point in the last act, A Doll's House is a play that might be turned into a very ordinary French drama by the excision of a few lines, and the substitution of a sentimental happy ending for the famous last scene…. But at just that point in the last act, the heroine very unexpectedly…stops her emotional acting and says: 'We must sit down and discuss all this that has

been happening between us.' And it was by this new technical feature...that
A Doll's House conquered Europe and founded a new school of dramatic
art. (*QI*, 212–213)

Shaw the young Fabian had hailed the play as a debunking of "the sweet
home, the womanly woman, the happy family life of the idealist's dream"
(*QI*, 151). Now, Shaw the veteran theater critic and dramatic innovator
saw Ibsen as a master innovator who had offered to late-Victorian society
not only a bold new anti-idealist philosophy but a new dramatic technique
by which to expound it. The Helmers' theatrical marriage was the tool for
presenting both.

The equation between marriage and theater that Shaw pointed out in
A Doll's House was not unique to Ibsen and Shaw, though *The Quintessence*
offers perhaps the most pithy and memorable setting forth of this idea.
The vision of theater as marriage, marriage as theater, was one that, with
numerous variations, became a recurring motif in the "new school of dramatic art" which Ibsen, by Shaw's account, had founded. Several prominent and influential English dramatists writing in the years following
Ibsen's London debut (not all of them admirers of Ibsen or of Shaw)
created plays that, like *A Doll's House*, depicted their protagonists' marriages in ways that emphasized the elements of scripting, staging, performance, and spectatorship within these relationships. In this book, I
examine the use of the theatrical marriage idea in works by Ibsen, Shaw,
Oscar Wilde, Arthur Wing Pinero, Henry Arthur Jones, and Elizabeth
Robins—dramatists identified by themselves or their observers, though
not always undisputedly, as leaders in Britain's New Drama movement.

Marriage in the Old Drama

The topics of marriage, love, gender, and sex were not, of course, anything
new in Late-Victorian London theaters—these had been staple subjects in
many of the best-known works throughout the century. Romantic cup-and-saucer comedies such as Tom Robertson's *Ours* (1866) and *School*
(1869) centered on the romances of young couples, culminating in their
marriages. Fallen-woman dramas such as English translations of the
younger Dumas's *La Dame Aux Camélias* (1852) and the many adaptations of Ellen Wood's sensational novel *East Lynne* (1861) centered on
women who, through transgression, lost their marriages (past, present, or
future), and whose consumptive and broken-hearted deaths offered a

tragic and inevitable close. Domestic comedies such as Tom Taylor's *Still Waters Run Deep* (1855) and *Victims* (1857) featured married couples in conflict, generally through the wife's social ambitions or extramarital flirtations, but ambitions and flirtations were quickly nipped in the bud, and wayward wives returned to the straight and narrow by the end of the third act. Cross-class alliances in Dion Boucicault's *Colleen Bawn* (1860) and Robertson's *Caste* (1867) were complicated by disapproving relatives and apparent deaths, but love and humble virtue triumphed in the end, and the supposedly dead spouses were startlingly resurrected.

These plays, popular in their own time and some of them still frequently revived in the closing years of the century, presented a strongly traditional vision of marriage. A wedding or a marital reconciliation or reunion represented a happy ending. To be excluded from the possibility of marriage, whether by transgression, death, or other circumstances, was tragic. If separations occurred, they generally resulted from external circumstances, such as accidents, parental interference, or military conflicts. Where real marital strife occurred, it could be easily explained as the sin or caprice of one spouse (most often the wife), as in *East Lynne* or *Still Waters*, and was readily resolved by death or reconciliation in the end. All the possibilities of married life, good and bad, were made to fit the rising and falling action of the well-made play.

These uncomplicated, idealized marriages dominated the British stage during the years when John Stuart Mill and Frances Power Cobbe were writing scathing exposures of domestic violence, women's economic dependence and political disempowerment, and the other aspects of marriage's dark side. During these same years, the Matrimonial Causes Act, the Married Women's Property Act, the Custody of Infants Act, and the debates surrounding them were making marked alterations in the theories defining marriage and in the practical realities of thousands of couples' lives. The Contagious Diseases Act and the outraged demands for its repeal furnished an official and very concrete image of the sexual double standard, and Charles Dickens, George Eliot, George Meredith, and Anthony Trollope were presenting readers with fictional bad marriages in all their excruciating nuance. In progressive theatrical circles, simplistic dramatic treatments of marriage and romance became a recognizable shorthand for the artistic and intellectual staleness and irrelevance of the mainstream theater. A. B. Walkley asked, "Are our playwrights addressing themselves to it [love] with sincerity, with veracity, with real insight? Or are they just 'muddling through' with it, repeating familiar commonplaces about it, not troubling to see the thing as it really is?" (*Pastiche and Prejudice*, 160). He ended his essay regretfully with the latter verdict. Shaw, in an 1895 review, lamented: "[W]ho on earth will ever know what Miss [Ellen] Terry can do if we are never to see her except in plays that date, in feeling if not in actual composition, from the dark ages before the Married Women's Property Act?" (*TN1*, 145).

Several factors help to explain this ideological time lag between the theater and the currents of British politics and literature on marriage as well as other issues. For much of the past century, theater had been considered more a popular amusement than an intellectual exchange or an art form. Dramatists generally wrote to the demands of actor-managers who controlled theatrical business. With slender compensation and no reliable international copyright laws in place, many found it easier and more lucrative to adapt French works by Scribe, Sardou, and Dumas *fils* than to attempt more original work. With playgoers, managers, and the censor to please, writers had little incentive to take risks or depart from established conventions, either in dramatic technique or in subject matter. The few mid-Victorian dramatists who successfully attempted innovation, the even fewer whose plays are known and even occasionally revived today, are those who, like Boucicault, had sufficient financial backing to become actor-managers themselves or, like Robertson and Gilbert, had the good fortune to meet with managers who treated them as collaborators, allowing them to direct their own plays and share in the profits.

Not until nearly the last decade of the century was there a concerted effort among dramatists, such as Shaw, Henry Arthur Jones, Arthur Wing Pinero, and Oscar Wilde, along with critics such as William Archer, A. B. Walkley, and J. T. Grein, and actors such as Elizabeth Robins, Mrs. Patrick Campbell, Janet Achurch, and Charles Charrington, to raise the intellectual and artistic quality of theatrical entertainment, alter the economic conditions that had slowed theatrical innovation in the past, and gain recognition for dramatic composition as serious and original literature. The New Drama movement, as this campaign came to be called, took the form of relentless negotiations with theatrical managers for fair royalties and authorial control over the staging and acting of plays. Participants wrote petitions and essays to rally support for improved copyright laws and the abolition of theatrical censorship. They advocated for a government-subsidized national theater as an alternative to the profit-driven organization of mainstream commercial theaters. They wrote, produced, and published plays (this last previously a rare practice) to attract and intelligently engage their audiences. The authors of New Drama aimed, as Shaw wrote in the preface to *Mrs. Warren's Profession*, to "fight the theatre...with plays" (*BH1*, 236).

The introduction of Ibsen's plays in London, though not the first manifestation of this movement, was an important catalyst, drawing admiration or disgust from playgoers, critics, and dramatists. Much of the discussion on *A Doll's House* and on subsequent plays such as *Ghosts* and *Hedda Gabler* focused on Ibsen's treatment of marriage, his challenge to the traditional theater's idealization of domesticity and romantic love. The debate gathered momentum from a recent controversy in the press. Mona Caird, in 1888, had published an essay in the *Westminster Review* declaring that "the present form of marriage...is a vexatious failure" and proposing that "The ideal marriage...should be *free*"—that is, more egalitarian, easier to dissolve, and tailored to the individual requirements of the couple, like other civil contracts ("Marriage," 197). Caird's essay, in the weeks that followed, provoked some thousands of letters to the *Daily Telegraph*, fiercely arguing the question: "Is Marriage a Failure?"[1] Though *A Doll's House* had been written nearly a decade earlier, the timing of its 1889 London production made it seem a part of the ongoing marriage debate. Shaw reinforced this association a few years later in *The Quintessence of Ibsenism*, twice repeating in his introduction on "Ideals and Idealists" that marriage "is a failure for many of us" (*QI*, 120).

Like Ibsen, numerous writers of New Drama in the years following discovered dramatic potential in the psychological tensions and legal problems of marriage. Whether they praised or opposed Ibsen's unorthodox dramatic structures and political perspective, their plays too became part of this discussion of the marriage institution and the possibilities for improving it. Some—Shaw and Robins, in particular—overtly used their plays to press agendas for marriage reform and other closely related political goals, such as voting rights and improved employment opportunities for women. Jones and Pinero had less interest in altering the political status quo, but recognized that more nuanced, sympathetic depictions of marital problems offered the possibility of more complex drama than earlier dramatists had produced, and that the public, in the midst of the "marriage failure" debate, would readily pay to see such plays.

Admittedly, studying marriages represented in plays (or in any literary genre) is not the same as studying the history of marriage in a given period. But studying depictions of marriage in literature, along with critical responses to these depictions, allows us to see what authors and their audiences considered the key difficulties of marriage in their time and the solutions they attempted to imagine. As Talia Schaffer has argued regarding the marriage plot in Victorian fiction, "Real marriage and its motives vary widely, and historians of the family have disagreed even about its most basic elements. But in the neater case study of the novel…marriage is a symbolic resolution to a cultural problem" (*Romance's Rival*, 3). Recent studies by Schaffer, Maia McAleavey, Esther Godfrey, and others have examined variations of the marriage plot in Victorian novels, showing ways in which authors used fictional unions to think through cultural problems such as class hierarchy, gendered power dynamics, and the desire for a vocation.

Drama, like the novel and other forms of entertainment, attempts to offer "symbolic resolutions" to the cultural problems of a given historical moment. But in the case of drama, the problems and their imagined solutions are amplified by being presented not on the page of a book to a lone reader (or even a vocal reader and a small group of listeners), but on the stage to an audience of hundreds. Discussions on marriage reform and related questions of gender roles and sexuality were carried on in many forums other than theaters, in some cases much earlier. But the theater as a social space and recreational venue offered unique opportunities in late-Victorian Britain for juxtaposing theory with practice, abstract with concrete, in the marriage debate. Couples, in attending mainstream evening theater performances together, put their own marriages on display even as they viewed and reflected on the marital strife of Lady Windermere and Paula Tanqueray. The question of what couples would feel comfortable viewing together was often a determining factor in business decisions for managers who, over the previous decades, had struggled to build respectable reputations. Actor-manager Charles Wyndham, for example, in staging Jones's *Case of Rebellious Susan*, demanded that Jones remove the play's ambiguous suggestions of the heroine's adultery because "married men will not bring their wives" to such a play (qtd. in Doris Jones, 135). More experimental plays, by contrast, such as Shaw's early works and the Ibsen plays that Robins performed and produced, were more often produced as matinées, a space for a primarily leisure-class female clientele, creating a uniquely feminine cultural milieu which A. B. Walkley mockingly dubbed "chocolate drama" (*Pastiche and Prejudice*, 68). Susan Torrey Barstow argues that the matinées and their female audiences contributed much to Ibsen's reputation as iconoclast and women's poet: seeing plays about women in the company of other women enabled female playgoers to "observe domestic, middle-class femininity as it was performed and critiqued" and created a sense of identification that was "not only individually but collectively transformative" ("Hedda is All of Us," 389). The audiences and performance spaces, as well as the content of the dramas, helped to shape theaters as places of discussion for marriage and "the woman question."

But, as I said at the outset, *A Doll's House* was not concerned merely with the personal experience or the legal arrangements of marriage, but with marriage *as* theatrical performance—with the idea that marriage and drama had each helped to shape the other, that marriage, like Nora's tarantella, was itself theatrical. Other prominent plays in the New Drama movement were also preoccupied with the links between marriage and theater, and with the theatricality of marriage relationships. This book attempts to outline some of the diverse and changing attitudes toward marriage, toward theater, and toward marriage as theater, attitudes reflected in plays written and produced in a moment when both institutions—theater and marriage—were undergoing significant transitions.

Defining Theatrical Marriage

By using such terms as "theatrical marriages" or the "theatricality of marriage" in describing the plays and productions on which this study focuses, I refer to several closely related and often overlapping phenomena. "Theatricality" has long been a versatile term, as Tracy Davis and Thomas Postlewait have shown; it has been used to signify, among other things, the Greek concept of mimesis, representation or imitation; the idea of showiness or excess, a "breakthrough into performance"; and the Roman idea of *theatrum mundi*, using theater as a metaphor for human life (*Theatricality*, 5–9). Davis and Postlewait also link theatricality with metadrama ("a play which comments upon the conventions of its genre") and metatheater ("a performance calling attention to the presentational aspects of theatre and its conventions in the moment of its transpiring") (*Theatricality*, 14–15). My discussion of marriage's "theatricality" makes some use of all of these ideas. When I describe Nora Helmer's marriage, for example, as "theatrical," I mean:

1. Literally, Nora's interactions with her husband consist largely of staged and scripted performances that he directs and she enacts, such as her tarantella. She incorporates music, dance, costumes, and

exotic characters, transforming their marriage into a miniature play within the play. Her roles emphasize her dependent, sensual femininity and his competent, dominant masculinity, a display of Judith Butler's gender performance writ large.
2. Both Nora and Torvald take the familiar theatrical conventions of domestic melodrama as a template for their own identities and their vision of each other. She sees herself as the threatened heroine in need of his heroic protection, and expects her life to culminate in a tragic sacrifice or a spectacular rescue. He envisions himself as the strong hero, ready to conquer any adversity. These visions, however, sincerely believed in, are ultimately contradicted by fact, and this clash between theatrical convention and unruly reality introduces an element of metadrama, allowing Ibsen simultaneously to use melodramatic devices and critique them.
3. Their marriage is for "the eyes of the world," a spectacle for an audience of neighbors and outsiders to enjoy, observe, and evaluate.
4. Because they are the central characters in a play about marriage, how their marriage develops determines what kind of play it is—and vice versa.

Ibsen, like the other dramatists whose work I will examine, was attempting to construct new, more socially relevant and intellectually challenging forms of drama by adapting and altering familiar ones which he considered stultifying, offering a theater which might be considered less "theatrical" by common definitions. Toril Moi, pointing to Ibsen as an early leader in the literary modernist movement, has argued that his modernism was largely defined by his "unmatched series of superbly sustained metatheatrical reflections," in which, paradoxically, "antitheatricalism is rejected" and, at the same time, "theatricality is criticized" (*Henrik Ibsen and the Birth of Modernism*, 9–10). I suggest that Ibsen's ambivalence toward theatricality is closely linked to his critique of traditional marriage. In revising familiar dramatic plots and devices, he attempted both to depict marriage as he saw it and to imagine modified and possibly improved versions of marriage. As dramatic and literary genres tend to be shaped by the assumptions and social codes of their time, so new kinds of art suggest the possibility of new ways of being and living. The New Drama plays tacitly asked: in a more egalitarian, more honest, less restrictive society, what might marriage look like? What might individual lives look like? And what might the theater look like?

Certainly, many of the aspects of theatrical marriage that I've described here are not unique to Ibsen or to New Drama, nor to the theater, nor to the Victorian period. As long as art and entertainment have existed, they have served to shape people's beliefs about marriage, gender roles, and sexuality (among other things), while also being shaped by these beliefs. And marriage has always been a kind of public performance for the approval and amusement of society, as the customary presence of witnesses at a wedding ceremony indicates, and as twenty-first-century fascination with celebrity weddings and politicians' private lives continues to demonstrate. J. L. Austin takes the "I do" of the marriage ceremony as the defining example of a performative utterance, a speech with a concrete, real-world effect. Eve Sedgwick, building on Austin's illustration, points to the essential role of the wedding guests or witnesses, those whose silent presence seals the validity of the performative "I do." Sedgwick thus unites performativity with performance, envisioning marriage as "a kind of fourth wall or invisible proscenium arch that moves through the world...continually reorienting around itself the surrounding relations of visibility and spectatorship" (*Touching Feeling*, 72). The angst inherent in the marriage performance and in the "marital proscenium," the image of an already-troubled marriage further strained by the relentless scrutiny of outsiders, is central to Victorian texts such as *Modern Love, Our Mutual Friend,* and *Middlemarch.* Thus, the turn-of-the-century dramas that I will discuss were in some senses merely catching up with a trend that had been visible in other literary genres decades before.

My claim, then, is not that the concept of marriage as theater originated with New Drama. Nor am I suggesting that until this time marriage had been considered, in some sense, private, and now suddenly became public, theatrical, under surveillance. It would be nearer the truth (though an oversimplification) to make the opposite claim: that marriage having always been carried on before an audience, and this publicity having been in general taken for granted, dramatists, novelists, and various social commentators were now beginning to openly question the rightness of society's role as the observer and arbiter of marital success. One late-Victorian marriage advice book, Edward John Hardy's *How to be Happy Though Married* (1885), concisely summed up the concept of theatrical marriage in the opening chapter, commenting, "The applause that is usually given to persons on entering the matrimonial stage is, to say the least, premature. Let us wait to see how they play their parts" (18).

If Hardy worried that the marriage spectators of society were too easily pleased, Mona Caird, writing a few years later, suggested the opposite problem: not only were those who observed their neighbors' marriages apt to be too critical—they had no right to claim that evaluative authority in the first place. In her controversial *Westminster Review* article, she envisioned the ideal marriage as an individualized contract, designed by the spouses themselves and dissoluble by their mutual decision, as both "free" and "private," without a need to satisfy the community's demands for conformity or respectability: "The matter [of marriage] is one in which any interposition, whether of law or of society, is an impertinence.... The idea of a perfectly free marriage would imply the possibility of any form of contract being entered into between the two persons, the State and society standing aside, and recognizing the entirely private character of the transaction" ("Marriage," 198).

The idea of a marriage carried on in private, apart from the scrutiny of family, friends, and acquaintances—like the idea of an authentic "real self" that should be separate from performance of any kind—had a persistent fascination for the authors of New Drama, even as they concluded such ideas to be impossible. Jones, Pinero, Shaw, and Wilde repeatedly depicted couples contracting marriages or pseudo-marriages that are in some way transgressive, unorthodox, or experimental, alternately defying public opinion, ignoring it, and hiding from it. Their protagonists cannot live with their marriage audience, yet they cannot live without it.

(Anti)-theatrical Victorians

This desire to escape marriage performance raises questions regarding the anti-theatrical perspectives that some scholars have attributed to the Victorians. Nina Auerbach, in *Private Theatricals*, presents anxious antitheatricality as a typical Victorian attitude, arguing that theater represented the antithesis of sincerity, "the primary source and metaphor for meretricious, life-destroying activity" (4). Theatricality, in Auerbach's account, was a destabilizing force to be earnestly avoided, yet at the same time an inescapable and curiously attractive "spirit of Victorian culture" (12). Rebecca Stern, similarly, suggests that the Victorians may have associated the rehearsed, imitative behaviors of stage performers with the repetitive movements of machines. During the Industrial Revolution and the generations following, she argues, the English came "to deem 'unnatural' anything that partook of mimicry or seemed in any way mechanical or constructed. If one's 'act' was too visibly rehearsed, the repetitions that made up proper, coherent identity were too reminiscent of the machines that had come to threaten nature in a more literal sense" ("Moving Parts," 425–426). In Stern's and Auerbach's analyses, theatricality severely strains the integrity of the subject; it is a temptation and a burden closely bound up with the promises and demands of modernity.

More recently, Lynn Voskuil has challenged this narrative of Victorian anti-theatricality, envisioning a more complex, less antagonistic connection between theatricality and authenticity; from her reading of the drama criticism of William Hazlitt and George Henry Lewes, she articulates a concept of "natural acting," a mode of authenticity taking shape through theatricality rather than in opposition to it. Victorians, Voskuil argues, "theatricalized the ideas and institutions they believed most authentic even as they authenticated the spectacles they made of themselves" (*Acting Naturally*, 3).

Shaw presented something akin to the idea of Voskuil's "natural acting" in an 1889 lecture to the Church and Stage Guild, "Acting, By One Who Does Not Believe In It." He pointed to anti-theatricality as the viewpoint of the typical theater critic, who views "the actor as a wretched imposter...a fellow that fights without courage, dares without danger, is eloquent without ideas" (*Platform and Pulpit*, 12–13). In contrast to this way of thinking, Shaw claimed that stage acting might offer a means of "self-realization" for an actor, an opportunity to embody aspects of one's individuality that cannot be expressed in everyday life (17). This kind of acting, he argued, was in fact "the final escape from acting, the ineffable release from the conventional mask which must be resumed as the artist passes behind the wing, washes off the paint, and goes down into the false lights and simulated interests and passions of the street" (16). Yet he also argued that "the street," the offstage world, can also offer opportunities for "self-realization." Rather than reinforce the dichotomy of real world versus unreal world, onstage versus offstage, he collapsed these distinctions. Both onstage acting and offstage life, he concluded, feature humans performing roles, roles which sometimes obscure or mask the person's true self and at other times allow for that self's truest expression.

Despite Shaw's outspoken rejection of the critics' equation of acting with artificiality, late-Victorian dramatists, including Shaw, often expressed ambivalence toward the idea of theatricality in the offstage world. They welcomed the opportunities for social change or self-fashioning that performed identities might offer, yet were unsettled by the seeming impossibility of identifying a "real self" in the midst of the roles adopted and enacted. A simple listing of Jones's major play titles gives an idea of his persistent fascination and distrust of the disguises and role-plays encouraged by the respectable community: *The Masqueraders, The Liars, The Hypocrites, Whitewashing Julia, Dolly Reforming Herself*, and so forth. This performance anxiety is visible even in the writings of Wilde. Though a relentless lampooner of Victorian "earnestness" and an unofficial patron saint of performance studies, in *De Profundis*, Wilde described his drama as a "personal...mode of expression," and his plays frequently center on characters seeking to avoid the public gaze (*OWII*, 29).

David Kurnick, in *Empty Houses*, examines the fiction of George Eliot, Henry James, William Makepeace Thackeray, and James Joyce—all novelists with unfulfilled ambitions for dramatic authorship—and claims that these authors' desire to write for theater signified "a desire for a palpable return to an embodied public and an impatience with the inward gaze of narrative fiction" (4). I make nearly the opposite claim for the New Drama of the 1890s: while Kurnick describes novelists attempting to move toward more public, theatrical modes of fiction, I see dramatists developing drama that in some respects attempted to emulate the privacy, the inwardness of the realist novel, shifting the stage's focus from spectacular catastrophes to more subtle psychological conflict, to individuals navigating between inner desire and conviction and the constraints of the outer world.[2] Significantly, several of the dramatists I discuss here (Ibsen, Robins, Shaw, and Wilde), before becoming known as dramatists in England, had written extensively in other genres more traditionally associated with individual expression—lyric poetry, novel, and essay, among them. The widely debated questions of marriage reform and women's role became central to the popular plays of the New Drama movement not only because such topics allowed plays to appear up to date and engaged with the issues of the day, nor because of the *frisson* of scandal promised by any suggestion of sex (though these were both undoubtedly factors), but because the idea of theatrical marriage presented an opportunity to dramatize the uncomfortable overlap between public and private, scriptedness and spontaneity, and performance and inner self.

In large part, New Drama authors' unease with theatricality, both onstage and in everyday life, may well have stemmed from their low opinion of the conventional theater of their time. Shaw impatiently posited in the preface to *Mrs. Warren's Profession*: "I have pointed out again and again that the influence of the theatre is growing so great that private conduct, religion, law, science, politics, and morals are becoming more and more theatrical, whilst the theatre itself remains impervious to common sense, religion, science, politics, and morals" (*BH1*, 236). If theaters were dominated by stereotyped, untruthful, shallow, and emotion-driven representations of life, then the theater's influence in society spelled disaster. Yet potential disaster might be converted to opportunity if, by transforming playwriting and theatrical performance, dramatists, actors, and other theater practitioners had the power to alter the outlooks and actions of their audience. If marriage is inevitably theatrical, Shaw suggested, then the quality of the play can break or make the marriage.

In the following chapters, I will examine a handful of plays that illustrate different perspectives and approaches to theatrical marriage, calling attention both to the frequent images of marriage as theater and to the ways in which plays modify standard dramatic genres by revising familiar theatrical conventions (and, along with them, the social and moral assumptions that underpin those conventions). The book is not designed as an exhaustive study of the works of any of the authors whose plays I discuss, most of whom had prolific playwriting careers extending over decades. Other scholars, in studying individual authors over the length of their careers, have ably shown how these authors' approaches to drama, as well as to marriage and related questions, evolved over time. In particular, Robert Gaines and the contributors to his edited collection *Bernard Shaw's Marriages and Misalliances* show Shaw's idea of marriage changing gradually from a cynical rejection of marriage as it was to a more constructive vision of marriage as it might be. Similarly, Sos Eltis and Kerry Powell show trajectories of development in the views on gender and sexuality presented in Wilde's plays, as Joan Templeton has done in analyzing Ibsen's depictions of women.

My aim, rather, is to show the comradeship, competition, and creative tension between these authors during the 1890s as they worked through a set of shared concerns regarding marriage depictions and theatrical reform. They had widely varying views regarding these two issues, and often debated heatedly through letters, reviews, and plays themselves, yet all agreed that better marriage and better theater were somehow linked. I endeavor to capture a critical moment in theatrical history and in each of the authors' professional lives. During this decade, Ibsen, in the final years of his career, rather suddenly gained attention in England. Wilde's instant success at West End comedy added luster to his already notorious persona as aesthete and poet, only to be speedily eclipsed by scandal. Veteran dramatists Pinero and Jones became recognized, though not universally admired, masters of the fashionable Society play. Shaw made his first obscure forays into playwriting. Robins, through her acting and producing of Ibsen's plays, gained a firsthand knowledge of the gender inequalities, in the theater and in society at large, that she would later seek to remedy as a playwright and suffrage activist. These authors challenged, revised, and built on one another's ideas, sometimes explicitly framing their plays as rewritings of earlier plays. By examining their works as a kind of ongoing conversation, I aim to highlight the complicated interpersonal dynamics that shaped *fin-de-siècle* marriage debates and theatrical changes.

While I seek to do justice to the totality of the performance event, examining the staging process and reception of the plays' early London productions, my project necessarily has a special concern for the narratives conveyed in the dramatic texts themselves, texts produced for reading as well as production, at a time when "dramatic literature" was considered by many a contradiction in terms. I aim to convey a sense of dramatists, in their texts and in the staging of them, in conversation with their critics, with earlier plays, and with the larger public.

In Chap. 2, I examine Ibsen's *Doll's House*, taking the play and its London responses as an illustration and starting point for my discussion of theatrical marriage. In the first half of the chapter, I discuss the drama itself, suggesting that Nora's soliloquies and her penchant for costumed role-playing, among other things, link her vision of marriage with the conventions of nineteenth-century theater, and how these conventions, marital and theatrical, are abruptly discarded in the final act. In the second half, I argue that the idea of marriage as performance became a frequently discussed theme in British responses to the play, particularly in the diverse adaptations, parodies, and sequels by London-based authors. Many of these writers, including Henry Herman and Henry Arthur Jones, Eleanor Marx, Thomas Anstey Guthrie, Walter Besant, and Bernard Shaw, attempted either to rewrite Nora's story to make it conform more neatly to the genre features Ibsen had rejected or to echo Ibsen's critique of the genre, sometimes in more explicit terms.

Chapter 3 looks at the drama of Oscar Wilde, which Wilde himself characterized as an unprecedentedly "personal" theatrical form. While some contemporary critics dismissed this style as an unoriginal rehashing of mid-century melodrama, irrelevant to the aims of the New Drama movement, others hailed Wilde's plays at once as a pattern for fashionable West-End plays and as a unique manifestation of Wilde's inimitable personality. Focusing on Wilde's first two commercially produced plays, *Lady Windermere's Fan* (1892) and *A Woman of No Importance* (1893), I argue that Wilde, like Ibsen, worked both through and in opposition to old performance genres. In the process, he developed his "personal" dramatic style, a style steeped in his celebrity persona, yet constructed from familiar ingredients. Like *A Doll's House*, his plays drew motifs and character types from familiar varieties of comedy and melodrama, often following the expected patterns only to reverse them at the last moment. Beyond his revision of popular theatrical formulas, Wilde also presented social performances such as afternoon calls and country house parties as genres to be parodied or reworked, often conflating these performances with the scenes more traditionally associated with the stage. In appropriating and blending scenes from the stage and the fashionable drawing room, he called attention to the rigid assumptions about marriage, gender, and morality on which these genres were based.

Chapter 4 focuses on Arthur Wing Pinero's problem play *The Second Mrs. Tanqueray* (1893), whose premiere followed that of *Lady Windermere's Fan* at George Alexander's fashionable St. James's Theatre, and which has been generally recognized as an exemplar of *fin de siècle* Society drama. Pinero, I argue, responded to Ibsen's challenge to idealized conventional marriage by depicting and ultimately dismissing alternative forms of union—unconventional marriages, sham marriages, and non-marriages. Whereas Ibsen criticizes the melodramatic behaviors and assumptions that he associates with traditional marriage relationships, Pinero implies that attempts to circumvent or discard these conventions are likely to prove even more theatrical and less successful.

Chapter 5 examines works by Henry Arthur Jones, who, like Pinero, is best remembered for fashionable West-End dramas and for his conservative opposition to Ibsen's iconoclasm. In plays such as *The Masqueraders* (1894) and *The Case of Rebellious Susan* (1894), he critiqued the metatheatrical images of marriage presented by Ibsen by focusing attention on the secondary characters who act as onstage spectators and critics of the central marital relationship. These confidants, *raisonneurs*, and other peripheral characters, serving as representatives of the outside world, uphold normative moral codes by critiquing and condemning the rebellious marital experiments of the plays' protagonists. Yet Jones, even while endowing these spectator characters with authority, undermined this authority by explicitly acknowledging the hypocrisy on which their judgments are based; his plays' defense of the status quo was at best an uneasy affirmation.

Chapter 6 offers a reading of Shaw's "Pleasant Play" *Candida* (1895), which he described as a reverse-gendered "counterblast" to *A Doll's House*, presenting a husband as doll or actor and the wife as director. While presenting a variation on Ibsen's metatheatrical marriage, Shaw also imitated and revised the romantic triangle and moralizing tone of Jones's *Masqueraders*, a play he had read and vehemently criticized shortly before beginning *Candida*. In *Candida*, Shaw associated marriage with the genre conventions of domestic comedy and seduction melodrama, as well as with quasi-theatrical public performances such as sermons, political speeches, and poetry recitation. Ultimately, *Candida*, like *A Doll's House*, suggests that the weaknesses of traditional marriage are closely related to those of traditional theater, and that the two institutions must be re-examined together. This comparison between the marriage relationship and theatrical performance is visible, with variations, in several of Shaw's subsequent plays, including *The Devil's Disciple* (1897), *Man and Superman* (1903), and *Getting Married* (1908). This last-mentioned, one of Shaw's most unapologetic discussion plays, carries especially telling echoes of *Candida*, with its wordy yet magnetic clergymen, its surprisingly chaste interlopers, and its relentless foregrounding of public performance in the form of costumes, rehearsed speeches and gestures, and the acknowledged presence of spectators (if not onstage, then in its close vicinity). *Getting Married*, I argue, in some ways brings to a conclusion the project Shaw had begun in his earlier plays, the project of redefining marriage and theater. If *Getting Married* does not stretch both institutions to their breaking points, it insists that those breaking points are in sight.

Chapter 7 examines Elizabeth Robins's suffrage play *Votes for Women!* (1907), in which the idea of marriage is de-centered and subordinated to broader questions regarding women's role in society. Robins, like Wilde and Pinero, depicts a fallen woman attempting to repair her life; rather than retiring to foreign exile or seeking rehabilitation in a wealthy marriage, however, she rejects her former lover's proposal and demands instead that he make amends by lending political support to the suffrage cause. A veteran actor and producer of Ibsen's plays, Robins viewed her play as an extension of Ibsen's exploration of women's experience. Where Ibsen had merely exposed marriage's failure to offer wives such as Nora and Hedda a constructive outlet for their energies and imaginations, Robins presented political activism as the needed outlet and an alternative to marriage. Robins's play also engages extensively with two issues sometimes mentioned but generally treated as peripheral by earlier dramatists:

the ways in which marriages are complicated by friendships, rivalries, enmities, or mentorships between women, and the problems entailed by the assumedly natural and obvious link between marriage and motherhood. Both of these ideas would become central in many of the plays written and performed by the Actresses' Franchise League members who followed Robins's example in using the theater as a platform for the suffrage message.

In concluding this study with an examination of Robins and her fellow suffrage dramatists, I aim to bring my argument full circle, not merely in focusing on a figure closely associated with the Ibsen performances with which this book began but also in re-examining the claims I took to be implicit in *A Doll's House* and in the New Drama movement more broadly. These plays implied that traditional theater and traditional marriage, each being partly responsible for the flaws of the other, must help to improve each other. More intelligent, authentic, and equitable relationships between men and women were shown to lead to life narratives better worth dramatizing, and more complex, intellectually challenging relationships portrayed onstage were presented as better models than the emotion-driven, stereotyped images of earlier Victorian drama. In *A Doll's House*, the discussion that transforms the play and the Helmers' marriage in the last act offered a possible example of how such new drama and new marriage might work—an example which seemed untheatrical or antitheatrical, "not a play," to many early London viewers. Robins echoed this claim, but broadened her play's focus. While the courtship and the seduction melodrama outlined early in her play mirror traditional assumptions regarding marriage as women's natural vocation and the automatic happy ending of drama, Robins's Vida Levering ultimately makes suffrage activism both her life vocation and her chosen genre of performance, a genre concerned not primarily with the marriages of individuals, but with cooperation between men and women—and between women and women—in society at large. In this way, *Votes for Women!* and the suffrage plays that followed it offered a resolution, or at least the hope of resolution, of many of the social and artistic problems that had persistently vexed the prominent marriage plays of New Drama. Political and economic equality promised the possibility of freer and more varied comradeship between men and women, romantic and otherwise, as well as dynamic and fulfilling life narratives for single women. Greater opportunities for women within the theater as actresses, managers, and dramatists enabled the perspectives of both genders to be represented onstage. Finally, the scripted and publicly displayed role of suffrage activist, as Robins depicted it for her heroine, offered a model for an authentic self realized not in opposition to theatrical performance, but through it.

NOTES

1. Jennifer Phegley estimates that the *Daily Telegraph* received about 27,000 letters on the topic in the second half of 1888 (*Courtship and Marriage*, 169).
2. Shaw, interestingly, was among the few critics to defend Henry James's play *Guy Domville* (1895) during its short run at St. James's Theatre, largely for its careful and restrained depiction of private thought and experience: "There is no reason why life as we find it in Mr James's novels—life, that is, in which passion is subordinate to intellect and to fastidious artistic taste—should not be represented on the stage. If it is real to Mr James, it must be real to others; and why should not these others have their drama[?]" (*TN1*, 6).

REFERENCES

Auerbach, Nina. *Private Theatricals: The Lives of the Victorians*. Cambridge, MA: Harvard University Press, 1990.
Austin, J. L. *How to Do Things with Words*. Edited by J. O. Urmson and Marina Sbisa. 2nd ed. Cambridge, MA: Harvard University Press, 1975.
Barstow, Susan Torrey. "'Hedda Is All of Us': Late-Victorian Women at the Matinee." *Victorian Studies* 43, no. 3 (2001): 387–411.
Boucicault, Dion. *The Colleen Bawn; or, The Brides of Garryowen*. London: T. H. Lacy, 1865.
Caird, Mona. "Marriage." *The Westminster Review*, December 1888.
Cobbe, Frances Power. "Wife-Torture in England." In *Criminals, Idiots, Women, and Minors: Victorian Writing By Women on Women*, edited by Susan Hamilton, 132–70. Peterborough: Broadview, 1995.
Davis, Tracy C., and Thomas Postlewait. "Theatricality: An Introduction." In *Theatricality*, edited by Tracy C. Davis and Thomas Postlewait, 1–39. Cambridge: Cambridge University Press, 2003.
Eltis, Sos. *Revising Wilde: Society and Subversion in the Plays of Oscar Wilde*. Oxford: Clarendon, 1996.
Gaines, Robert, ed. *Bernard Shaw's Marriages and Misalliances*. New York: Palgrave Macmillan, 2017.
Godfrey, Esther. *The January-May Marriage in Nineteenth-Century British Literature*. New York: Palgrave Macmillan, 2009.

Hardy, Edward John. *How to Be Happy Though Married: Being a Handbook to Marriage*. London: T. Fisher Unwin, 1885.
Ibsen, Henrik. *A Doll's House*. Translated by William Archer. London: T. Fisher Unwin, 1889.
Jones, Doris Arthur. *Taking the Curtain Call: The Life and Letters of Henry Arthur Jones*. New York: Macmillan, 1930.
Jones, Henry Arthur. *Representative Plays by Henry Arthur Jones*. Edited by Clayton Hamilton. 4 vols. Boston: Little, Brown, & Co, 1925.
McAleavey, Maia. *The Bigamy Plot: Sensation and Convention in the Victorian Novel*. Cambridge: Cambridge University Press, 2015.
Mill, John Stuart. *The Subjection of Women*. Edited by Stefan Collini, 117–218. Cambridge: Cambridge University Press, 1989.
Moi, Toril. *Henrik Ibsen and the Birth of Modernism: Art Theater, Philosophy*. Oxford: Oxford University Press, 2008.
Phegley, Jennifer. *Courtship and Marriage in Victorian England*. Oxford: Praeger, 2012.
Robertson, Tom. *Plays by Tom Robertson*. Edited by William Tydeman. Cambridge: Cambridge University Press, 1982.
Schaffer, Talia. *Romance's Rival: Familiar Marriage in Victorian Fiction*. Oxford: Oxford University Press, 2016.
Sedgwick, Eve. *Touching Feeling: Affect, Pedagogy, Performativity*. Durham, NC: Duke University Press, 2003.
Shaw, Bernard. *Our Theatres in the Nineties*. 3 vols. London: Constable, 1932.
———. *Platform and Pulpit*. Edited by Dan H. Laurence. New York: Hill & Wang, 1961.
———. *The Bodley Head Bernard Shaw: Collected Plays with Their Prefaces*. Edited by Dan H. Laurence. 7 vols. London: The Bodley Head, 1970.
———. *The Quintessence of Ibsenism*. In *Shaw and Ibsen: Bernard Shaw's The Quintessence of Ibsenism and Related Writings*, edited by J. L. Wisenthal, 97–237. Toronto: University of Toronto Press, 1958.
Stern, Rebecca F. "Moving Parts and Speaking Parts: Situating Victorian Antitheatricality." *ELH* 65 (1998): 423–49.
Taylor, Tom. "Still Waters Run Deep." In *Plays by Tom Taylor*, edited by Martin Banham, 23–58. Cambridge: Cambridge University Press, 1985.
Templeton, Joan. *Ibsen's Women*. Cambridge: Cambridge University Press, 1997.
Voskuil, Lynn. *Acting Naturally: Victorian Theatricality and Authenticity*. Charlottesville, VA: University of Virginia Press, 2004.
Walkley, A. B. *Pastiche and Prejudice*. London: Heinemann, 1921.
Wilde, Oscar. *The Complete Works of Oscar Wilde*. 12 vols. New York: Doubleday, 1923.
Wood, Ellen. *East Lynne*. New Brunswick, NJ: Rutgers University Press, 1984.

CHAPTER 2

Doll and Director: Ibsen's Old and New Drama

Actress Elizabeth Robins, encountering Ibsen's *Doll's House* for the first time in a Novelty Theatre performance in June 1889, was thrilled both by the boldness of the play's ideology and by the emotional power of the characters and acting. The one element with which she found fault in the production, however, was Nora's tarantella, which she described nearly forty years later as "a piece of theatricalism, Ibsen's one concession to the effect-hunting that he had come to deliver us from" (*Ibsen and the Actress*, 13). William Archer and Harley Granville-Barker concurred with Robins's assessment, criticizing Nora's dance as the play's "flawed streak," as "Ibsen's last concession to…the theatrical orthodoxy of his earlier years" ("The Coming of Ibsen," 167; *WAI*, 214). The tarantella, they agreed, was an embarrassing irrelevance, simply an opportunity for the lead actress to display her well-shaped legs.

Yet the "theatrical orthodoxy" of the tarantella, which struck Ibsen's most enthusiastic admirers as jarringly old fashioned, was an essential component in the play's critique of traditional marriage, a critique that led some of these same commentators to hail the play as "an event that was to

---

An early version of this chapter was published in 2016 in *Theatre Survey* under the title "Performing Marriage: *A Doll's House* and its Reconstructions in Fin-de-Siècle London." The material is republished here with the permission of Cambridge University Press.

© The Author(s) 2020
M. Christian, *Marriage and Late-Victorian Dramatists*, Bernard Shaw and His Contemporaries,
https://doi.org/10.1007/978-3-030-40639-4_2

change lives and literatures" ("Ibsen and the Actress, 9–10). The criticisms directed at the tarantella by Robins, Archer, and other early London spectators—conventionality, shallowness, artificiality—bore a striking resemblance to charges of a different sort: namely, those leveled against the marriage institution by contemporary social critics and women's rights advocates who hailed Ibsen as "the Woman's Poet" ("Nora," 23; "Nora, by Ibsen," 3). Traditional marriage and traditional theater were alike accused of patterning themselves after rigid customs rather than fact or probability, of perpetuating simplistic assumptions about human behavior (in particular, about gender relations), privileging display over authenticity, and glossing over problems not easily resolved. Since long before the nineteenth century, marriage, like death, had served as a central structuring device for a variety of dramatic genres: the wedding of young lovers signified comedy's happy ending by default, while the death of one or both lovers or the seduction of the young woman, and her consequent exclusion from marriage and domesticity, were the expected unhappy conclusions of seduction melodrama. Thus, to question the rightness of marriage was to destabilize theatrical tradition in lasting ways.

A Doll's House was just such a destabilizing force, a play that exposed the problems of marriage and theater simultaneously. It sharply critiqued the nineteenth-century veneration of domesticity, and it also departed from Victorian theatrical conventions, in both the structure of the well-made play and the plot devices and character types of domestic melodrama. I suggest that *A Doll's House* presents marriage itself as a theatrical performance, a play within the play, the kind of spectacle that Eve Sedgwick would later describe as a perpetual performance behind the "marital proscenium" (*Touching Feeling*, 72). The Helmers' marriage is metatheatrical, endowing the protagonists with what Lionel Abel has termed "a playwright's consciousness" and "an acute awareness of what it means to be staged" (*Metatheatre*, 57–58). In the play, marriage and theater are each to some degree held responsible for the other's shortcomings, with the suggestion that if either institution is to be improved, then assumptions about both must be re-examined. In Judith Butler's terms, the play not only presents gender and other socially constructed identities as performed spectacles but also asks what it might look like to revise these traditional performances—both social and theatrical—so as to call attention to their constructedness (*Gender Trouble*, 190).[1] It was this double attack on marriage law and theatrical custom that made the play such an epoch-making event for women's rights and for theatrical reform in late-Victorian Britain.

In this chapter, I call attention to the ways in which *A Doll's House* connected dramatic convention with marriage reform, associating rigid gender assumptions with rigid dramatic conventions and finally rejecting both. This connection is especially evident, I suggest, in the tarantella and the play's other explicitly metatheatrical devices, in which the act of performance is brought to the consciousness of characters and audience.

This idea of marriage as theater and theater as a school for marriage exerted a particular fascination on early English audiences and became a prominent theme in English criticism of the play, particularly the criticism that took the form of what we would now call fanfics—adaptations, parodies, and sequels published by writers as diverse as Bernard Shaw, Henry Herman, and Henry Arthur Jones; *Punch* humorist Thomas Anstey Guthrie (under the pseudonym "F. Anstey"); novelist and historian Walter Besant; socialist leader Eleanor Marx; and dramatist Israel Zangwill. These fictional responses took a practical approach to criticism, showing rather than telling what Ibsen meant or what he ought to have written. While these rewritings primarily responded to Ibsen's challenge to traditional marriage, whether with attacks or support, they were also concerned with the play's departure from theatrical norms, taking Ibsen's unresolved ending as an invitation to a conversation about dramatic structure, acting, and playwriting. In these dramas or short stories, the authors offered alternative narratives of the Helmer marriage using conventional genre frameworks, including domestic melodrama, moral cautionary tale, comedy, and farce, often revising these genres. Ibsen's critique of marriage, as these adaptations illustrated, posed a serious challenge to nineteenth-century theatrical conventions, making narratives of marriage and desire increasingly difficult to contain within traditional genre categories, revealing a need for new kinds of drama.

Wife and Husband, Dancer and Director

Nora's tarantella is a convenient starting point because as a compact play within the play, managed and performed by husband and wife, it presents the intersection of theater and marriage at its most literal. The dance of the Capri fisherwoman is at once a theatrical display and a miniature portrait of the Helmers' marital relationship. It presents marriage itself metatheatrically, as a spectacle that draws attention to the act of performance. Errol Durbach calls attention to the tarantella's genre affiliations, its associations with the theater Archer and Robins condemned as "orthodox." "The tarantella," he declares, "leaps straight out of the melodramatic entr'acte," a form privileging music, emotion, and visual display (*A Doll's House: Ibsen's Myth of Transformation*, 70). In appropriating the familiar spectacular convention, he argues, Ibsen also subverts it; ironically, the "effect-hunting" virtuoso display becomes a scene heavy-laden with social meaning.

A play within a play was hardly a new strategy in the late nineteenth century. The motif forms a prominent part in several Shakespeare plays, including *A Midsummer Night's Dream*, *The Taming of the Shrew*, and *Hamlet*. Tracy Davis and Thomas Postlewait, as well as Lionel Abel, point to *Hamlet* as the defining example of a play within a play and of a hero exhibiting "dramatic self-consciousness," both devices exemplifying Elizabethans' "new modern consciousness about the dramatized nature of identity and society" (*Theatricality*, 15–16). By the late nineteenth century, however, dramatists and managers were attempting different strategies for staging plays within plays, largely prompted by changes in theatrical architecture. A. B. Walkley commented on the difficulties of staging scenes such as Hamlet's Mousetrap play in a modern proscenium theater. He praised theater practitioners who innovated in such scenes, for example, by having the internal play onstage and allowing the audience-characters to sit among the playgoers in the auditorium. "The result," he claimed, "is a curious blend of sensations; you feel yourself both spectator and actor, at a play and in a play." Hence, the innovation was "much more than a mechanical change," a "psychological" one as well (*Pastiche and Prejudice*, 119–120). In adapting an old dramatic technique to new building structures, Walkley argued, authors and managers disturbed the comfortable fourth-wall habit of spectatorship, the assumed separation between the play and the outside world. Ibsen, writing in a time of artistic and technical transition in the theater, helped develop fresh uses for the play within the play. In presenting Nora's dance performance, he forced an uncomfortable sense of identification between the audience in the seats and the audience—in particular, the husband—onstage.

The preparation and performance of the dance supply a secondary structure to the play, an ironically frivolous counterpoint to Krogstad's blackmail and Nora's efforts to stave it off. It is a performance of which the playgoers in the auditorium see only the preparation and rehearsal, the final performance taking place offstage at the neighbors' party. The roles played by Nora and Torvald in preparing the dance offer insights into the functions that each fulfills as wife and husband. That is, Nora serves as the dancing entertainer, and Torvald, besides being chief spectator, positions himself as producer and director. He selects the piece, coaches Nora as she rehearses, and coordinates her exit on the evening of the party. In describing the performance afterwards to Christina Linden,[2] he assumes the tone both of critic and stage manager:

> She dances her tarantella with wild applause, and well she deserved it.... Ought I to let her stop after that—to weaken the impression? Not if I know it. I took my sweet little Capri girl—my capricious little Capri girl, I might say—under my arm; a rapid turn round the room, a curtsey to all sides, and—as they say in novels—the lovely apparition vanished! An exit should always be effective. (*DH*, 95)

He points out the flaws of her performance, admitting that "there was, perhaps, a little too much nature in her rendering of the idea—more than was, strictly speaking, artistic" (*DH*, 95). He claims authority not only to evaluate Nora's dancing but also to define "natural" and "unnatural." Like George du Maurier's hypnotist-impresario Svengali, who would fascinate London audiences in the following decade, Torvald sees his wife's performance as a showcase for his skill as stage manager and proprietor of a gifted prima donna.

Yet, as Archer and (more recently) Austin Quigley have pointed out, in the case of the Helmers, this directing is a mutual process, a point that neither Nora nor Torvald acknowledge, even in the final discussion scene (*WAI*, 16; *The Modern Stage and Other Worlds*, 103). Nora, while apparently submitting to Torvald's infantilizing supervision, uses her dance as a means of manipulating him. To flatter his sense of masculine capability, she exaggerates her own dependence, repeating, "I can't get on without your help" and "I can't dance to-morrow if I don't rehearse with you first" (*DH*, 45, 80). Yet, as she dances, she disregards Torvald's commands to dance "slower" and "not so violently"; in this way, she can simultaneously rebel against his directorship and reinforce her image of childish ineptitude (*DH*, 81). Even as she acts the parts of Italian peasant and incompetent female, the dance offers Nora an opportunity to momentarily let down her hair (literally and figuratively) and break free from the civilized restraints of Torvald's society.

Nora's tarantella performance carries an erotic suggestion that becomes increasingly explicit in the third act. In their Norwegian home, proverbially associated with chilly respectability, Torvald creates a miniature Italy, a northerner's fantasy of a space for uninhibited sensuality. Torvald tipsily spells out the dance's sexual implications after their return from the party: "I see you have the tarantella still in your blood—and that makes you all the more enticing" (*DH*, 98). The dance stages his sexual fantasy, an almost literal sample of the couple's bedroom relationship.

The tarantella is evidently only one of the many child-wife masquerades in Nora's repertoire. Torvald's directorship is also a matter of routine, for Nora begs him to "direct me as you used to do" (*DH*, 81). Considering their relationship in retrospect in the final act, Nora compares herself to a street performer and Torvald to the spectator who pays to be entertained: "I seem to have been living here like a beggar, from hand to mouth. I lived by performing tricks for you" (*DH*, 114). They have a marriage that, like many mid-nineteenth-century melodramas, consists of visual spectacle and predetermined character types.

THE MELODRAMATIC PERSPECTIVE

The Helmers' theatrical outlook shapes not only the way Nora entertains her husband but their perceptions of themselves and each other. Their idyllic visions of married life echo the values reinforced in mid-nineteenth-century drama. Such sentimental comedies and melodramas—plays that largely dominated London theaters in the 1880s, and in which Ibsen pioneer Janet Achurch reportedly excelled as an "emotional" actress prior to her 1889 *Doll's House* venture[3]—generally featured beautiful heroines, courageous heroes, and a clear trajectory of rising and falling action with a tidy resolution at the end.

A Doll's House appears to promise just such a clear trajectory, not only to the audience but to the characters themselves, for, as Durbach points out, the Helmers implicitly rely on melodramatic conventions as the shaping forces of their own lives (*A Doll's House: Ibsen's Myth of Transformation*, 65). As Krogstad's blackmail threats escalate, Nora's expectations vacillate between last-minute deliverance and pathetic suicide. Her romantic fantasies are made explicit in her monologues, in which she vents her misery and anticipates conventional stage crises and rescues. She envisions

Krogstad's betrayal even as she declares it to be "nonsense" (*DH*, 44). She predicts her husband's miraculous self-sacrifice, repeating three times that "he would do it, in spite of all the world" (*DH*, 62). Like the tarantella, these monologues are a familiar device in mid-nineteenth-century theater. As John Northam has noted, Ibsen had been proud to eliminate such speeches from his earlier realist play, *The League of Youth* (1869), yet he gave Nora seven of these speeches (*Ibsen's Dramatic Method*, 15). Nora reveals more of her melodramatic fantasies in her conversation with Christina, whom Archer disparaged as a stock confidant—like the tarantella, an outdated theatrical device (*WAI*, 214). Having saved her husband's life with the money she secretly borrowed, Nora describes to Christina a tender future scene in which she will triumphantly claim the title of savior (*DH*, 21). The familiar theatrical techniques through which Nora makes these revelations highlight the conventional theatricality of the content she reveals and of the Helmers' general perspective on their family life.

Torvald's expectations are no less theatrically conditioned than Nora's. He describes himself as a hero who has "shoulders…broad enough to bear the whole burden" (*DH*, 61). In his more tipsy, amorous moods, his role-playing becomes elaborate. He envisions the holiday party as a scene of romantic intrigue. "When we're among strangers," he explains to Nora, "do you know why I speak so little to you, and keep so far away?…Because I am fancying we love each other in secret, that I am secretly betrothed to you, and that no one guesses there is anything between us" (*DH*, 98). Ironically, to perform his marriage relationship before third persons, Torvald must perform singleness. The departure from the party becomes, in his imagination, the happily-ever-after conclusion to a romantic comedy: "And then, when we have to go…I imagine you are my bride, that our marriage is just over, that I am bringing you for the first time to my home, and that I am alone with you for the first time" (*DH*, 98–99). As Joan Templeton has said, these speeches offer telling commentary on the sexuality of a manly man who is most aroused by the fantasy of his wife as passive virgin bride ("The Doll House Backlash," 33). They also construct a bizarre inversion of Sedgwick's marital proscenium. That is to say, the Helmers' marriage might, like all marriages, "exist in and for the eyes of others" (*Touching Feeling*, 72). Yet while the "others" at the party see an unexceptional married couple, Torvald envisions himself and his wife as secret lovers who must conceal their affection. The social and artistic conventions of sentimental romance have so permeated his consciousness that, to keep his marriage happy or even functional, he must imaginatively refashion it in the image of these conventions.

Torvald and Nora reimagine their ordinary bourgeois married life after the pattern of sensational theater. Shaw later alleged in the preface to *Three Plays for Puritans* that many English playgoers shared this tendency, having been long exposed to drama and fiction preoccupied with romantic love: "If the conventions of romance are only insisted on long enough...then, for the huge compulsorily schooled masses who read romance or nothing, these conventions will become the laws of personal honor.... Nay, why should I say will be? They *are*. Ten years of cheap reading have changed the English from the most stolid nation in Europe to the most theatrical and hysterical" (*BH2*, 26–27). Ibsen's two leading characters illustrate the sentimental mindset Shaw described, showing not only the faultiness of conventional marriage but also romantic drama's importance in shaping those conventions.

Unmaking the Well-Made Play

Theatrically conditioned assumptions underpin the Helmer marriage. By the third act, however, these assumptions have collided with the couple's prosaic characters and circumstances, and their relationship is unraveling in consequence. Not surprisingly, Torvald's heroic declarations are discarded as soon as Krogstad's blackmail threatens his reputation, and Nora's sacrificial aspirations culminate in a hysterical suicide attempt that rescues no one.

In the midst of the IOU crisis, the clash between fantasy and fact is dramatized by the husband's and wife's ludicrously mismatched speeches and responses. As Torvald reads Krogstad's incriminating letter, Nora delivers her last anguished soliloquy: "Never to see him again. Never, never, never. Never to see the children again. Never, never.... Oh no, no, no, not yet. Torvald, good-bye! Good-bye my little ones!" (*DH*, 105–106). Envisioning her husband as a savior about to brave disgrace for her sake, she poises herself to prevent this sacrifice, luxuriating in her emotional excess. Torvald, however, far from sacrificing himself chivalrously, berates her like an ordinary man aghast at his own sudden danger. These incongruities play out in the resulting dialogue:

HELMER: What is this? Do you know what is in this letter?
NORA: Yes, I know. Let me go! Let me pass!

HELMER:	*(holds her back)* Where do you want to go?
NORA:	*(tries to get free)* You sha'n't save me, Torvald.
HELMER:	*(falling back)* True! Is it true what he writes? No, no, it cannot be true.
NORA:	It is true. I have loved you beyond all else in the world.
HELMER:	Pshaw—no silly evasions.

* * *

NORA:	Let me go—you shall not save me. You shall not take my guilt upon yourself.
HELMER:	I don't want any melodramatic airs. (*DH*, 106)

The scene reads, as Durbach says, like a "farcical breakdown of Scribean theatrical convention" (*A Doll's House: Ibsen's Myth of Transformation*, 65). For Nora, swept away by the pathos of her husband's anticipated heroism, the uppermost facts of the situation are her love and her need to prevent his self-sacrifice. Torvald, however, has no sacrificial intentions to prevent. Contemplating the mundane facts of debt, forgery, and possible imprisonment, he sees her protestations simply as ploys for sympathy.

As the melodramatic conventions disintegrate, so do the couple's theatrical assumptions about their marriage. Nora, while saving her husband's life, has jeopardized his career through her unwitting felony. Perhaps more significant, she has jeopardized his manly self-reliance as he discovers that he owes his recovered health to her years of labor. In Torvald's eyes, Nora has ceased to be an ideal wife and become "a hypocrite, a liar...a criminal," and "an unprincipled woman" (*DH*, 107). The romantic marriage ideal, in short, can no longer be the template for their life narrative, and the marriage must consequently either dissolve or continue on some other model. Torvald, clinging to his respectability, can envision no alternative but a retreat behind the marital proscenium in a hollow imitation of their old ideal married life. "[W]e must live," he says, "as we have always done; but of course only in the eyes of the world.... Henceforward there can be no question of happiness, but merely of saving the ruins, the shreds, the show of it!" (*DH*, 108). Torvald's tirade, unjust as it is, illustrates a problem that Ibsen treated seriously both in *A Doll's House* and later in *Ghosts*: the absurdity of an unhappy marriage maintained merely as a façade—the painful consequence of an exclusive preoccupation with the respectability that must constantly be performed. As Torvald's marriage is transformed, so is his relation to outsiders; once intrusive observers from whom he conceals his affection as a "secretly betrothed" lover, these third persons are now the all-important "world," forcing him to act as husband despite his estrangement from his wife.

When Krogstad's second letter arrives, more theatrics ensue, this time with the parts reversed. For Torvald, the recovered IOU signals the melodramatic rescue, just as the earlier threatening letter marked, for Nora, the melodramatic catastrophe. He repeats, "we are saved," a stock phrase appropriate to a happy ending (*DH*, 109–110). Enamored of the heroic character that he repudiated five minutes before, he comes to believe he has saved his wife as she expected. "You may rest secure," he assures her; "I have broad wings to shield you" (*DH*, 111). Nora's misery and her affection for him—which he has just dismissed as irrelevant—are now uppermost in his mind: "Oh, Nora, they must have been three awful days for you!...And in your agony you saw no other outlet but—no; we won't think of that horror" (*DH*, 110). He now accurately comprehends Nora's suicidal frenzy of five minutes earlier as he views the situation from the same theatricalized perspective. As he welcomes theatrical closure, his belief in the rightness of his marriage returns. His rescued heroine is again his "scared little song-bird," his "bewildered, helpless darling" (*DH*, 111, 112).

The play-acting, however, is again one sided, despite Torvald's attempts to prompt her with "Don't you hear, Nora?" (*DH*, 110). For Nora has discarded her faith in happy endings and happy marriage, and she greets her husband's rejoicings with curt, brief sentences. Though Torvald may no longer feel it necessary to "come to an understanding" about the failures of their marriage, it is Nora's turn to say they must "come to a final settlement" (*DH*, 108, 112).

The well-made fragmentation that concludes Ibsen's blackmail plot was most vividly highlighted, perhaps, by Henry Arthur Jones and Henry Herman in *Breaking a Butterfly* (1884), an adaptation that painstakingly restored the dramatic continuity that Ibsen had interrupted. Years later, Jones recalled the adaptation as one of the "transgressions of my youth and ignorance," an attempt to turn *A Doll's House* into a "sympathetic play," knowing "nothing of Ibsen, but...a great deal of [Tom] Robertson and H. [J.] Byron" (qtd. in Richard Cordell, *Henry Arthur Jones and the Modern Drama*, 52). Written and produced in 1884, five years before Ibsen's unadapted original play made its English debut at the Novelty Theatre, *Breaking a Butterfly* follows the contours of Ibsen's plot for the first two acts, with Flora the child-wife hiding her secret, and Dunkley the creditor threatening to expose her forgery. The abrupt break from the original comes at the end of the second act, when Flora's husband, Humphrey Goddard, does what Torvald has failed to do: he shields his wife by claiming guilt for her crime. Following this "miracle," the final act unfolds according to the same melodramatic expectations that were rudely deflated by the Helmers. In *Breaking a Butterfly*, Ibsen's lopsided half-crisis and half-resolution are fused into one tender scene, so that the husband forgives at the same moment the wife protests his sacrifice:

FLORA: Humphrey, you shall not do it.... The innocent must not suffer for the guilty!
HUMPHREY: In this case the innocent must suffer for the innocent. Thank God, no burden has yet fallen upon me in my life but I have been able to take it up and bear it like a man....
FLORA: Let me go! Throw me off, and don't mind what becomes of me! I'm not worth your caring for!
HUMPHREY: Hush! Hush!...All you did was for the best. (*Breaking a Butterfly*, 64–66)

The lines are essentially a scrambled and paraphrased version of Ibsen's dialogue, with a few jarring passages removed. This is the scene that Nora anticipated, that Torvald in retrospect would have preferred. Humphrey shows himself the heroic protector, and Flora has all of Nora's winsome childishness with none of her unruly adult qualities—her independent thinking and sexual manipulation. Their marriage is so ideally uncomplicated that when the forged note is retrieved, the play is over. Humphrey closes the curtain by declaring: "Nothing has happened, except that Flossie was a child yesterday: to-day she is a woman" (*Breaking a Butterfly*, 76). Herman and Jones turned *A Doll's House* into a representative specimen of the genre Ibsen was rejecting, rendering Ibsen's moment of transition doubly striking.

Serious Discussion: New Drama, New Marriage

This transition, when Nora orders her husband to sit down for the discussion, repudiates the structure imposed by Herman, Jones, and their peers. Shaw and Archer saw this scene not only as a change of direction within the plot of one play but also as a defining event in dramatic history, in which Ibsen stood on "the threshold of the essential drama," in which he "conquered Europe and founded a new school of dramatic art" (*WAI*,

214; *QI*, 213). Ibsen, in fact, takes care to call attention to the abrupt departure from custom as the Helmers sit down to talk, for Nora comments on the novelty of their situation at some length:

NORA: *(after a short silence)* Does not one thing strike you as we sit here?
HELMER: What should strike me?
NORA: We have been married eight years. Does it not strike you that this is the first time we two, you and I, man and wife, have talked together seriously?
HELMER: Seriously! Well, what do you call seriously?
NORA: During eight whole years and more—ever since we first met—we have never exchanged one serious word about serious things.... I say that we have never yet set ourselves seriously to get to the bottom of anything. (*DH*, 113)

In case viewers (like Torvald) might overlook the seriousness of the occasion, Nora repeats the word *serious* or *seriously* four times.

Shaw, in *The Quintessence of Ibsenism*, took her speech as a turning point between old theater and new, the introduction of the so-called discussion scene, an innovation marking the shift from domestic melodrama to problem play, when Nora "very unexpectedly...stops her emotional acting and says: 'We must sit down and discuss all this that has been happening between us'" (*QI*, 213). The well-made play, Shaw said, followed the pattern of exposition, situation, and unravelling, whereas the new problem play, of which *A Doll's House* was the prototype, followed the trajectory of exposition, situation, and discussion (*QI*, 213). This innovation, Shaw argued, signaled a change in theater's function: rather than simply presenting a formulaic story, drama would henceforward offer a forum for discussing problems and ideas, with the plot's events serving mainly as a pretext for debate, being gradually "overspread" and "assimilate[d]" into the conversation (*QI*, 219). The discussion scene, deemed anti-theatrical by older dramatic standards, gradually became accepted as part of a new set of theatrical conventions. Later critics have likewise taken this scene to effect a significant change in dramatic structure, though some have questioned the success of that change.[4]

While critics have seen Nora's repeated insistence on the new "seriousness" as a disruption to the well-made play, Nora herself is more interested in disrupting her marriage and contrasting it with the marriage she wishes to have. Until now, she has viewed her relationship with Torvald as a melodrama propelled by emotion; now, a new theatrical convention offers a new model for envisioning her marriage and herself. She pursues what is, if only for the moment, an experiment with this other kind of marriage, one that, like the new theater, centers on conversation rather than on feeling and sensory excitement. In explaining the flaws in their marriage, Nora implicitly describes the marriage that she would accept as genuine. She declares that she has modeled her opinions after Torvald's (*DH*, 114). By contrast, the new kind of marriage would allow her to form opinions independently, as she is doing at that moment. Their home has been a "playroom" (*DH*, 114). A real marriage would make space for "serious" reflection. Throughout their marriage her husband has directed her to dance, to dress, to come or go. She now takes initiative for the first time, ordering him to sit down and listen.

Kristin Ørjasæter, examining this indirect description of better marriage, credits many of Ibsen's claims to the influence of his longtime friend, Norwegian feminist Camilla Collett. Collett, she explains, argued for marriage as "a union between two equal partners" who are dedicated to "personal growth" and have "mutual duties to respect and guide each other" ("Mother, Wife, and Role Model," 24–25). Many of Nora's arguments in the final scene of *A Doll's House*, she suggests, might be read as echoes of Collett's claims. More broadly, Joan Templeton sees the play as a part of a larger conversation on women's rights. She points out that among Ibsen's British audiences, the play's critique of conventional marriage and its call for women's education and independence would be familiar from the writings of Mary Wollstonecraft, John Stuart Mill, and Harriet Martineau ("The Doll House Backlash," 32). In the discussion scene, Ibsen dramatized a debate European intellectuals had carried on for decades past.

Nora concludes that she cannot form this more equitable marriage until she has become "a fit wife." To become one, she leaves in order to "stand quite alone" and "know [her]self" (*DH*, 115). Here again, Ørjasæter suggests, Ibsen may be showing Collett's influence, in particular, with her insistence that women must do "substantial inner work" to develop the self-respect and capability for clear thought needed to participate in the more egalitarian marriage she advocated ("Mother, Wife, and Role Model," 29). Nora asserts that a true marriage between herself and Torvald could only happen through the "miracle of miracles," and her slamming door cuts short Torvald's hopeful musings (*DH*, 122, 123).

With this grim conclusion, Ibsen's play stops short of dramatizing the positive side of the marriage argument. Though it has depicted the flaws of fixed gender hierarchy, it can do little more than speculate about what a marriage between equals, without these flaws, might look like.

THE OTHER DISCUSSION SCENE

While numerous critics have examined the discussion scene at the end of the last act, few have noted the similar discussion with which the act opens, between Christina Linden and Nils Krogstad. The conversation's immediate outcome is the opposite of Nora's, ending with an engagement where Nora's ended with a de facto divorce. This contrast has led some scholars to characterize Christina as simply a foil to Nora, a "womanly" woman juxtaposed to the "New Woman" (Ørjasæter is an exception).[5] Yet in structure and dialogue, the two discussions have much in common. Like Nora, Christina initiates the conversation by dictating her interlocutor's movements, directing him to prepare physically for the discussion; she tells him twice to "come in" to the room, and he reluctantly complies, as Torvald will later do when told to "sit down" (*DH*, 87–88, 112). Also, like Nora, Christina states that they have "a great deal" to say to each other and that he has "never really understood" her (*DH*, 88). In taking initiative in this scene, assuming the masculine functions of proposing and (presumably) breadwinning, Christina anticipates the departures Nora will later make from her prescribed gender role. At the same time, as Ørjasæter observes, Christina's intended union with Krogstad is "based on mutual acceptance of their need for each other," offering hope for the better marriage that the Helmers can only achieve through a "miracle" ("Mother, Wife, and Role Model," 33). Here, as in the play's close, discussion is used to interrupt the melodramatic trajectory that, until now, has set the pattern for marriage and for the play itself.

Archer dismissed Krogstad and Christina as stock characters, relics of the obsolete theatrical tradition from which Ibsen was departing. In his introduction to the play in his 1906 collection of Ibsen's works, he exclaimed "How impossible, in [Ibsen's] subsequent work, would be such figures as Mrs. Linden, the confidant, and Krogstad, the villain!" (*WAI*, 214). Early in the play, this evaluation seems accurate; the two fulfill traditional, almost mechanical, dramatic functions. Christina listens to Nora's backstory, facilitating the play's exposition, and Krogstad threatens Nora with ruin, raising both terror and the expectation of rescue. In their final conversation, however, their efforts to help or harm Nora are set aside as they examine their own pasts, presents, and futures. When the Helmers are re-introduced at the end of the conversation, confidant and villain appear to have traded intentions. Krogstad is eager to retrieve the blackmailing letter, while Christina is determined to leave it to reveal the numerous secrets of Nora's marriage. The marriage of villain and confidant, with its calm optimism and unorthodox gender performance, defies melodramatic convention nearly as boldly as the Helmers' final separation.

The challenge Christina and Krogstad posed to these dramatic stock types might be measured by the alterations Ibsen's English bowdlerizers made. Jones and Herman, in *Breaking a Butterfly*, evidently thought Christina and Krogstad unconventional enough to need significant revision. Their secondary characters, confidant Agnes Goddard and villain Philip Dunkley, remain confidant and crook throughout. They are also kept safely separate, with no thought of romance between them, and they, like Flora and Humphrey, strictly follow orthodox gender roles. Christina's task of recovering the IOU is delegated not to Agnes, but to her comic admirer, Dan Birdseye. These revisions illustrate the extent to which Ibsen had disrupted the conventions of the well-made play. Ibsen's secondary characters, as well as the central couple, are used to challenge Victorian assumptions about marriage and theater, and Jones and Herman and others who adapted the play responded to this challenge in a variety of ways.

Remodeling the Doll's House: Parodies and Adaptations

Breaking a Butterfly was an early instance of what Kerry Powell calls "the epidemic temptation to rewrite Ibsen" (*Oscar Wilde and the Theatre of the 1890s*, 77). More succumbed to this temptation a few years later, when actual Ibsen plays began appearing on London stages.[6] Some writers, offended by the plays' unflattering depictions of family, duty, and other ideals, wrote corrective adaptations or punished the offending characters in sequels, restoring the moral balance. Ibsen's supporters, led by Shaw and Archer, pressed the Ibsenite campaign forward with dramatic polemics as well as essays. Still other adaptations were frank caricatures, aiming for a laugh at the expense of admirers and detractors who seemed to take the plays far too seriously.

Not surprisingly, most of the adaptations of *A Doll's House* hotly debated the play's criticisms of traditional marriage. In attempting to counter or reinforce these criticisms, some rewritings followed Ibsen's example in presenting marital problems as metatheatrical spectacles and, in some degree, held theater responsible for these problems. This relationship was made explicit in "A Doll's House Repaired," an alternative ending written by Eleanor Marx in collaboration with playwright and novelist Israel Zangwill. As Bernard Dukore and Rachel Holmes have both noted, Marx had been one of Ibsen's early English supporters, having hosted and starred in a private 1883 performance of *A Doll's House* (also featuring young Bernard Shaw as Krogstad), and by 1890 had published translations of *An Enemy of the People* and *The Lady from the Sea* ("Karl Marx's Youngest Daughter," 309; *Eleanor Marx: A Life*, 334–337). The "repaired" parody, published in the socialist monthly paper *Time* in March 1891, is a caustic satire on Ibsen's attackers and their ideal of "womanliness," a sanitized reworking in which Nora is made to remain in the doll's house and to apologize for the sin of working for her living. The script was published with a snide introduction presenting the alterations as "in accord with Ibsen's real intentions" ("A Doll's House Repaired," 251). That is, the authors eliminated the supposed inconsistencies of character of which Ibsen's critics had complained, preserving Nora's childish dependence and Torvald's masculine authority to the end. Crediting Jones and Herman as a precedent, Marx and Zangwill rewrote the story essentially from Torvald Helmer's point of view, as he would have preferred it. As Bernard Dukore explains, they mocked Torvald's values by making those values central to the play's conclusion ("Karl Marx's Youngest Daughter," 321). In the final discussion scene, the lines are virtually swapped: Zangwill and Marx put Nora's recriminations into Torvald's mouth (with modifications), and Torvald's remonstrances into Nora's. Whereas Ibsen's Nora reproaches Torvald for infantilizing and controlling her, the "Repaired" Torvald scolds Nora for having put up an infantile front while secretly thinking for herself. Echoing the declaration of Ibsen's Nora, "I've lived by performing tricks for you," the "Repaired" Torvald concludes:

> You lived by playing tricks on me.... Here you have been an actress, just as at home you were your papa's infant phenomenon. And the children, in their turn, will grow up actors. I thought it real when you were only playing before me, just as the children did when we took them to the pantomime. That has been our marriage.... You were never the helpless, silly song-bird I

took you for. When I thought you my little lark, my squirrel, you were deceiving me. (A Doll's House Repaired, 248)

Torvald directs his rebuke not primarily against Nora's lying and forgery, but against the feminine role-playing that he himself has encouraged. Marx and Zangwill exaggerate Torvald's arrogance to the point of caricature, making him openly flaunt his gullibility as he condemns her, even as he underscores the theatrical nature of Nora's wifely submission.

They likewise stress the importance of the "eyes of the world" in the Helmers' increasingly cynical marriage performance, wickedly parodying of the original Torvald's appeal to "duty":

NORA: Consider what the world will say.
TORVALD: The world! The world will know nothing unless you again forget yourself, and forsake your holiest duties.
NORA: My holiest duties? What are my holiest duties?
HELMER: Do you ask that? To keep up appearances. ("A Doll's House Reapaired, 250)

The revisions, according to Marx's sarcastic preface, were calculated to "satisfy the English sense of morality" by preventing the wife's departure and rebuking her insubordination ("A Doll's House Repaired, 251). The husband banishes her to the guest room but maintains the nominal marriage, preserving the family's reputation.

The "Repaired" ending, like Ibsen's original, makes use of melodramatic gestures. But Marx and Zangwill not only exploit these gestures far more abundantly but also continue to employ them in the closing lines of the play, instead of dropping them when the blackmail threat is withdrawn. As Torvald berates Nora for her forgery, she does not, like Ibsen's Nora, stand silent, comprehending her husband's true character for the first time. Rather, she "*sinks shrieking on the floor at his feet,*" then "*rises and stands with clasped hands.*" Later, as he orders her to the guest room, Nora "*sinks on her knees* while *catching hold of his coattails*" ("A Doll's House Repaired," 243–252). Dukore suggests that in deploying melodramatic movements, the writers "imply that the social views and dramatic technique of the earlier period, which this scene parodies, are what respectable English theatergoers prefer" ("Karl Marx's Youngest Daughter," 313). I would add that the parodists not only invoke the views and

techniques but also conflate them: Marx and Zangwill suggest that to be melodramatic, in the judgment of Ibsen's hostile critics, is to be womanly.
A more light-hearted perspective on marital metatheatricality appeared in F. Anstey's (Thomas Anstey Guthrie's) *Nora; or, The Bird-Cage*, originally published in *Punch* and afterwards compiled with several other parodies in *Mr. Punch's Pocket Ibsen* (1893), a collection of cartoonish skits lampooning Ibsen's "magnificently impenetrable obscurity" (*Mr. Punch's Pocket Ibsen*, 5). When Nora, preparing for her final departure, is asked how she intends to educate herself, Anstey makes her reply, "I shall *begin* with a course of the Norwegian theatres. If *that* doesn't take the frivolity out of me, I don't really know what *will*!" (*Mr. Punch's Pocket Ibsen*, 85). The remark mocks the gloom and didacticism that had become synonymous with Ibsen's name in England and, at the same time, attributes to these didactic plays the real-world marital consequences of the wife abandoning her home. The idea is reinforced when Nora, having exited, returns a moment later, "*looking rather foolish*," according to the stage directions. Torvald exclaims, "What? Back already? Then you *are* educated?", to which Nora replies, "The Norwegian theatres are all closed at this hour—and so I thought I wouldn't leave the cage till to-morrow—after breakfast" (*Mr. Punch's Pocket Ibsen*, 86–87). Anstey jokingly turns the idea of marriage as theater on its head; rather than escaping from an unhealthily theatrical marriage, theater is presented as a cause of the wife's departure and the destination of her (unsuccessful) escape. If life inside the doll's house is theatrical, Anstey implies, life outside it may be still more so.

This conclusion suggests an insight on the ways in which English theatergoers responded to Ibsen's theatrical innovations. By the early 1890s, Ibsen's dramas, in rejecting popular genre conventions, had become recognized by English playgoers as a genre with its own conventions. Anstey stresses this in all his parodies with references to recurring motifs in Ibsen plays. In making her confession to Rosmer, Rebecca West offers the preamble, "A long time ago, before the play began—in Ibsenite dramas, all the interesting things somehow *do* happen before the play begins" (*Mr. Punch's Pocket Ibsen*, 31). Hedwig Ekdal and Hedda Gabler are prevented from their suicides by the inefficient pistol, "that fatal Norwegian weapon which, in the Ibsenian drama, *never* shoots straight" (*Mr. Punch's Pocket Ibsen*, 164). In revising the devices of domestic melodrama, Ibsen created another genre, purportedly a more realistic one. Anstey questions this claim, highlighting what he considered the absurdities of Ibsen's plots and strategies.

The idea of Ibsenian drama as a new genre was considered more seriously in two *Doll's House* sequels published in 1890 by Walter Besant and Bernard Shaw, imagining events twenty years after Nora's departure, titled, respectively, "The Doll's House—and After" and "Still After the Doll's House." Besant's sequel attacked Nora's departure as heartlessly selfish and imagined its consequences, culminating with the suicide of Nora's daughter, Emmy. Shaw's sequel to Besant's narrative defended Nora, placing the blame for Emmy's death on the respectable society that has ostracized Emmy and the entire Helmer family as a result of Nora's rebellion. Besant presents the middle-aged Nora as a fashionable novelist who "laugh[s] scornfully" at the mention of her family's misery—her former husband's drunkenness, her sons' forgery and recklessness, and her virtuous daughter's poverty ("The Doll's House—And After," 321). Nora's New Woman identity is described as a pose directed toward spectators, intended to be watched and studied:

> She threw aside...all the conventions, and openly, not secretly, in the sight of all, she began to live the life of perfect freedom. She wrote novels also, which the old-fashioned regarded with horror. In them she advocated the great principle of abolishing the family, and making love the sole rule of conduct. She even related in these works her own adventures. ("The Doll's House—And After," 320)

In Besant's description, the New Woman's philosophy is simply a righteous cloak for her selfishness. Nora's independent life is enacted "in the sight of all" and becomes material for lucrative novels. By the mid-nineties, Besant's arrogant Nora had become a stock type familiar from Sydney Grundy's *New Woman* (1894), Henry Arthur Jones's *Case of Rebellious Susan* (1894), and Arthur Wing Pinero's *Notorious Mrs. Ebbsmith* (1895). The New Woman, as these plays depicted her, showed her independence by dressing mannishly and mouthing emancipatory jargon. Nora, Besant suggests, has left the dramatic scenario of the happy marriage, but her departure has created a new dramatic scenario, the emancipated woman's defiance of society.

Shaw reinforced this idea in his sequel to Besant's sequel, though he contradicted what he called Besant's "representative middle class evangelical verdict on the play" (*CLS1*, 239). "Still After the Doll's House" is a discussion in which Nora converses with the ex-forger Krogstad, now the husband of Christina, who has reformed him into a prosperous but secretly reluctant moral paragon. Their argument chiefly examines the causes of Emmy's suicide, along with some general remarks regarding hypocrisy and respectability. Krogstad, resenting the wife who makes him a "puppet," recalls Nora's declaration of independence and complains: "A woman can [leave her husband] and be made a heroine of, if she is only pretty enough. But the very set that makes a heroine of you would join my set in hounding me out of the place as a blackguard if I did such a thing" ("Still After the Doll's House," 137). Shaw, like Besant, suggests that Nora, in quitting her husband, is viewed as a "heroine"—no longer a melodramatic heroine, but a heroine of another genre, the New Woman narrative. Though Shaw certainly viewed this narrative from a very different perspective from Besant's, he acknowledged a few grains of truth in the stereotypes dramatized by Grundy, Jones, and Pinero. In *The Philanderer* (1893), the "unwomanly" women of the Ibsen Club have obviously picked up Ibsen phrases as the latest literary fashion. Like Besant, Shaw suggests that Nora's independent life, with the speeches and physicality that accompany it, has ironically become a matter of performance and spectatorship, just as her marriage once was—a specimen of the Ibsenian genre. When quitting the melodrama of her marriage, Ibsen's Nora wishes to escape into some unperformed, absolute reality—to leave the "playroom," to "stand quite alone" (*DH*, 114, 115). But, as Besant and Shaw both suggest, her departure from the doll's house is as much a drama as her life there ever was.

A Doll's House, associating the Helmer marriage with theatrical performance, had implied a connection between the problems of conventional marriage and those of conventional theater, and this idea was taken up and examined in the English afterlives of the play. As critics responded with approval or indignation to the play's critique of marriage, these adaptations also called attention to the ways in which the Helmer separation departed from theatrical custom and became a custom in itself.

Conclusion

A few years after the London debut of *A Doll's House*, Shaw complained that while politics, private behavior, and other areas of life were becoming increasingly "theatrical," "the theatre itself remains impervious to common sense, religion, science, politics, and morals" (*BH1*, 236). *A Doll's House* acknowledged the real-world theatricality on which Shaw insisted, and this emphasis on theatricality was an important part of the appeal that led Shaw and others to welcome the play as a drama that was not "impervious"—a play that, by challenging conventional codes of morality, served to "greatly deepen the sense of moral responsibility" (*QI*, 199). *A Doll's House* presented marriage as a weighty example of "theatrical" conduct, showing a couple who treat their marriage as a dance, a series of poses. In presenting marriage metatheatrically, linking it with the acts of rehearsal and performance, and with specific theatrical genres, the play implied that theater was partly to blame for marital problems like the Helmers'. Traditional theatrical genres reinforced standards of "manly" and "womanly" behavior, encouraged sentimentality, and uncritically accepted marriage as the necessary narrative endpoint, the *sine qua non* of the happy ending.

The discontents of the Helmer marriage are addressed through discussion—a conversation in which the partners are bent on understanding and making themselves understood, in which preconceived assumptions about each other are evaluated and in some cases discarded. For Torvald, sitting down to converse with his wife—or rather, to hear her talk—is a jarring experiment in re-defining the married state. It posed a similar challenge to spectators: in contrast with more traditional performances, it postponed resolution, requiring audiences to consider as well as feel.

In this way, the discussion scene was presented as a starting point for better marriages and better theater. If marriage and human conduct in general are becoming "theatrical," as Shaw asserted, taking stage performance as their lenses on life, then the quality of the performance became a momentous question. Melodrama, dance, and domestic comedy have failed as models, the play suggested; better to take a discussion play as pattern. If theater and other arts are among the ways in which societies articulate identities, then new genres might offer new ways of understanding and living life.

This idea received a variety of responses from the authors who attempted to rewrite *A Doll's House*. Marx and Zangwill reinforced Ibsen's critique of romantic theater by caricaturing the melodramatic sentimentality of the conventional ideal woman. Anstey and Herman and Jones erased or mocked the dramatic innovations that were becoming recognized as the "Ibsen" genre, suggesting that this new kind of drama, and not traditional romantic theater, was leading to marital discontent. Besant and Shaw elaborated on the idea of a "New Woman" dramatic genre by depicting the theatricality of Nora's life as a mature woman. *Doll's House* sequels broadened the public discussion of Ibsen's works, as Archer, Shaw, and their associates were eager to do. These sequels also suggested that the widely acknowledged turning point in theatrical conventions might have long consequences for marriage and society. In the following years, this link between theatrical change and social change would be taken up, challenged, and debated in the plays of Jones, Shaw, and other dramatists in England.

NOTES

1. I am indebted for this idea to the anonymous reader who reviewed an abridged version of this chapter for publication in *Theatre Survey*, as well as to Unni Langås's observations regarding Judith Butler's concept of performed gender and its relevance to Nora.
2. Archer's anglicization of "Kristine Linde." Since I am primarily concerned with the play as it was performed and received in London in the 1880s and 1890s, all quotations and names are as they appeared in Archer's translation, published by T. Fisher Unwin, which was the English version most readily available to the English dramatists and critics whose writings I discuss here. It is also identical to the text used by Janet Achurch and Charles Charrington with the company at the Novelty Theatre production in 1889, with the exception of a few passages that were removed to shorten the performance and afterwards restored by Archer.
3. As Bernard Ince has documented in "Before Ibsen," Janet Achurch's longest-running and most frequently played roles in her early acting years included ingénues in adapted French dramas and sentimental fallen-woman characters such as Lady Isabel Carlyle in Ellen Wood's *East Lynne*, Rachel Dunbar in Sydney Grundy's *Rachel*, and Mercy Merrick in Wilkie Collins's *New Magdalen*.
4. P. F. D. Tennant, reviewing the French plays that figured prominently in Ibsen's repertoire during his years as stage manager and artistic director in Bergen and Christiania, concludes that "it is in fact only the natural fluency of the dialogues which distinguishes [Ibsen's 'reckoning' scenes] from the scenes we find with Augier and Dumas *fils*" (*Ibsen's Dramatic Technique*, 84).
5. See Durbach, *A Doll's House: Ibsen's Myth of Transformation*, 44; Northam, *Ibsen's Dramatic Method: A Study of the Prose Dramas*, 27; Quigley, *The Modern Stage and Other Worlds*, 106; Unni Langås, "What Did Nora Do? Thinking Gender with A Doll's House," 158.
6. In addition to the *Doll's House* rewritings discussed below, a partial list of Ibsen-based English pieces includes Mrs. Hugh Bell's *Jerry-Builder Solness* (1893), J. M. Barrie's *Ibsen's Ghost* (1891), and *Beata* (1892), Austin Fryers's tragic prequel to *Rosmersholm*. Some more widely known original

plays of the decade—in particular, Shaw's *Candida* and Wilde's *Ideal Husband*, also contain significant re-workings of Ibsenian ideas (the Ibsen motifs in *Candida* will be discussed in Chap. 6; for an analysis of *An Ideal Husband* and its echoes of Ibsen's *Pillars of Society*, see Kerry Powell, *1890s*, 81–88).

REFERENCES

Abel, Lionel. *Metatheatre: A New View of Dramatic Form*. New York: Hill & Wang, 1963.
Anstey, F. *Mr. Punch's Pocket Ibsen*. New York: Macmillan, 1893.
Archer, William. *William Archer on Ibsen: The Major Essays, 1889–1919*. Edited by Thomas Postlewait. Westport, CT: Greenwood, 1984.
Besant, Walter. "The Doll's House—And After." *The English Illustrated Magazine* (January 1890): 315–25.
Butler, Judith. *Gender Trouble: Feminism and the Subversion of Identity*. New York: Routledge, 1999.
Cordell, Richard. *Henry Arthur Jones and the Modern Drama*. Port Washington, NY: Kennikat, 1968.
Davis, Tracy C., and Thomas Postlewait. "Theatricality: An Introduction." In *Theatricality*, edited by Tracy C. Davis and Thomas Postlewait, 1–39. Cambridge: Cambridge University Press, 2003.
Dukore, Bernard. "Karl Marx's Youngest Daughter and 'A Doll's House.'" *Theatre Journal* 42, no. 3 (1990): 308–21.
Durbach, Erroll. *A Doll's House: Ibsen's Myth of Transformation*. Boston: Twayne, 1991.
Granville-Barker, Harley. "The Coming of Ibsen." In *The Eighteen-Eighties*, edited by Walter de la Mare, 159–97. Cambridge: Cambridge University Press, 1930.
Holmes, Rachel. *Eleanor Marx: A Life*. New York: Bloomsbury, 2014.
Ibsen, Henrik. *A Doll's House*. Translated by William Archer. London: T. Fisher Unwin, 1889.
Ince, Bernard. "Before Ibsen: The Early Stage Career of Janet Achurch 1883–89." *Theatre Notebook* 67, no. 2 (2013): 66–102.
Jones, Henry Arthur, and Henry Herman. *Breaking a Butterfly*. Privately Printed, 1884.
Langås, Unni. "What Did Nora Do? Thinking Gender with A Doll's House." *Ibsen Studies* 5, no. 2 (2005): 148–71.
Marx, Eleanor, and Israel Zangwill. "A Doll's House Repaired." *Time* (March 1891): 239–53.
"Nora." *The Englishwoman's Review*, January 15, 1883.
"Nora, by Ibsen." *Women's Penny Paper*, March 30, 1889.

Northam, John. *Ibsen's Dramatic Method: A Study of the Prose Dramas*. Oslo: Universitetsforlaget, 1971.

Ørjasæter, Kristin. "Mother, Wife, and Role Model: A Contextual Perspective on Feminism in A Doll's House." *Ibsen Studies* 5, no. 1 (2005): 19–47.

Powell, Kerry. *Oscar Wilde and the Theatre of the 1890s*. Cambridge: Cambridge University Press, 1990.

Quigley, Austin E. *The Modern Stage and Other Worlds*. New York: Methuen, 1985.

Robins, Elizabeth. *Ibsen and the Actress*. New York: Haskell House, 1973.

Sedgwick, Eve. *Touching Feeling: Affect, Pedagogy, Performativity*. Durham, NC: Duke University Press, 2003.

Shaw, Bernard. *Bernard Shaw: Collected Letters, 1874–1897*. Edited by Dan H. Laurence. Vol. 1. 3 vols. New York: Viking, 1965.

———. "Still After the Doll's House." In *The Works of Bernard Shaw*, vol. 6, 125–37. London: Constable, 1931.

———. *The Bodley Head Bernard Shaw: Collected Plays with Their Prefaces*. Edited by Dan H. Laurence. 7 vols. London: The Bodley Head, 1970.

———. *The Quintessence of Ibsenism*. In *Shaw and Ibsen: Bernard Shaw's The Quintessence of Ibsenism and Related Writings*, edited by J. L. Wisenthal, 97–237. Toronto: University of Toronto Press, 1958.

Templeton, Joan. "The Doll House Backlash: Criticism, Feminism, and Ibsen." *PMLA* 104, no. 1 (1989): 28–40.

Tennant, P. F. D. *Ibsen's Dramatic Technique*. Cambridge: Bowes & Bowes, 1948.

Walkley, A. B. *Pastiche and Prejudice*. London: Heinemann, 1921.

CHAPTER 3

Wilde's Personal Drama

When Oscar Wilde's engagement to Constance Lloyd was announced in January 1884, the *Nottingham Evening Post* proclaimed, "Bunthorne is to get his bride," echoing *Patience*, the operetta in which Gilbert and Sullivan had lampooned Wilde and the Aesthetic movement two years before ("Metropolitan Notes," 2). The *Edinburgh News* echoed the joke while reporting on Wilde's wedding in late May, jocosely grumbling that "The concluding chorus of 'Patience'—'No one now is Bunthorne's Bride'— was *not* performed in lieu of the Wedding March" ("Occasional Notes," 2). Judging by anecdotal evidence, the marriage that began as a sequel to a comic opera became increasingly theatrical with time. Attending the theater together during their engagement, the couple found their box the object of stares from fellow spectators, and even cast members stole glimpses through holes in the curtain (*Constance*, 82). Eleven years later, on April 1, 1895, the night before the opening of the first of the three trials that were to shatter both their lives, Oscar and Constance spent a final playgoing evening at St. James's Theatre, seeing *The Importance of Being Earnest* in the company of Lord Alfred Douglas. As Constance's biographer Franny Moyle describes it, the outing was a desperate attempt to convince the scandal-hungry public that "If Oscar Wilde's wife had no issue with his relationship with Bosie Douglas, then neither should anyone else" (*Constance*, 263). The effort proved vain. Like Lord and Lady Windermere, the Wildes found that "The world has grown so suspicious of anything that looks like a happy married life" (*OW7*, 56–57).

© The Author(s) 2020
M. Christian, *Marriage and Late-Victorian Dramatists*, Bernard Shaw and His Contemporaries,
https://doi.org/10.1007/978-3-030-40639-4_3

To describe Wilde's marriage as theatrical is perhaps redundant, since, by his own admission, Wilde had virtually lived onstage from the outset of his adult life. First, he proclaimed his artistic doctrines on the lecture platform, carefully managing his own spectacle of celebrity. As Aestheticism was widely mimicked onstage and in the press, in many observers' minds, Wilde became the velvet-clad real-life counterpart of *Patience*'s Bunthorne and of George du Maurier's "Maudle" cartoons. Later, he became known as successful poet, critic, and dramatist. In the courtroom, his accusers cast him as sexually deviant even as he acted the part of brave nonconformist and poised wit.[1] His marriage drew notice both as a performance in its own right and as a completing of Wilde's grand life-spectacle: Bunthorne had his bride, the House Beautiful its hostess, the author his literary helpmeet, the accused man his loyal ally, and the sex criminal his deceived victim.

In recent years, Wilde has become almost an honorary founding father of the performance studies field. Kerry Powell, in *Acting Wilde*, sweepingly declares that "Wilde was among the first to discern that life is a continuum of performance" and that "late-twentieth-century theories of performance can be seen as an elaborate footnote to Wilde, who produced art, including the art of life, in performative terms without the benefit of a theory of performance to guide him" (*Acting Wilde*, 1–3). Other scholars have used his life and works as starting points to articulate broad theories of performance and theatricality. Sharon Marcus, in her analysis of *Salomé*, identifies Wilde, Bernhardt, and the chief characters in the play as examples of Victorian "theatrical celebrity," defining celebrity as being theatrically structured around the asymmetrical relationship between viewers and performers ("Salomé!!," 999–1018). Lynn Voskuil, in presenting her concept of Victorian "natural acting"—that is, theatrical performance that is not opposed to authenticity, but renders authenticity itself theatrical—identifies the Sibyl Vane episode of *Dorian Gray* as an exemplary illustration of the idea, joking that Lord Henry Wotton might be employed as "Judith Butler's stage manager" (*Acting Naturally*, 19). Wilde, in addition to being a master showman himself, has become useful as a point of contact between the nineteenth and the twenty-first centuries, allowing scholars to adapt modern theories of performativity into tools for examining Victorian art and society.

It is no surprise, then, that studies of Wilde's plays have frequently called attention to parallels between Wilde's own marriage and those of his characters. Carol Schnitzer, for example, examining *An Ideal Husband* (1895), points to the husband's shameful secret and the wife who worships his integrity, describing Sir Robert's plight as "a transposition into more acceptable terms of Wilde's own trepidation about his secret homosexual life," expressing his "desire to continue with his double life and to retain the love of his wife in spite of it" ("A Husband's Tragedy," 25). In *The Importance of Being Earnest*, the "Bunburying" jokes have been widely read as sly allusions to secret homosexual subculture, especially in Algernon's insistence that "A man who marries without knowing Bunbury has a very tedious time of it" (*OW8*, 24).[2] Others, such as John Clum, looking at the plays more generally, have pointed out resemblances between Constance and the idealistic young female characters such as Lady Chiltern, Lady Windermere, and Hester Worsley and identified Wilde himself with his women and men with pasts, who dazzle with their wit while struggling to conceal disreputable secrets (*The Drama of Marriage*). Wilde's plays, by these assessments, offer a sort of coded autobiography dramatizing the tensions between Wilde's marriage, sexuality, and celebrity persona.

Such biographical readings take encouragement from some of Wilde's own comments, suggesting some connection between his plays and his life. As Herbert Beerbohm Tree, producing *A Woman of No Importance*, prepared to play Lord Illingworth, Wilde said of the character: "He is certainly not natural. He is a figure of art. In fact, if you can bear the truth, he is MYSELF" (qtd. in Hesketh Pearson, *Beerbohm Tree*, 65). Later, during his time in prison, he sorrowfully boasted in *De Profundis*: "I took the drama, the most objective form known to art, and made it as personal a mode of expression as the lyric or sonnet" (*OW11*, 29). Though Wilde did not specify what he meant by "personal" drama, or what traits he shared with Lord Illingworth or any other character, he claimed to allow for more self-expression in his plays, more reflection of the creator's personality, than the "objective" dramatic realism that was being developed by leaders of the New Drama movement.

In the previous chapter, I argued that *A Doll's House* highlights the problems of traditional marriage by likening it to traditional theater, and that Nora's departure signals a rejection of both—a desire for a "true self" that is separable from performance or theatricality. Wilde's plays, preoccupied with the acting of social roles within marriage and other contexts, frequently convey a similar performance angst, yet also suggest alternative ways of envisioning performance and audience. Through shrewd characters such as Mrs. Erlynne, Wilde implies that the authenticity of marriage or singleness, purity or impurity, might be viewed, not as avoidance of a scripted role, but as the onus to choose among available forms of theatricality.

For some early viewers, Wilde's drama seemed to offer little that was personal or original; rather, they seemed like rehashings of mid-century melodrama and eighteenth-century comedies of manners. His early Society comedies, *Lady Windermere's Fan* and *A Woman of No Importance*, attracted frequent comparisons with mid-century English and French plays. But it was in large part through and in opposition to old performance genres that Wilde developed his "personal" dramatic style, a style steeped in his personality yet constructed from recognizable ingredients. He drew motifs from familiar varieties of comedy and melodrama, often following expected patterns only to reverse them at the last moment. Viewing life itself in theatrical terms, he presented social performances such as afternoon calls and country house parties as genres to be parodied or reworked, often conflating these performances with scenes more traditionally associated with the stage. In blending scenes from stage and drawing room, he called attention to the rigid assumptions about marriage and morality that underpinned these genres. In revising familiar scenes, he attempted to reimagine a theater in which these assumptions might be, if not openly rejected, at least destabilized.

Even as Wilde reshaped the English theater into a more "personal" art, the theater shaped his image in important ways. In some eyes, he was an inveterate novelty-monger trying yet another publicity stunt. In others, he was an artist attempting a challenging new project. For years, he had been a theatrical character and topic under the names of Reginald Bunthorne, Maudle, and numerous others. Now he took control of his theatrical image. Under the names of Lord Illingworth, Mrs. Erlynne, and Oscar Wilde, he declared himself star character and creator of a unique theatrical form.

Wilde in the Role of Dramatist

By the time Wilde began to write plays for the commercial theater, he had been a well-known figure in the literary world for more than ten years, first as adored and ridiculed figurehead of the Aesthetic movement, then as controversial critic, essayist, and novelist. Hence, announcements of *Lady Windermere's Fan* early in 1892 invited much speculation: surely a play by Wilde, the supremely unconventional man, would be something extraordinary. One first-night critic remarked on this contagious curiosity in the

Pall Mall Gazette: "At some theatres you hear about Irving, or Hare, or Arthur Roberts, or Nellie Farren, but on Saturday night nobody thought very much about actor or actress. In all directions you heard Oscar Wilde—just as, a fortnight ago, in all directions you heard influenza" ("Mr. Oscar Wilde's Play," 1). Audiences came prepared to be dazzled, amused, and perhaps shocked.

For many, the play's chief shock was its ordinariness—a play featuring an ostracized fallen woman, a marital squabble, an arrested elopement, and an allowance of mistaken identities and hide-and-seek. The baffled *Pall Mall Gazette* critic exclaimed: "Is 'Lady Windermere's Fan' a huge joke? We all know that Mr. Wilde is a desperate humourist, and the idea of leaving the world to think he had written a novel, original, daring play and then writing one that has no novelty, originality, or daring may have been too much for him" ("Mr. Oscar Wilde's Play," 1). *The Standard* concurred: "It was felt that [Wilde] would regard the trespass and disregard of the canons of play-writing as a first necessity.... As a matter of fact, the canons have been respected" ("St. James's Theatre," 3). Wilde seemed, to most, either to be following the common English practice of imitating the French melodramas of Dumas *fils* or else reintroducing the eighteenth-century comedy of manners (Lady Windermere's dodge behind Lord Darlington's curtains in Act III drew comparisons with the screen scene in *A School for Scandal*).

Paradoxically, even as *Lady Windermere's Fan* and Wilde's later plays were labeled as rehashings of outworn theatrical conventions, they were also viewed as uniquely representative of Wilde, described in terms Wilde would later echo in speaking of his "personal" drama. The *Pall Mall Gazette* critic, regarding *Lady Windermere's Fan*, reported, "I do not remember ever being at so personal a first night. The influence of the society cynic seemed all over the house.... And when the curtain fell the cry was 'Author!' Oscar's spirit had been so pervasive that we wished at last to see him in the flesh" ("Mr. Oscar Wilde's Play," 1). The plentiful epigrams were taken as echoes of Sheridan and also as a self-promotional display of Wilde's wit. The seductions, family secrets, and intercepted letters were at once simple melodramatic imitations and a Wildean nose-thumbing at the very idea of theater as creative art. Charles Brookfield and J. M. Glover would later mock this combination of imitation and self-reference in *The Poet and the Puppets*, their burlesque of *Lady Windermere's Fan*. The show's prologue featured a "poet," a caricature of Wilde, in the process of writing a play, consulting a fairy who served as his muse:

POET: Well, you know I have a new idea. I've invented Art and Flowers and Fairies. Now I'm thinking of inventing plays and actors and actresses. I'm sure they'd be a delightful resource when one is bored.
FAIRY: What kind of plays and actors?
POET: Oh, they must be well-known ones. I can't afford to invent anything that isn't well-known and successful. (*The Poet and the Puppets*, 219)

Brookfield and Glover, like numerous critics, suggested that whatever pre-existing material Wilde might borrow, his real theme would always be Oscar Wilde.

Wilde himself echoed this tongue-in-cheek assessment of his plays in his insistence on drama as a "personal" art form rather than an "objective" one. He argued that in reusing familiar theatrical plots and recreating them in his own image, he transformed not only those particular plots but also the nature of theater itself. As his critics grew amused or exasperated at his seemingly lazy and narcissistic style, Wilde claimed these traits as his chief literary legacy. In this rejection of an "objective" dramatic method, he echoed the declaration his chief speaker had made years earlier in "The Decay of Lying":

> All bad art comes from returning to Life and Nature, and elevating them into ideals. Life and Nature may sometimes be used as a part of Art's raw material, but before they are of any real service to Art they must be translated into artistic conventions. The moment Art surrenders its imaginative medium it surrenders everything. As a method Realism is a complete failure, and the two things that every artist should avoid are modernity of form and modernity of subject-matter. (*OW5*, 61–62)

Reliance on facts and on the conditions of everyday life, his speaker implies, tends to stifle invention and the personality of the inventor.

With this dismissal of dramatic realism and endorsement of a "personal" dramatic approach that privileged self-expression over subject matter, it is no surprise that Wilde came into conflict with Archer, Shaw, and other leaders of the New Drama movement, or that his work occupies an anomalous position in the late-nineteenth-century dramatic canon. To theatrical leaders who deprecated familiar stage conventions, Wilde's plays seemed retrogressive. J. T. Grein, an early champion of Ibsen's plays, labeled Wilde "an English Sardou" ("Wilde as Dramatist," 236). A. B. Walkley assessed his plays as "all style and no sincerity" (*OW7*, ix). Archer, in his treatise on British dramatic history from the Elizabethans to the 1920s, allotted Wilde two pages at the end of his chapter on pre-Ibsen drama of the 1880s (Pinero and Jones have, between them, seventeen pages in this chapter and twenty in the next). He explained that though Wilde's major plays were produced between 1892 and 1895, "they were unaffected, or very slightly affected, by the new influences," and so "may be called essentially the drama of the 'eighties'" (*The Old Drama and the New*, 303). Whether Wilde was a century ahead of his time, as some recent performance theorists argue, or a decade behind it, as Archer claimed, he did not fit the narrative of dramatic history Archer envisioned.

Nor was this narrative of much interest to Wilde. He disdained the forms of "objective" theatrical realism—material, social, philosophical, psychological—that Archer, Shaw, and Ibsen's supporters were laboring to develop and the anti-idealism that Shaw praised in *The Quintessence of Ibsenism*. To Wilde, realism and idealism were alike fair game. Regarding critics who invoked Shakespeare's exhortation to "hold the mirror up to nature," he quipped in "The Decay of Lying" that such critics "forget that this unfortunate aphorism...is deliberately said by Hamlet in order to convince the bystanders of his absolute insanity in art-matters" (*OW5*, 34–35). To Wilde, the New Drama movement's emphasis on truth and reality was simply another set of ideals, and often a damaging one.

Yet for all his avowed scorn for the theater as a "mirror to nature," Wilde's practices as a dramatist reflect a concern for lifelikeness in both script and performance. The painstaking revisions for each of his major plays show an attention to plot and character nuance belying the careless writerly persona he publicly cultivated.[3] When the characters of *Lady Windermere's Fan* gave him difficulty, he wrote in frustration to George Alexander, "I can't get a grip of the play yet: I can't get my people real" (*Oscar Wilde: A Life in Letters*, 134). Shaw evidently recognized the intricacy behind the breeziness when, in reviewing *An Ideal Husband*, he quipped: "They [Wilde's critics] protest that the trick is obvious, and that such epigrams can be turned out by the score by any one lightminded enough to condescend to such frivolity.... The fact that his plays, though apparently lucrative, remain unique under these circumstances, says much for the self-denial of our scribes" (*TN1*, 9).

Wilde's theoretical dismissal of "modernity of subject-matter" likewise contrasts with the settings of his major plays. His most successful plays are set in contemporary English high Society. The fashionable venues in which these plays were produced, George Alexander's St. James's Theatre and Herbert Beerbohm Tree's Haymarket, specialized in spectacles that carefully imitated the opulent surroundings of wealthy playgoers. (Many of the Society plays of Arthur Wing Pinero and Henry Arthur Jones, which I will examine in subsequent chapters, were produced in these same theaters.) In such productions, the society (lowercase *s*) of British people, or of humanity in general, was conflated with Society (capital *S*) of the elite. Wilde was aware of this conflation, and he readily used, highlighted, and mocked it. Depicting the upper-class social world allowed Wilde to examine the notion of performed identity and its tensions with the authentic self. As Leonore Davidoff has argued, British high Society was founded on the desire for stable identity in a shifting socio-economic environment, serving as a tool for "the traditional aristocratic elite [who] were obsessively concerned with the question of access to their ranks" (*The Best Circles*, 15). In a changing nation, Society was viewed as a controllable space in which people could be reliably evaluated, included or excluded based on their fitness or unfitness. Yet this idea of knowable identity, simultaneously condemning theatrical artifice and making it all but necessary, becomes a chief target of critique in Wilde's plays.

To some viewers, the onstage Society gatherings—dinners, house parties, dances—were the plays' most credible elements, a saving grace in the eyes of some critics who dismissed Wilde's plots as dull and unreal. The *Pall Mall Gazette* reviewer, after complaining of the predictable plot of *Lady Windermere's Fan*, conceded that the play's "clever pictures of impossible Society people" offered a "pleasanter side," adding, "Indeed, if they were not so preternaturally witty, his duchess and two or three of his young men would fairly represent some of the fashionable modern cynics" ("Mr. Oscar Wilde's Play," 1).

Even as they pleased Wilde's audiences, these depictions of Society and the people who maneuvered their way through it formed an essential element of Wilde's "personal drama." *The Era* commented, "Mr. Oscar Wilde is a representative man in 'society.' At one period he was regarded as the 'Apostle of the Beautiful.'…From mere externals Mr. Wilde passed to the higher efforts of poet, essayist, and novelist, and now he figures in the world of fashion as a successful dramatist" ("Lady Windermere's Fan," 11). Even as his personality was seen by early audiences to infuse the plays, so the act of writing plays added a new dimension to his public persona. Charles Brookfield made this notion explicit as he burlesqued *Lady*

Windermere's Fan. Early in *The Poet and the Puppets*, in the birthday ball of "Lady Winterstock" (Lady Windermere's burlesque counterpart), the poet-narrator who represents Wilde comes onstage to sing about his playwriting debut to one of Sullivan's tunes from *Patience*, Archibald Grosvenor's "Silver Churn":

> A Poet lived in a handsome style,
> His books had sold, and he'd made his pile,
> His articles, stories, and lectures, too,
> Had brought success as everybody knew.
> But the Poet was tired of writing tales
> Of curious women and singular males;
> So soon as he'd finished his Dorian Grey [sic],
> He set to work at a four-act play. (*The Poet and the Puppets*, 232–233)

The scene depicts the burlesque pseudo-Wilde in a setting often associated with Wilde himself, in a fashionable drawing room entertaining guests with his wit. At the same time, the grouping of the "Poet" with fawning female admirers closely replicates the prototype scene in *Patience*. Brookfield and Glover simultaneously parodied Wilde's play and previous parodies of Wilde himself, depicting the poet as both author and stage-hogging star. The burlesque includes a grimly humorous touch: Wilde's dandy tempter, Lord Darlington, is rechristened "Lord Pentonville," a possible foreshadowing of Wilde's imprisoned future. This part was acted by Brookfield himself, who three years later would assist the Marquess of Queensberry in collecting the evidence that would lead to Wilde's conviction. Yet whatever veiled personal hostilities the piece contained, it encapsulated the central claim of many responses to the play: in depicting aristocratic Society onstage, Wilde was depicting himself at the center of that Society.

Wilde's representations of this upper-crust world structure his marriage plots and his exploration of theatrical convention. He shows the routines of high Society—morning calls, evening dances—as inherently theatrical activities and as sites of tension for the strained marriages or would-be marriages of the protagonists. The calls, balls, and receptions that his characters stage manage offer both a frame for the plays' action and a drama in their own right, sometimes almost crowding out the plot. It is in the eyes of this Society that the central characters carry out their courtships, seductions, and marital quarrels. Marriages are a source of social stability, yet are perilously unstable in themselves, as the problematic marital reconciliations—the official "happy endings"—suggest. In questioning the centrality of marriage as social foundation, Wilde undercuts the melodramatic suppositions upon which many of his plot motifs are grounded. His chaste wives and husbands are no longer unquestionably "good." His sexually experienced characters are not automatically unmarriageable or destined for death or tragedy. The glitteringly blasé script of Society is played in ironic counterpoint to the melodramatic tropes the plays abundantly borrow. Society and melodrama vie for the right to classify people as good or bad, charming or tedious. These competing categories form a crucial conflict in Wilde's Society dramas.

GOOD HOSTESS AND BAD GUESTS

In the opening scene of *Lady Windermere's Fan*, the formal script of upper-class social intercourse is invoked in the first few lines. Lady Windermere, in agreeing to be "at home" to Lord Darlington, tells her butler, "I'm at home to anyone who calls" (*OW7*, 9). The young wife, in receiving a male visitor, signals that the visit will be an innocent one, suggesting some vague anxiety in this need to openly display her innocence. This anxiety is reinforced a moment later when she greets Lord Darlington: "No, I can't shake hands with you. My hands are all wet with these roses" (*OW7*, 10). She holds her admirer at a distance while offering an excuse to prevent seeming unfriendliness. These few bland statements exemplify the tact and adroitness that have allowed Lady Windermere to become a successful, well-liked, and respectable Society hostess.

As a wealthy upper-class woman, Lady Windermere is one of what Davidoff terms the "specialised personnel" who during the nineteenth century served as gatekeepers of social acceptance (*The Best Circles*, 16). Davidoff argues that these functions were delegated to women, the wives of aristocrats and prominent politicians, because these women were believed to offer "a haven of stability, of exact social classification" to balance the social mixing to which men were exposed in the public sphere. Women's comparative ignorance of people of other ranks and backgrounds was deemed their chief qualification (*The Best Circles*, 16). In depicting Lady Windermere, Wilde exaggerates this qualifying ignorance. Her ignorance will bring her close to ruin, yet it also marks her, in the eyes of her acquaintances, as a "good woman," so good that her virtue sanitizes even questionable guests.

Lady Windermere's equation of virtue with social protocol also sets up her behavior as a foil to her husband's and Mrs. Erlynne's, as she learns from the Duchess of Berwick: "He goes to see her continually, and stops for hours at a time, and while he is there she is not at home to anyone" (*OW7*, 28). The echo of Lady Windermere's own phrase at the opening of the act underscores the contrast between her own carefully guarded innocence and her husband's seeming guilt. The Duchess's nieces, who live opposite Mrs. Erlynne's house, prove a dangerous audience for Windermere's apparent transgression: "Well, they're always at the window.... They *see* him. They can't help it—and although they never talk scandal, they—well, of course—they remark on it to everyone" (*OW7*, 28–29). The Duchess's perpetual self-contradictions—her nieces "never talk scandal" but "remark on it to everyone"—highlight the hypocrisy of the Duchess, the nieces, and the Society for which they speak, and they also mark the disconnect between report and fact. The nieces' story, like the nieces themselves, who never appear onstage, take on a reality independent of fact. The story becomes the reality of the Windermere's fashionable world, the people who, in evaluating their marriage, virtually determine its course. The fact that the duchess later repudiates most of her early statements—Mrs. Erlynne "must be all right" and the nieces are "always talking scandal"—reinforces the degree to which high Society's realities are constructed and performed to meet the demands of an audience (*OW7*, 73). The "right" thing to say, for the Duchess (and for Society, in general), is determined by appearance, not accuracy. Lord Windermere, failing to realize this fact, precipitates the crisis in his marriage. Reviewers were quick to notice this. Moy Thomas, writing for *The Graphic*, exclaimed: "The hero of *Lady Windermere's Fan*...is in fact presented as a model of romantic generosity; yet he deliberately and persistently treats his beautiful young wife in a way which stamps him as either an idiot or a brute" ("Mr. Oscar Wilde's New Play at the St. James's Theatre," 274). However blameless his conduct may ultimately prove, he fails to participate in his wife's public show of marital fidelity.

This theatrical reading of the situation—adultery as faulty social performance—is reinforced by Lady Windermere's reaction to the rumors. In her early speeches, she staggers under the emotional injury of his apparent betrayal. She protests, "He loves *me!* He loves *me!*" as she vainly attempts to dismiss the report, and as she confronts her husband moments later, her reproach is: "[Y]ou who have loved me, you who have taught me to love you...pass from the love that is given to the love that is bought.... I feel stained, utterly stained. You can't realize how hideous the last six months seem to me now—every kiss you have given me is tainted in my memory" (*OW7*, 34, 36). As the first shock hardens into a settled resentment, however, she dwells less on private pain and more on the public humiliation of appearing as a wronged wife, credulous enough to be ignorant of "what every one in London knows already" (*OW7*, 92, 35). Her husband's request that she invite Mrs. Erlynne to her birthday party seems "a triumph" for her rival, simultaneously permitting her husband's adultery and putting her permission on display for her guests (*OW7*, 40). To comply is to publicly forfeit her status as loved wife of a faithful husband, as well as her position as high Society's defender of morality.

Unable to prevent this public insult, she plans to answer it with another, equally public: "[Y]ou gave me this fan to-day," she tells her husband; "it was your birthday present. If that woman crosses my threshold, I shall strike her across the face with it" (*OW7*, 44). In planning to strike Mrs. Erlynne, making her husband's gift the instrument of punishment, she not only plans revenge on Mrs. Erlynne for her supposed injury but also repudiates the real shame of being seen as the naïve, unwitting victim. It is an act of self-vindication as well as retaliation. In making "an example" of one transgressive woman, thus frightening others away, she hopes to reestablish herself as moral arbiter and virtuous hostess. The Duchess has praised her for her "select" parties, for "mak[ing] a stand" against the mixing of respectable and unrespectable people. By her attack on Mrs. Erlynne, she means to continue to earn this admiration, declaring, "There is not a *good* woman in London who would not applaud me" (*OW7*, 44).

Her intended gesture carries a suggestion of chivalric romanticism: having no knightly defender, she must challenge her assailant on her own behalf (a motif that Wilde would use again in *A Woman of No Importance*). In *Tess of the D'Urbervilles*, published the previous year, Tess similarly defies the interloper who threatens her marriage, slapping Alec D'Urberville with her glove, a gesture the narrator calls "the recrudescence of a trick in which her armed progenitors were not unpractised" (*Tess of the D'urbervilles*, 452–453).[4] Yet Lady Windermere's would-be chivalry in her own defense carries a whiff of slapstick, which interrupts the situation's dramatic tension. Charles Brookfield, in his burlesque *The Poet and the Puppets*, played up this suggestion. His "Lady Winterstock," threatened by a visit from "Mrs. Earlybird," proclaims:

I'll keep mamma outside at any hazard.
Should she come here—I'll land her o'er the mazzard. (*The Poet and the Puppets*, 226)

The ludicrous blend of proper English and slang deflates Lady Windermere's righteous anger, even as the daughter's prudish aversion to "my mamma—this low enchantress" undermines the pathos of the seemingly betrayed wife (*The Poet and the Puppets*, 225). In Brookfield's parody, the knightly attack is reduced to a cockney fistfight between two ladies in evening gowns.

The first act ends, as it begins, with commonplace instructions to a servant—instructions heavy with suggestion regarding the play's relational dynamics. Still heated from her altercation with her husband, Lady Windermere directs the butler: "Parker, be sure you pronounce the names of the guests very distinctly to-night. Sometimes you speak so fast that I miss them. I am particularly anxious to hear the names quite clearly, so as to make no mistake. You understand, Parker?" (*OW7*, 45). This piece of social scripting lends symmetry to the one-act tragedy with which the play begins. The loyal wife has been turned against her husband. The tactful Society hostess has been reduced to threats of violence. Lady Windermere's humiliating loss of control culminates in the anticlimax in Act II when, at Mrs. Erlynne's arrival, her nerves and hands fail her, and she cannot carry out her threat.

As the hostess loses power to enforce morality in her marriage, her party, or even her own fingertips, the guests come to dominate the stage. These guests afford Wilde an opportunity to poke fun at the vapid silliness of the high Society pageant. Different caricatures bring their individual dramas to the forefront by turns. The matchmaking Duchess pairs off her taciturn daughter with the Australian millionaire, Mr. Hopper. Lady Plymdale bullies her helpless lover, Mr. Dumby. Lord Augustus dithers and fawns over Mrs. Erlynne. This scene, like the party scenes in Wilde's later plays, offered a flattering mirror and an animated fashion magazine to wealthy playgoers, and fantasy material for those in cheaper seats. Shaw, reviewing a similar party scene in *An Ideal Husband*, suggested that the actors might be trying too hard to please the more middle-class viewers, betraying their own social naïveté in the process: "There is no doubt that these glimpses of expensive receptions in Park Lane, with the servants announcing titles *ad libitum*, are enormously attractive to social outsiders (say ninety-nine hundredths of us); but the stage reproduction is not convincing: everybody has an outrageous air of being at a party; of not being used to it; and, worst of all, of enjoying themselves immensely" (*TN1*, 11). Some of the actors evidently missed the expressions of boredom and weariness, even when characters openly declared them.

The Windermeres' guests serve as an onstage audience or Greek chorus to observe and narrate the seeming triangular relations of their hosts and Mrs. Erlynne. They are the "every one in London" who know of the husband's supposed misconduct. Lady Windermere confides to Lord Darlington, "I feel that every woman here sneers at me as [Mrs. Erlynne] dances by with my husband" (*OW7*, 67). And on this point, at least, Lady Windermere is right. Lady Plymdale, the chief sneerer, salts Lady Windermere's wound by observing, "My dear Margaret, what a handsome woman your husband has been dancing with! I should be quite jealous if I were you! Is she a great friend of yours?" (*OW7*, 76). Other female guests add that Mrs. Erlynne is a "fascinating woman" and "just a little too attractive" (*OW7*, 77, 73). The men regard Lord Windermere's apparent attachment with amusement, remarking, "Windermere knows that nothing looks so like innocence as an indiscretion," and "Yes, dear Windermere is becoming almost modern. Never thought he would" (*OW7*, 77). Regarding Lady Windermere's hospitality to her husband's supposed mistress, opinions vary from "Lady Windermere has that uncommon thing called common sense" to Lady Plymdale's "It takes a thoroughly good woman to do a thoroughly stupid thing!" (*OW7*, 77, 66). In their eyes, Lady Windermere is countenancing her husband's affair, presenting a respectable front that covers but does not conceal the transgressions underneath. The entire second act is an elaborate metatheatrical layering of appearances and realities: the thin pretense of marital harmony, the open secret of strife and seeming adultery, and, beneath these competing illusions, the truth of Mrs. Erlynne's motherhood, past misconduct, and blackmailing attempts at rehabilitation.

Tempter and Fallen Woman: Rewriting Badness

These contradictions between seeming and reality, and fashionable Society's indifference to the contradiction, become the crux of Lord Darlington's argument as he urges Lady Windermere to leave her marriage. In denouncing her husband's infidelity, Lord Darlington exclaims, "you would have to be the mask of his real life, the cloak to hide his secret"—claims that the evening's events appear to substantiate (*OW7*, 68).

When Lady Windermere hesitates, he hints at future concealments, still more shameful: "In a week you will be driving with this woman in the park. She will be your constant guest—your dearest friend" (*OW7*, 71). Certainly manipulative seducers were nothing new in Victorian drama. The villains of Tom Taylor's *Still Waters Run Deep* (1855) and *Victims* (1857) profited (in every sense) from the vanity of other men's wives, and Sir Francis Levison preyed upon Lady Isabel's unfounded jealousies in Ellen Wood's popular novel *East Lynne* (1861) and its numerous stage adaptations. Some of Lord Darlington's lines—his protestations of lasting love and his assertions of the husband's unworthiness—might have come from *East Lynne* almost verbatim.

Yet Lord Darlington is a modified tempter. He appears more sincere than earlier seducers in his professed affection and his indignation against the husband. After his love is rebuffed, his first-act cynical wit is replaced by musings about the "purity and innocence" of a "good woman" (*OW7*, 113). He is, as Kerry Powell puts it, a "dandy whose armor of wit and cynicism has been pierced by love" (*Oscar Wilde and the Theatre of the 1890s*, 18). The casting decision, as well as the play's text, evidently played against the attractive wickedness of the stock seducer, for several reviewers commented on Nutcombe Gould's unfitness for the role. The comic paper *Judy* chaffed George Alexander for "putting Mr. Nutcombe Gould, with his kind, homely, wouldn't-hurt-a-fly sort of face, in the character of a wife stealer" ("The Call Boy," 100). By blending the characters of seducer, dandy, and sentimental lover, Wilde used the character stereotypes and moral absolutes of melodrama even as he pushed against them.

Lord Darlington, attempting to persuade Lady Windermere to elope with him, directly addresses the issue of marriage as a performance, a conflict between false role-playing and one's "real self." He argues that in leaving her husband and refusing to mask his misconduct, Lady Windermere could achieve a more "real," less artificial life. He berates her for "dragging out some false, shallow, degrading existence that the world in its hypocrisy demands," insisting on the need to live "one's own life, fully, entirely, completely" (*OW7*, 70). Echoing Ibsen, he urges her, "Be yourself!," implying that by exiting her marriage performance (and eventually marrying him), she might enter a pure, performance-free, authentic selfhood; he urges her, like Nora, to assert her identity not as wife or mother, but as a human being (*OW7*, 71).

Lady Windermere eventually succumbs to this logic. Though her immediate reason for leaving—her husband's apparent infidelity—is different from Nora's, she justifies her choice in similar terms. She protests that her husband has "never understood" her and adds: "He may do as he chooses now with his life. I have done with mine as I think best, as I think right. It is he who has broken the bond of marriage—not I. I only break its bondage" (*OW7*, 81–82). Wilde reframes the melodramatic seduction within Ibsen's logic of individualism, turning it into a debate about marriage, morality, social convention, and identity.

The idea of escaping performance by leaving her marriage, however, is an idea rejected by Mrs. Erlynne, who in the last two acts becomes the play's chief speaker. Her response to Lady Windermere's display of individualistic bravado is on several points strikingly conventional. She appeals to sentiment ("your husband loves you"), pragmatism ("You haven't got the kind of brains that enables a woman to get back"), and maternal duty ("Your place is with your child") (*OW7*, 100). Her pleas might easily have come from the mouth of Torvald Helmer. Yet Mrs. Erlynne's arguments contain another strain that counters Lord Darlington's vision of authentic post-marital life. Mrs. Erlynne presents a luridly theatricalized picture of a transgressive woman's life outside the pale of Society: "You don't know what it is to…[be] afraid every moment lest the mask should be stripped from one's face" (*OW7*, 99). Far from being an escape from disparaging public scrutiny, and from the need to perform respectability in order to shield her husband, Mrs. Erlynne argues that life outside her marriage would bring Lady Windermere under far more contemptuous scrutiny and oblige her to act respectability on her own behalf, under nearly impossible circumstances. Mrs. Erlynne rejects the concept of a "real self" separable from performed identities, and she has found empowerment in that rejection, learning to adopt many roles and play them well. But she argues that Lady Windermere is incapable of this sort of deliberate theatrical maneuvering. That Lady Windermere finally yields, not to this pragmatic argument, but to the more traditional appeal of motherhood, marks the limits of Lady Windermere's New Woman defiance—Nora is not swayed by such considerations. But Mrs. Erlynne's insistence on the inherent theatricality not only of marriage, but of the fallen woman who is shut out from marriage, is presented as a defining element in Mrs. Erlynne's character, becoming a central issue in the play's last act.

In the first three acts, Mrs. Erlynne's story closely resembles that of Lady Isabel Carlyle in *East Lynne*, who, having mistakenly suspected her husband of infidelity and left him for a lover, afterwards returns in disguise, overwhelmed with remorse, to meet her children, who do not recognize her.[5] The despairing monologues of Isabel are repeatedly echoed by Mrs. Erlynne. "Oh!" exclaims Isabel (in T. A. Palmer's stage adaptation of the novel), on being deserted by her seducer, "My punishment is hard to bear—but I have deserved it, all my future life spent in repentant expiation can never atone for the past, never, never" (*East Lynne*, 324–325). Mrs. Erlynne, desperate to rescue her daughter from social ruin, likewise soliloquizes: "How bitterly I have been punished.... No; my punishment, my real punishment is to-night, is now!" (*OW7*, 83). To Lady Windermere, she speaks in a similar vein: "One pays for one's sin, and then one pays again, and all one's life one pays.... As for me, if suffering be an expiation, then at this moment I have expiated all my faults, whatever they have been" (*OW7*, 100). Mrs. Erlynne's penitent language mirrors that of Lady Isabel and of Victorian fallen women generally, so much so that Kerry Powell has argued that except for the play's last act, "Wilde comes perilously close to letting his delinquent-mother character subside into mere imitation" (*Oscar Wilde and the Theatre of the 1890s*, 24). As marriage is the default happy ending in Victorian drama, exclusion from marriage and consequent social (and sometimes literal) death is the expected ending for women such as Lady Isabel and Mrs. Erlynne. Yet even in the conventional earlier acts, Wilde subtly pushes against the moral vision of the play's melodramatic prototypes. While Lady Isabel laments that even a lifetime of "repentant expiation" cannot pay for her sin, Mrs. Erlynne asserts that her sufferings have "expiated all [her] faults," implying that society's punishment of sexually transgressive individuals like Lady Isabel and Mrs. Erlynne (and Wilde himself) may be unjustly severe.

The End of Good and Bad

In the last act, Mrs. Erlynne discards her Lady Isabel persona entirely, with its remorseful speeches and tearful reunions, and chooses not to reveal her identity to her daughter. Like Lady Windermere's role of virtuous wife and Lord Darlington's as seducer, Mrs. Erlynne finds the chastened fallen woman and repentant mother to be theatrical roles that do not suit her. "Oh," she tells Lord Windermere, "don't imagine I am going to have a pathetic scene with her, weep on her neck and tell her who I am, and all that kind of thing. I have no ambition to play the part of a mother.... [H]ow on earth could I pose as a mother with a grown-up daughter?" (*OW7*, 140). She repudiates dramatic gestures of penance:

I suppose, Windermere, you would like me to retire into a convent or become a hospital nurse or something of that kind, as people do in silly modern novels. That is stupid of you, Arthur; in real life we don't do such things—not as long as we have any good looks left, at any rate.... And besides, if a woman really repents, she has to go to a bad dressmaker, otherwise no one believes in her. And nothing in the world would induce me to do that. (*OW7*, 141)

In having Mrs. Erlynne eschew the trappings of the fallen woman, Wilde suggests that shame is inherently theatrical, involving its own costumes and gestures, preoccupied with the gaze of real or imagined others—an idea that affect theorists such as Eve Sedgwick and Sara Ahmed have echoed and discussed in recent decades.[6] This shame is the performance that respectable Society, in the persons of Lady and Lord Windermere, demands from Mrs. Erlynne. Lady Windermere, early in the play, plans to strike her across the face at her party, publicly exposing and expelling her from "good" Society. In the final act, Lord Windermere similarly attempts to prompt expressions of remorse, reminding her of her "innocent" girlhood.

Yet all attempts at shaming fail. Lady Windermere, Lord Windermere, and Lord Darlington all disgustedly describe Mrs. Erlynne as "shameless," and, however misguided their scorn, the adjective proves accurate. Instead of adopting the markers of shame—repentance, religion, and good works—as means of moral restoration, Mrs. Erlynne deflates these acts to the level of sentimental poses. If marriage is emptied of its moral and romantic significance and becomes simply a role one plays to ensure social belonging, the same thing happens to the tragedy of seduction and the consequent suffering. Wilde emphasizes Mrs. Erlynne's refusal of false role-playing through stage directions as well as dialogue. In avoiding the "pathetic scene" with her daughter, she speaks with "*a note of deep tragedy*" and "*reveals herself*" (*OW7*, 140). Her refusal of the motherly role is itself a piece of what Lynn Voskuil terms "natural acting," authenticity not opposed to theatricality, but theatrically constructed ("Wilde and Performativity, 356–364). While Lady Windermere, like Nora, has envisioned a life of unperformed authenticity in the absence of a script or an audience, Mrs. Erlynne recognizes the impossibility of such an escape and learns to maneuver among the role-playing possibilities available to her. To her, the formal manners of a Society lady, the mask of the adventuress, the tears of the long-lost mother, the shameful gestures and dress of the fallen woman, and the proud refusal of any of these roles are all equally theatrical poses. She seeks not to escape performance in marriage or out of it, but embraces the theatricality of her marriage to Lord Augustus, taking it as the most suitable role. Like her author, she regards identity and reality as inherently theatrical.

Mrs. Erlynne gives a final twist to the familiar fallen-woman narrative when, in the final moments of the play, she secures an engagement with Lord Augustus. A rich and aristocratic marriage, once the happy ending of good characters and the haven from which bad ones were excluded, is awarded to the woman with the past. Thus, dramatic tradition, along with Lady Windermere herself, declares Mrs. Erlynne to be "a very good woman" (*OW7*, 155). Yet there is an irony in this inversion. Mrs. Erlynne's marriage with Lord Augustus, which causes theatrical convention and London Society to class her as "good," has been achieved by manipulating a silly man, whereas the one action that causes Lady Windermere (and most likely the audience) to admire her "goodness"—her generous self-sacrifice to save Lady Windermere's reputation—confirms her "badness" in the eyes of Lord Windermere and all the men in the third act. In having his adventuress declared "good" by dramatic standards, Wilde challenges Society's classification of "good" and "bad."[7]

The play ends, like a mid-Victorian domestic comedy, with the formation of a new marriage and a reconciliation of the existing one. Yet the official happy ending is an uneasy conclusion, for the harmony is founded on deception and ignorance—Lady Windermere's ignorance of Mrs. Erlynne's true identity, Lord Windermere's ignorance of his wife's near-elopement with Lord Darlington, Lord Augustus's readiness to believe any explanation Mrs. Erlynne invents, and Mrs. Erlynne's silence regarding her own secrets and everyone else's.

Equally significant, both marriages must be carried on in the absence of spectators—at least, the sharply critical spectators of London high Society. Mrs. Erlynne insists that her married life with Lord Augustus must be lived "out of England," and the Windermeres prepare to retire to Selby. Throughout the play, characters are pressed by the demands of observant Society, yet also desire to escape its gaze. The Duchess of Berwick advises Lady Windermere to take her apparently wandering husband to Aix or Homburg, where he will be out of Mrs. Erlynne's reach, away from the view of the chattering Saville girls, and where only Lady Windermere "can watch him all day long" (*OW7*, 29). Lady Windermere, angered and humiliated by her husband's seeming infidelity, contemplates leaving

England with Lord Darlington and ultimately forming a new marriage with him, away from the scandals of her husband's philandering and her own elopement. Even submissive Lady Agatha Carlisle, newly engaged to Mr. Hopper, consents to return with him to Australia, away from London Society and from her domineering mother, until the Duchess vetoes the plan, declaring that "Grosvenor Square would be a more healthy place to reside in," despite many "vulgar people" there (*OW7*, 75). This ubiquitous performance anxiety culminates with the final exodus of both principal couples from London, though the season is not yet over. Reputations have been narrowly saved and marriages salvaged, but marriage performance within the context of London Society is abandoned.

Performance Minus Audience

If *Lady Windermere's Fan* is a marriage-audience play, Wilde's next Society drama, *A Woman of No Importance* might be called its opposite. That is, not only are the protagonists not married (nor even supposed to be), but the peripheral characters can hardly be regarded as an "audience" for anyone. In the first act and the early part of the second, Wilde virtually inverts the hierarchy between major and minor characters in a manner that calls to mind Alex Woloch's description of characters "jostl[ing] for limited space within the same fictive universe," involving both author and audience in a "dynamic flux of attention" (*The One Vs. The Many*, 13). The banter of party guests, which occupies the periphery at Lady Windermere's ball, takes center stage at the Hunstanton Chase house party. The play's first two acts are dominated by the chatter of Lady Hunstanton and her guests. Lady Caroline conscientiously nags her fourth husband, Sir John Pontefract. The politician Mr. Kelvil extols "the beauty of our English home-life" while avoiding his wife and eight children (*OW7*, 188). Archdeacon Daubeny bemoans his absent wife's poor health. Mrs. Allonby complains of her husband's good temper. Lady Stutfield agrees with everyone. Lady Hunstanton, the easy-going hostess, tosses out irrelevant anecdotes of other people's elopements and misalliances.

During these early scenes, the guests who will become most central to the plot—Lord Illingworth; the young bank clerk, Gerald Arbuthnot; Hester Worsley, the American heiress; and Mrs. Arbuthnot, Gerald's mother and Lord Illingworth's erstwhile mistress—are kept in the background. Hester and Gerald have only a few minutes onstage in which to make their romantic attachment evident. Lord Illingworth engages in verbal fencing matches with Mrs. Allonby but does little else. Mrs. Arbuthnot does not even appear until the second act. William Archer took this privileging of supernumeraries over protagonists, of wit over story, as a symptom of Wilde's laziness, bad editing, and lukewarm interest in theater:

> He regards prose drama (so he has somewhere stated) as the lowest of the arts.... [H]e amuses himself by lying on his back and blowing soap-bubbles for half an evening, and then pretending, during the other half, to interest himself in some story of the simple affections such as audiences, he knows, regard as dramatic.... Mr Wilde will one day be more sparing in the quantity and more fastidious as to the quality of his wit. ("A Woman of No Importance," 228)

Yet the play's bizarre structure, with the verbose and virtually plotless first act, highlights the question implicit in the play's title: who *is* of importance, or of no importance, in the play? Lady Hunstanton and her aristocratic guests are far more important socially than the Arbuthnots, but the plot relegates them to the background. They contribute little or nothing to the narrative of Lord Illingworth's past liaison with Rachel Arbuthnot and their struggle for the affection of their illegitimate son. Being ignorant of this liaison, the Hunstanton visitors can hardly offer the relevant (though inaccurate) commentary that the Windermere party guests provide for their hosts' relationships, marital and extramarital. Formally, the aristocrats may be considered secondary characters. Yet with their banter and anecdotes, contrasted with the heavy moral rhetoric of Hester and the Arbuthnots, they frequently upstage the protagonists. The system of Society, in its attempt to classify persons by rank, economic worth, and moral probity, is depicted as a failure, and the early scenes consequently give a sense of elegant, leisured chaos.

Even when Lady Hunstanton and her guests do contribute information regarding the main characters—Lord Illingworth's possible choice of wife, for example, or Gerald's appointment as Lord Illingworth's secretary— the information is riddled with digressions regarding large feet and French governesses. Rather than fleshing out the main characters and commenting on their stories, as the minor characters do in *Lady Windermere's Fan*, Lady Hunstanton and her guests compete with the protagonists, not only for stage time but also for the audience's interest.

A Perfect Shame

As unimportant Mrs. Arbuthnot's story unfolds alongside this "Society," she appears as a strange foil to Mrs. Erlynne, her fellow fallen woman. She is in many ways the model penitent that Lord Windermere would have preferred Mrs. Erlynne to be. She has adopted with a vengeance the life of maternal devotion and self-chastisement that Mrs. Erlynne pointedly rejects. Instead of parrying the condemnations of the moralists around her, she takes masochistic pleasure in endorsing Hester's pronouncement that "A woman who has sinned should be punished" and that "She shouldn't be allowed to come into the society of good men and women" (*OW7*, 280). Like Mrs. Erlynne, Mrs. Arbuthnot has lived outside the boundaries of the reputable world. But rather than trying to work her way back across this boundary, as Mrs. Erlynne does, Mrs. Arbuthnot seems bent on cementing her separateness. Though she has taken the nominal role of wife or widow without any legal foundation, affixing "Mrs." to an assumed surname, she avoids what she considers "good" Society. "What have women who have not sinned to do with me, or I with them?" she asks (*OW7*, 307). In the 1893 Haymarket production, her performance of shame was reinforced by costume as well as speech. Her black gown, surrounded by the bright colors of Lady Hunstanton and her guests, was described by *Sketch* as standing out "in grim, sombre majesty against the brilliant dresses of the butterfly women" (qtd. in *Theatre and Fashion*, 26). Her clothes visually marked her suffering, separateness, and self-condemnation.

Ironic, then, that there seems to be little condemnation available for this self-professed sinner. Mrs. Erlynne's very name provokes reactions of "*That* woman" (*OW7*, 65). Mrs. Arbuthnot, by contrast, is dismissed as "a woman of no importance" (*OW7*, 204). Her entrance in the second act, in the midst of Hester's denunciation of the English aristocracy, goes unnoticed for several minutes. Even when she is seen, she rouses so little curiosity that the talk promptly turns back to Hester's tirade. To most of Lady Hunstanton's guests, Mrs. Arbuthnot is merely Gerald's mother, or "the lady in black velvet" (*OW7*, 241). Those who don't ignore Mrs. Arbuthnot naïvely praise her. Lady Hunstanton eagerly seeks out her company, speaking of her with gushing admiration as "the sweetest of women," "so good," and "a sweet saint" (*OW7*, 192, 295). The earnest Hester, too, declares, "You are so different from the other women here. When you came into the drawing-room this evening, somehow you brought with you a sense of what is good and pure" (*OW7*, 279). With their ignorant approval or indifference, Lady Hunstanton and her guests unconsciously heighten the irony, for the audience knows that this uninterestingly "good" woman, if her past were known, would instantly become the target, not only for censure but also for the salacious fascination of the whole party. At the same time, this insistence on Mrs. Arbuthnot's virtue and her ordinariness allows Wilde again to deconstruct the rigid moral dichotomy of good and bad, as he has already done through Lady Windermere's affirmation of Mrs. Erlynne's "goodness." But this time, the one who clings to that dichotomy most tenaciously is the fallen woman herself.

Mrs. Arbuthnot's rigid moral perspective leads her to view her own situation as a simple seduction drama, with Lord Illingworth as seducer and herself as betrayed victim. This dramatic lens colors her language as she confronts Lord Illingworth: "Are you talking of the child you abandoned? Of the child who, as far as you are concerned, might have died of hunger and of want?" (*OW7*, 245). Lord Illingworth, in her eyes, is "the man who spoiled my youth, who ruined my life, who has tainted every moment of my days" (*OW7*, 247). Later, narrating Lord Illingworth's misdeed to her son, she dilates on her suffering (in third person, without revealing herself as the woman in the story): "[H]er life was ruined, and her soul ruined, and all that was sweet, and good, and pure in her ruined also.... She is a woman who drags a chain like a guilty thing. She is a woman who wears a mask, like...a leper. The fire cannot purify her. The waters cannot quench her anguish. Nothing can heal her!" (*OW7*, 289). The story, as Mrs. Arbuthnot tells it, is a traditional fallen-woman narrative, aligning her with Hetty Sorrel, Hester Prynne, Lady Isabel Carlyle, and numerous others. She takes melodramatic rhetoric to extremes, out-Isabeling Lady Isabel in her agony.

Her lamentations clash with the flippant quips of Lady Hunstanton and her guests. They clash perhaps even more strikingly with the prosaic facts of Mrs. Arbuthnot's situation, for, in comparison with other fallen women of Victorian fiction, her fall seems to have left few external consequences. She accuses Lord Illingworth of leaving their child to starve, yet she apparently has money enough to live in her own house with at least one servant (though playgoers never learn how). The son she calls "child of my shame" sees no shame in himself or her until she points it out to him (*OW7*, 311). She speaks of being chained and leprous, but she has kept her secret so successfully that her neighbors fear no sinful contagion from her or her son. In all these points, her life contrasts markedly with Mrs. Erlynne's.

This irony is not lost on Lord Illingworth, who meets Mrs. Arbuthnot's reproaches matter of factly. Charged with having "abandoned" his son, he replies, "You forget, Rachel, it was you who left me. It was not I who left you.... As for saying I left our child to starve, that, of course is simply untrue and silly. My mother offered you six hundred a year" (*OW7*, 245–246). When she complains, "You don't realize what my past has been in suffering and in shame," he counters with, "I think Gerald's future considerably more important than your past.... But don't let's have a scene" (*OW7*, 247). Lord Illingworth offers her an alternative lens through which to interpret her past and his, a worldly, amoral perspective not unlike Mrs. Erlynne's, which, if adopted, would greatly mitigate her guilt and her misery. But she clings to her melodramatic moral vision. The result is a collision of ideas which Archer praised as "the most virile and intelligent—yes, I mean it, the most intelligent—piece of English dramatic writing of our day" ("A Woman of No Importance," 229). The dialogue is a lopsided melodrama reminiscent of the scenes between Nora and Torvald in the third act of *A Doll's House*, in which one spouse's heroics or lamentations are cut short by the other. Here again, old drama and new come into awkward contact in a scene that might aptly illustrate Lionel Abel's concept of metatheater, presenting two characters with a "playwright's consciousness," each attempting to shape the action into a different kind of play (*Metatheatre*, 57). One sees the action as a seduction melodrama in which a man's failure to marry his child's mother necessitates a miserable ending. The other sees a Society comedy in which one's marital status or sexual history, if skillfully concealed or wittily joked about, need make little difference.

Two Seduction Scenes

This contest between Mrs. Arbuthnot's melodramatic perspective and Lord Illingworth's more worldly-wise one continues in the third act as the parents struggle for the son's loyalty. In the two parent-and-son scenes that symmetrically bookend the act, Gerald is first invited to adopt his father's aesthetic, hedonistic views on marriage, family, and Society, and then is urged by his mother to renew his embrace of traditional morality. Each parent tries, with varying degrees of subtlety, to turn Gerald against the other. Lord Illingworth repeatedly affirms Mrs. Arbuthnot's value according to conventional morals, and then promptly goes on to challenge the standard. "Your mother is a thoroughly good woman," he concedes,

"But good women have such limited views of life, their horizon is so small, their interests are so petty, aren't they?" (*OW7*, 258). As alternative to traditional "goodness," he presents an aesthete's manifesto: "[T]o be modern is the only thing worth being now-a-days.... A man who can dominate a London dinner table can dominate the world. The future belongs to the dandy.... A well-tied tie is the first serious step in life" (*OW7*, 259–260). In his series of epigrammatic counsels, he explains the belief system that underpins the Society represented in Lady Hunstanton's house party, which has dominated the play thus far.

Mrs. Arbuthnot counters Lord Illingworth's dandy philosophy by classifying him, as she classifies herself and all people and things, within a rigid framework of good and evil. She labels Lord Illingworth "a bad man," expecting this claim to win the debate easily, since she has raised her son to be "a good man" (*OW7*, 286, 249). Gerald, who has hitherto uncritically accepted his mother's viewpoint, now reviews it in the light of Lord Illingworth's lesson. He first tries to resolve the tension between the familiar old philosophy and the attractive new one as a gender-based difference of perspective: "I suppose you think him bad because he doesn't believe the same things as you do. Well, men are different from women, mother. It is natural that they should have different views" (*OW7*, 286). Mrs. Arbuthnot persists, pointing to Lord Illingworth's seduction of a young girl as proof of his badness, and insists that though the action was done twenty years ago, "what this man has been, he is now, and will be always"—a declaration that Lord Illingworth unwittingly confirms as, offstage, he reenacts his past seduction in his attempt to kiss Hester (*OW7*, 286–287). Gerald, unable either to condemn Lord Illingworth or to reject outright his mother's standard of good and evil, transfers the condemnation to the unnamed victim: "I dare say the girl was just as much to blame as Lord Illingworth was" (*OW7*, 289). His words, however true or untrue they may be of his mother, are instantly contradicted as Hester, Lord Illingworth's new prey, screams out her indignation.

Lord Illingworth's attempt to kiss Hester, as first-night reviewers were quick to note, is a stereotypical stage device that might have been copied and pasted from *Black-Eyed Susan*, *The Octoroon*, or any number of Victorian melodramas. Moy Thomas, reviewing the play for *The Graphic*, joked: "'Let me see,' said a spectator in the stalls to his neighbor, on the first night, 'in what French melodrama is it that we have a mother who stays the uplifted arm of her illegitimate son by exclaiming, 'Hold, Henri, he is your father?' The answer was, 'Ask, rather, in what French melodrama is it not?'" ("A Woman of No Importance," 475). But this predictability makes it an intriguing foil for the other seduction scene with which the act opens, in which Gerald is the object. Lord Illingworth kisses Hester on a whim, on a dare. Though he finds Hester "decidedly pretty," she never holds his attention for long (*OW7*, 197). Throughout the play's dialogue, he never attempts to speak to her. She is merely a difficult trophy that he hopes to add to his collection of sexual conquests. In one important point, the attempted kiss differs from its melodramatic prototypes: it is done offstage, as if Wilde were determined to get it over with. For Boucicault, the altercation between virtuous maiden and wicked lord would have been the main event of the act. For Shaw, it would have been an opportunity for ten minutes' vigorous debate on the practical merits and demerits of puritanism (along the lines of the "duel of sex" in *You Never Can Tell*). For Wilde, the purely physical heterosexual seduction attempt is too uninteresting even to be shown onstage. Wilde was aware of the scene's typicality; in fact, as Herbert Beerbohm Tree later recalled, he rather harped on it: "People love a wicked aristocrat who seduces a virtuous maiden, and they love a virtuous maiden for being seduced by a wicked aristocrat. I have given them what they like, so that they may learn to appreciate what I like to give them" (qtd. in Hesketh Pearson, *Beerbohm Tree: His Life and Laughter*, 67).

What Wilde "liked to give," apparently, was another seduction scene altogether, this time with Gerald as the object. Lord Illingworth's interest in Gerald is more serious. Even before he knows Gerald to be his son, he expresses a wish for lasting companionship. "My dear boy," he says in the first act, "It is because I like you so much that I want to have you with me" (*OW7*, 196). Throughout the play, as their kinship is discovered by both, Lord Illingworth's desire increases, until he at last proposes marriage to his son's mother in the hopes of being reconciled to his son. One need not read a specifically homosexual or incestuous meaning into the story (though some have[8]) to recognize the attraction between the older man and the younger as a form of seduction. It is a spiritual or intellectual seduction not unlike the one shown in the opening chapters of *The Picture of Dorian Gray*, in which Lord Henry Wotton gradually converts Dorian to dandyism and narcissism. Wilde mentioned *Dorian Gray*, in fact, as a source for his play (though, as he mentioned this in connection with the "wicked aristocrat who seduces a virtuous maiden," he might have had Sibyl Vane in mind more than Lord Henry) (*Beerbohm Tree: His Life and Laughter*, 67). Nevertheless, the author underscores this resemblance between the two lords, placing some of Lord Henry's lines almost verbatim into Lord Illingworth's mouth: "Remember that you've got on your side the most wonderful thing in the world—youth! There's nothing like youth.... Youth has a kingdom waiting for it. Every one is born a king, and most people die in exile, like most kings. To win back my youth, Gerald, there is nothing I wouldn't do—except take exercise, get up early, or be a useful member of the community" (*OW7*, 256). Some critics took this self-quotation as a symptom of Wilde's mental drying-up; the *Hearth and Home* reviewer remarked, "At one period, I had serious thoughts of going home quietly, and escaping from dialogue which I already knew almost by heart" ("At the Play," 788).

But the scene is not a simple clone from Wilde's earlier novel. As Sos Eltis has justly pointed out, Lord Henry Wotton's cold manipulativeness is humanized in Lord Illingworth by his affection and unfulfilled paternal longing (*Revising Wilde*, 111–112). Wilde softens his cynicism in the sidelong inquiry, "You have missed not having a father, I suppose, Gerald?" (*OW7*, 257). Yet the father quickly turns cynical again as he begins to poison the son's mind against the mother, insinuating, "A mother's love...is often curiously selfish" (*OW7*, 258). The scene revises the mentor-and-disciple dynamic of *Dorian Gray*, casting the two characters as father and son rather than simple acquaintances. For the purpose of theatrical adaptation, the family tie offers a socially acceptable explanation for audience and censor, a reassuring alternative to the homoerotic suspicions attached to Wilde's novel. Mrs. Arbuthnot, Basil Hallward-like in her obsessive devotion, completes the familial love triangle. Gerald's intellectual seduction is not taken to extremes and followed to its long-term consequences as Dorian's is. Gerald's new enthusiasm for the dandy's hedonism is cut short at the end of the act by the more conventional seduction attempt which precipitates Gerald's return to his mother's strict moral code. Even so, the scene, in which Lord Illingworth gradually wins his son's allegiance with epigrams and arguments, is a fascinating psychological drama in itself.

The contrast between the melodramatic mother's perspective and the dandy father's is perfectly encapsulated in these two seduction scenes: the formulaic attempt on the young woman and the subtle pursuit of the young man. The two scenes in essence propose a redefinition of theatrical seduction along the lines of the redefinition of marriage offered in *A Doll's House*, exchanging one based on hysterical emotion, simple physical attraction, and pre-defined speeches and gestures, for another based on talk and intellectual rapport.

In the end, it is the old drama and the old seduction that claim control of Gerald and the play. The sensational ending of the act, with Hester's panicked accusation, Gerald's heroic threat of revenge, Mrs. Arbuthnot's shriek of "Stop, Gerald, stop! He is your own father!", and the astonished tableau on which the curtain falls, presents a concrete enactment of Mrs. Arbuthnot's melodramatic mental landscape, just as the witticisms of the country house party have, throughout the past three acts, created the play in Lord Illingworth's image (*OW7*, 292). Lord Illingworth's high Society virtually disappears from the final act. The scene shifts to Mrs. Arbuthnot's house, whence Lord Illingworth is at last expelled, and where Gerald and Hester forgive Mrs. Arbuthnot, condemn Lord Illingworth, and confirm their own future marriage.

Morality with a Vengeance

Some reviewers, seeing this triumph of the "good" characters, took the play as a lesson on the rewards of virtue. Moy Thomas concluded, "So far as there is a serious purpose in Mr. Wilde's play, it appears to be that of rebuking the rich and idle class of Society for its love of pleasure, its cynicism, its mean profligacy, its contempt of principle, its hatred of enthusiasm, its profound disbelief in the existence of anything better than itself" ("A Woman of No Importance, 475). *The Era* suggested that the play's lesson might be not so much against the wickedness of the aristocracy, but against their dullness: "Lord Illingworth…points in his own person the moral that vice, if endowed with sufficient sententiousness, may become as wearisome as the most 'preachy' variety of virtue" ("The London Theatres," 9).

Others suspected a touch of ridicule in the hackneyed good characters and charming bad ones. Archer described the play as a melodramatic caricature that risked turning into the thing it travestied. He dubbed Mrs. Arbuthnot, in adapted Wildean phrase, "the Unreasonable eternally lamenting the Unalterable," suffering from "a stubborn determination to be unhappy, for which Lord Illingworth can scarcely be blamed" ("A Woman of No Importance," 229). Sardonically assessing the third-act ending, he wrote:

It would be a just retribution if Mr Wilde were presently to be confronted with this tableau, in all the horrors of chromolithography, on every hoarding in London, with the legend "Stay, Gerald! He is your father!" in crinkly letters in the corner. Then, indeed, would expatriation—or worse—be the only resource of his conscience-stricken soul. His choice would lie between Paris and prussic acid. ("A Woman of No Importance," 229)

Yet Archer recognized the satire in Mrs. Arbuthnot's extravagant self-lacerating morality and its ultimate triumph in the play, a mocking response to viewers who, the previous year, had complained of Mrs. Erlynne. For those who condemned Wilde's earlier fallen woman as heartless, Wilde now presented an anti-Erlynne who has wallowed in sorrow, self-reproach, and motherly devotedness for twenty years.

The contrast is completed in the play's ending. Mrs. Erlynne eagerly accepts the aristocratic marriage proposal that she has obtained through flattery and maneuvering, which will make her "a good woman" in the eyes of her world. But Mrs. Arbuthnot rejects the offer of the man who once refused to marry her, arguing that the marriage ceremony that would officially undo her wrong would be a fresh crime. When Gerald appeals first to justice, then to Society's demands, and then to religion, she insists that the marriage would be a false performance with God as the chief audience:

> I [will not] ever stand before God's altar and ask God's blessing on so hideous a mockery as a marriage between me and George Harford. I will not say the words the church bids us to say. I will not say them. I dare not. How could I swear to love the man I loathe, to honour him who wrought you dishonor, to obey him who, in his mastery, made me to sin? No; marriage is a sacrament for those who love each other.... No, Gerald, no ceremony, Church-hallowed or State-made, shall ever bind me to George Harford. (*OW7*, 307–308)

She argues that a wedding ceremony can include all legally recognized and religiously sanctioned steps and yet be invalid if the people involved do not "mean" it, or if they are not the people qualified to perform those steps (in this case, "those who love each other")—an idea similar to the one J. L. Austin would later propose in his theory of performative speech acts. In Austinian terms, Mrs. Arbuthnot's lack of affection for Lord Illingworth would render her speech act doubly hollow.

Lord Illingworth's proposal is itself hardly an expected prelude to a traditional dramatic ending, for he makes not even a superficial pretense of being motivated by conscience, social propriety, or any affection for Mrs. Arbuthnot herself. He goes out of his way to disavow such motives: "I don't admit it is any duty of mine to marry you. I deny it entirely. But to get my son back I am ready—yes, I am ready to marry you, Rachel—and to treat you always with the deference and respect due to my wife" (*OW7*, 324–325). Lord Illingworth cares not for his relationship with his prospective wife, but only with his son. It is a proposal in which marriage itself is de-centered.

The awkward, strained link between Lord Illingworth's high Society and Mrs. Arbuthnot's world is snapped as Mrs. Arbuthnot, like Hardy's Tess, slaps her one-time lover with a glove, delivering the punishment that Lady Windermere had once attempted and failed to execute. Lord Illingworth is expelled from the Arbuthnot home, and the Arbuthnots prepare to emigrate to America. On the surface, it is a straightforward, idyllically happy ending for the "good" characters. The young lovers prepare to marry, and the stained mother is forgiven and reunited with son and daughter-in-law (*OW7*, 179). Lord Illingworth is banished from the life of his son, and Hester's convenient wealth ensures that Gerald need owe him nothing. Mrs. Arbuthnot, in her last word, declares Lord Illingworth "A man of no importance" (*OW7*, 331).

Yet their departure might be read as equally a release for the elegant Hunstanton world from its disruptively serious characters. Throughout the play, Lady Hunstanton's guests have repeatedly referred to Hester and Mrs. Arbuthnot as dampers on their enjoyment. Lady Caroline grumbles, regarding Hester and American women in general, "Why can't they stay in their own country? They are always telling us it is the Paradise of women" (*OW7*, 179). Lord Illingworth, as he prepares to exit, contemptuously summarizes the play's action from the perspective of aristocratic Society: "It's been an amusing experience to have met amongst people of one's own rank, and treated quite seriously too, one's mistress and one's [bastard]" (*OW7*, 329). As the good characters escape wicked Society, the urbane community of Lord Illingworth, Lady Hunstanton, and the rest is freed from its preachy misfits, and the routine of tea and table talk can continue undisturbed.

A Woman of No Importance re-creates the performance anxiety of marriage and sexual propriety in *Lady Windermere's Fan*, exaggerating it to absurdity. While Lord and Lady Windermere, to repair their marriage, must flee to the countryside to escape London's too-observant Society, Mrs. Arbuthnot, Gerald, and Hester forsake the English countryside and England in order to escape a Society that scarcely observes them at all.

CONCLUSION

In his first two Society dramas, Wilde juxtaposed the melodramatic plot conventions of sexual temptation and fall, past secrets, and long-lost parents and children with the scripts and settings of upper-class social events. In old-fashioned melodrama and *fin-de-siècle* Society alike, to be married, apparently married, or at any rate a possible future candidate for marriage is essential to belonging. Wilde presents two female protagonists who flout this rule: Mrs. Erlynne makes an aristocratic marriage in spite of her apparent ineligibility, and Mrs. Arbuthnot, when given the opportunity to do the same, refuses. Mrs. Erlynne circumvents the restrictions of melodramatic fallen women and is successfully assimilated to high Society, while Mrs. Arbuthnot, in effectively divorcing herself from Lord Illingworth and his Society, merely embraces a slightly milder and more tolerant version of the melodramatic perspective to which she, along with Hester, has subscribed throughout the play. Both women resolve their dilemmas not by attempting to escape from theatrical display, but from recognizing the essential theatricality of their worlds and adopting the most suitable roles available.

Wilde's rejection of objective reality in favor of a reality that is constructed and performed was perhaps most explicitly stated in the first of his three trials in 1895. When interrogated regarding his "Phrases and Philosophies for the Use of the Young," Wilde offered what he claimed as his "philosophical definition of truth": Truth, he declared, was "something so personal that...the same truth can never be apprehended by two minds"—hence his aphorism that "A truth ceases to be true when more than one person believes in it" (qtd. in Merlin Holland, *The Real Trial of Oscar Wilde*, 76). The theater seems an improbable medium for arguing such a doctrine, being generally assumed to be among the most collective art forms, aiming to establish a consensus, a common understanding of a play's narrative among several performers and numerous spectators. Such a maxim would appear doubly out of place amid the theatrical realism of the late nineteenth-century dramatists, in which dramatists' espousal of "truthful portraiture of modern life" presupposed some objective truth to be depicted (Henry Arthur Jones, *The Renascence of English Drama*, 89).

Wilde, in challenging the values of realism and objectivity in the theater, developed a dramatic approach which, like his conception of truth, was unapologetically "personal." In his audiences' estimation as well as his own, his drama was an expression of his experience and personality. At the same time, his plays blurred the clear divide between life and drama, actors and audience, in ways that, as Kerry Powell has suggested, would later be developed into nonmimetic dramatic theory and practice by Brecht, Artaud, and post-modern dramatists such as Tony Kushner and Sarah Kane (*Acting Wilde*, 173). However unorthodox this may have appeared to his contemporaries, the dramatic form offered Wilde a uniquely appropriate venue for offering his idea of reality and identity as performances: the scripted dialogue, actors, and plots with a careful blend of hackneyed stock devices and innovative variations of his Society dramas enabled him to present with particular vividness the claim that he had already made in his fiction, reviews, and essays.

NOTES

1. For performance-oriented readings of Wilde's trials, see Shoshana Felman, "Oscar Wilde's Performance on the Witness Stand"; and Kerry Powell, *Acting Wilde: Victorian Sexuality, Theatre, and Oscar Wilde*.
2. For discussions of *Earnest* and its possible allusions to homosexual identity and subculture, see Christopher Craft, *Another Kind of Love: Male Homosexual Desire in English Discourse, 1850–1920*; and Powell, *Acting Wilde: Victorian Sexuality, Theatre, and Oscar Wilde*.
3. For analyses of Wilde's plays and their development through early drafts, see Sos Eltis, *Revising Wilde: Society and Subversion in the Plays of Oscar Wilde*; and Powell, *Acting Wilde: Victorian Sexuality, Theatre, and Oscar Wilde*.
4. Alan Bird, in *The Plays of Oscar Wilde*, suggests that the subtitle of *Lady Windermere's Fan—A Play about a Good Woman*—might itself be an echo of *A Pure Woman*, the subtitle of *Tess*. Like Hardy, Wilde invokes a familiar moral ideal in order to subvert it and call for a redefinition (*The Plays of Oscar Wilde*, 113).
5. Powell suggests that Wilde may have signaled the resemblance to *East Lynne* even in the name of the erring mother, Mrs. Erlynne (Powell, *Oscar Wilde and the Theatre of the 1890s*, 31).
6. In particular, Ahmed describes shame, especially when publicly acknowledged, as a social performance sometimes used symbolically to cancel out a past shameful action: "[P]ublic expressions of shame try to 'finish' the speech act by converting shame to pride.... [W]hat is shameful is passed over in the enactment of shame" (*The Cultural Politics of Emotion*, 120).

7. As Sos Eltis has pointed out, Lady Windermere's final judgment of Mrs. Erlynne's "goodness" marks not only the young woman's increased experience and discernment but also the limits of that discernment: she no longer automatically dismisses Mrs. Erlynne as "bad" simply based on her sexual past, but she continues to use simplistic moral labels, which Mrs. Erlynne herself has discarded, and she would probably withdraw her verdict of "goodness" if she knew Mrs. Erlynne's relation to herself (Eltis, *Revising Wilde: Society and Subversion in the Plays of Oscar Wilde*, 82).
8. See, for example, Patricia Behrendt and John Clum. Both cite Lytton Strachey's facetious synopsis, written after seeing Beerbohm Tree's 1907 revival of the play: "Mr. Tree is a wicked Lord, staying in a country house, who has made up his mind to bugger one of the other guests—a handsome young man of twenty. The handsome young man is delighted; when his mother enters, she sees his Lordship and recognizes him as having copulated with her twenty years before, the result of which was—the handsome young man. She appeals to Lord Tree [*sic*] not to bugger his own son. He replies that it is an additional reason for doing it (oh! he is a *very* wicked Lord)" (qtd. in Patricia Behrendt, *Oscar Wilde: Eros and Aesthetics*, 156; and Clum, *The Drama of Marriage: Gay Playwrights/Straight Unions from Oscar Wilde to the Present*, 34).

REFERENCES

Abel, Lionel. *Metatheatre: A New View of Dramatic Form*. New York: Hill & Wang, 1963.
Ahmed, Sara. *The Cultural Politics of Emotion*. New York: Routledge, 2004.
Archer, William. "A Woman of No Importance." In *Victorian Dramatic Criticism*, edited by George Rowell, 228–31. London: Methuen, 1971.
———. *The Old Drama and the New*. Boston: Small, Maynard, & Co., 1923.
"At the Play." *Hearth and Home*, May 4, 1893.
Austin, J. L. *How to Do Things with Words*. Edited by J. O. Urmson and Marina Sbisa. 2nd ed. Cambridge, MA: Harvard University Press, 1975.
Bird, Alan. *The Plays of Oscar Wilde*. New York: Barnes & Noble, 1977.
Brookfield, Charles H. E., and J. M. Glover. *The Poet and the Puppets*. In *Victorian Theatrical Burlesques*, edited by Richard W. Schoch, 216–46. Burlington, VT: Ashgate, 2003.
Clum, John M. *The Drama of Marriage: Gay Playwrights/Straight Unions from Oscar Wilde to the Present*. New York: Palgrave Macmillan, 2012.
Craft, Christopher. *Another Kind of Love: Male Homosexual Desire in English Discourse, 1850–1920*. Berkeley: University of California Press, 1994.
Davidoff, Leonore. *The Best Circles: Women and Society in Victorian England*. Totowa, NJ: Rowman & Littlefield, 1973.

Eltis, Sos. *Revising Wilde: Society and Subversion in the Plays of Oscar Wilde.* Oxford: Clarendon, 1996.
Felman, Shoshana. "Oscar Wilde's Performance on the Witness Stand." *Yearbook of Comparative and General Literature* 55 (2009): 300–16.
Gilbert, W. S. *Patience: Or, Bunthorne's Bride.* In *The Complete Annotated Gilbert and Sullivan*, edited by Ian Bradley, 265–354. Oxford: Oxford University Press, 1996.
Grein, J. T. "Wilde as Dramatist." In *Oscar Wilde: The Critical Heritage*, edited by Karl Beckson, 236. London: Routledge, 1970.
Hardy, Thomas. *Tess of the D'Urbervilles.* Oxford: Clarendon, 1983.
Holland, Merlin. *The Real Trial of Oscar Wilde.* New York: Harper Perennial, 2003.
Jones, Henry Arthur. *The Renascence of the English Drama.* London: Macmillan, 1895.
Kaplan, Joel H., and Sheila Stowell. *Theatre and Fashion: Oscar Wilde to the Suffragettes.* Cambridge: Cambridge University Press, 1994.
"Lady Windermere's Fan." *The Era*, February 27, 1892.
Marcus, Sharon. "Salomé!! Sarah Bernhardt, Oscar Wilde, and the Drama of Celebrity." *PMLA* 126, no. 4 (2011): 999–1018.
"Metropolitan Notes." *The Nottingham Evening Post*, January 16, 1884.
Moyle, Franny. *Constance: The Tragic and Scandalous Life of Mrs. Oscar Wilde.* London: John Murray, 2011.
"Mr. Oscar Wilde's Play." *The Pall Mall Gazette*, February 22, 1892.
"Occasional Notes." *Edinburgh News*, June 5, 1884.
Palmer, T. A. *East Lynne.* In *Female Playwrights of the Nineteenth Century*, edited by Adrienne Scullion, 295–346. London: Everyman, 1996.
Pearson, Hesketh. *Beerbohm Tree: His Life and Laughter.* London: Methuen, 1956.
Powell, Kerry. *Acting Wilde: Victorian Sexuality, Theatre, and Oscar Wilde.* New York: Cambridge University Press, 2009.
———. *Oscar Wilde and the Theatre of the 1890s.* Cambridge: Cambridge University Press, 1990.
Schnitzer, Carol. "A Husband's Tragedy: The Relationship Between Art and Life in Oscar Wilde's An Ideal Husband." *The Victorian Newsletter* (Spring 2006): 25–29.
Sedgwick, Eve. *Touching Feeling: Affect, Pedagogy, Performativity.* Durham, NC: Duke University Press, 2003.
Shaw, Bernard. *Our Theatres in the Nineties.* 3 vols. London: Constable, 1932.
"St. James's Theatre." *The Standard*, February 22, 1892.
"The Call Boy." *Judy: The Conservative Comic*, March 2, 1892.
"The London Theatres." *The Era*, April 22, 1893.
Thomas, W. Moy. "A Woman of No Importance." *The Graphic*, April 29, 1893.
———. "Mr. Oscar Wilde's New Play at the St. James's Theatre." *The Graphic*, February 27, 1892.

Voskuil, Lynn. *Acting Naturally: Victorian Theatricality and Authenticity.* Charlottesville, VA: University of Virginia Press, 2004.

———. "Wilde and Performativity." In *Oscar Wilde in Context*, edited by Kerry Powell and Peter Raby, 356–64. Cambridge: Cambridge University Press, 2013.

Walkley, A. B. "Introduction." In *The Complete Works of Oscar Wilde*, 7: ix–xiv. New York: Doubleday, 1923.

Wilde, Oscar. *Oscar Wilde: A Life in Letters.* Edited by Merlin Holland. London: Fourth Estate, 2003.

———. *The Complete Works of Oscar Wilde.* 12 vols. New York: Doubleday, 1923.

Woloch, Alex. *The One vs. the Many: Minor Characters and the Space of the Protagonist in the Novel.* Princeton: Princeton University Press, 2004.

Wood, Ellen. *East Lynne.* New Brunswick, NJ: Rutgers University Press, 1984.

CHAPTER 4

Pinero's Old-Fashioned Playgoer

On the eve of Aubrey Tanqueray's wedding in Arthur Wing Pinero's *The Second Mrs. Tanqueray* (1893), confidant Cayley Drummle takes leave of the prospective bridegroom by saying: "I'm merely a spectator in life; nothing more than a man at a play, in fact; only, like the old-fashioned playgoer, I love to see certain characters happy and comfortable at the finish… Then, for as long as you can, old friend, will you—keep a stall for me?" (*AWP1*, 79). In likening his friendship to the experience of playgoing, Cayley suggests an affinity with the play's audience as he, like them, observes the unfolding events of his friend's married life. The remark might also be read more broadly as a comment on the type of relationship the New Drama movement's leaders envisioned between play and audience, theater and community.

The Second Mrs. Tanqueray followed *Lady Windermere's Fan* at St. James's Theatre, and, like its Wildean predecessor, was recognized as a defining example of the Society drama. Yet, Pinero's position in British theater history has long been debated. Critics and theater historians have alternately labeled him a fearless leader of the New Drama movement, a reluctant follower, and a reactionary holder-back. His aim, as he himself articulated it in a letter to William Archer, was re-establishing the status of drama as an art form and "popularizing a rational, observant, home-grown play" (*Collected Letters*, 135). He viewed this project as a matter of national prestige, writing original English plays (i.e., not translated from French or

© The Author(s) 2020
M. Christian, *Marriage and Late-Victorian Dramatists*, Bernard Shaw and His Contemporaries,
https://doi.org/10.1007/978-3-030-40639-4_4

Norwegian) that would gain respect for English theater—an aim that caused friction with some of Ibsen's London advocates. Pinero argued that the Ibsenites had done English drama a disservice by putting a foreign dramatist at the forefront of the dramatic revival. He complained to Archer that by holding up Ibsen's plays as "the Perfect drama," Archer and others were "discrediting native practice" (*Collected Letters*, 135). He also opposed the practice of having Ibsen's work and other experimental plays produced by small private groups such as J. T. Grein's Independent Theatre and the Stage Society, arguing that such plays and productions contributed little to what he considered the chief aims of theatrical reform—improving the production quality, drama content, and audiences' tastes in mainstream commercial theaters. The ventures of Shaw, Grein, Archer, and the Ibsenites, Pinero insisted, at best improved theatrical quality for a tiny minority of theatergoers. The majority, he predicted, would reject *A Doll's House* for vaudeville and other unedifying entertainment. Pinero wished to improve the quality of acting, production, and playwriting but not at the expense of commercial viability. Only in this way, he argued, could intelligent theater be made accessible for theatergoers and financially rewarding for dramatists.

Many contemporaries expressed admiration of these efforts. Clayton Hamilton, twenty years after the event, declared that "The modern English drama was ushered into being on the night of May 27th, 1893," the opening night of *The Second Mrs. Tanqueray* ("Introduction," 3). Archer credited Pinero as a leader in the movement to make drama a "mirror of real life" and to dignify play texts as "dramatic literature" (*The Old Drama and the New*, 206, 309). Allardyce Nicoll likewise praised him for naturalistic dialogue and "intimate treatment of life's problems" (*British Drama*, 360).

Shaw's judgment was sharply opposite, deriding Pinero as "a humble and somewhat belated follower of the novelists of the middle of the nineteenth century," one who "has never written a line from which it could be guessed that he is a contemporary of Ibsen, Tolstoi, Meredith, or Sarah Grand" (*TN1*, 45). Regarding Pinero's "pseudo-Ibsen" problem plays, Shaw asserted, the supposed problems were limited to "naughty ladies" and "foregone conclusions of the most heartwearying conventionality concerning sexual morality" (*BH2*, 18).

Shaw's verdicts, as he himself acknowledged, were characteristically vehement and might be best taken with a generous spoonful of salt as one dramatist's dismissal of another whose tastes and methods differed from his own.[1] Nevertheless, his complaints call attention to the ethical assumptions—much opposed to Shaw's—that govern Pinero's plays, and that drew criticism from other observers, even those who hailed Pinero as a theatrical reformer. Archer regretfully judged that "some of Sir Arthur's best work is marred by a failure to keep abreast of moderately enlightened political and philosophic thought" (*The Old Drama and the New*, 290). Hamilton Fyfe agreed, concluding that Pinero "was contented with the old ways" and with his "conventional" way of thinking (*Sir Arthur Pinero's Plays and Players*, 151). In sum, the inherent conservatism of Pinero's plays, particularly on gender issues, led numerous contemporaries to judge that, while such an attitude did not nullify his contributions to the New Drama, it was an unfortunate drawback, an inevitable *but* that must follow any litany of his accomplishments.

More recent scholars, while in general concurring with the claims of these early critics, have also presented a more complex picture of Pinero's contributions to late-Victorian theater and to the social debates of his day. Susan Carlson, Rudolf Weiss, Heather Anne Wozniak, and Michael Meeuwis, among others, have called attention to elements of his dialogue and characterization that complicate the moral rigidity suggested by the plays' outlines. They also consider factors of the Victorian theatrical world that may have shaped the plays, as well as being shaped by them. While earlier critics tended to conclude that Pinero had made important contributions to drama *but* was reactionary on social questions of marriage and gender, these later scholars have considered ways in which his views, reactionary and otherwise, enabled him to navigate the changing theatrical scene of the late nineteenth and early twentieth centuries and make his particular contributions to it. The metatheatrical elements in plays such as *The Second Mrs. Tanqueray*, for example, demonstrate the ways in which Pinero modifies the genres of problem play and comedy of manners and discusses the social performances of fallen and unfallen women, as well as calling attention to the role of fashionable theaters and actor-managers as moral arbiters for the community.[2] In examining the ways in which Pinero used theatrical marriage to comment on social debates and on the theaters for which he wrote, I build on the work of these recent critics.

In the previous chapters, I argued that both Ibsen and Wilde criticized traditional marriage by representing it metatheatrically—that is, by presenting marriage as a play within the play with a husband and wife who conceive their relationship in theatrical terms. In this chapter, I suggest that Pinero used similar metatheatrical devices to present a more conservative perspective on marriage and gender. His plays supported the norms of male authority, female purity and submission, domesticity, and respectability—the values that Ibsen and Wilde had most explicitly challenged—by insisting that successful marriages, like successful plays, must satisfy Society. This is not to say that Society's standards are represented as always right. Audiences (of the marriages and of the plays) receive their share of criticism from Pinero. Yet, the audience's approval, right or wrong, must be won, for to defy their judgment is social (and occasionally literal) death for the observed couples.

Pinero reinforced this dictum by depicting couples who defy and are punished for it. Unlike the respectable and apparently ideal marriages in *A Doll's House* and *Candida*, the marriages in Pinero's social problem plays are often, in one way or another, deliberately unconventional. Some are sham marriages or experimental alternatives to legal marriage. Aubrey Tanqueray, for example, repudiates the sexual double standard by marrying Paula Ray, a woman with a promiscuous past. Agnes Ebbsmith envisions her unwedded partnership with Lucas Cleeve as practical free-love propaganda. Being openly unconventional, these marriages or pseudo-marriages attract scrutiny from acquaintances, and much of the drama consists of couples' efforts to invite or escape this critical inspection. If traditional marriage is to be compared, in Ibsen's plays, to a tarantella or a melodrama, then, Pinero responds, these less-traditional alternatives are no less theatrical, being always observed by "the eyes of the world."

THE WORLD OF ST. JAMES'S

The powerful "world" is personified in Pinero's plays by the friends and neighbors who observe the marriage and serve as an onstage audience to the conjugal spectacle. These secondary characters comment on the marital strife of the protagonists, occasionally attempting to influence events with advice or other intervention. Their efforts to interpret or evaluate the marriage performance mirror the desires of the larger audience in the auditorium, who are invited at once to view the friend and adviser characters as part of the drama's narrative, identify with them as fellow-spectators, and critique their faulty assessments of the marriage under observation.

Cayley Drummle, the self-proclaimed "old-fashioned playgoer" in *The Second Mrs. Tanqueray*, embodies many qualities characteristic of these onstage spectators. In dramatic function, he is in some ways very "old-fashioned" indeed, but these old fashions are revised. Pinero uses dramatic conventions from mid-century melodramatic tradition in ways that defamiliarize those conventions and even the basic practices and assumptions of spectatorship. Cayley fills the role of confidant, a staple function in adapted nineteenth-century French plays, filling the audience in on the details of Aubrey's and Paula's past lives and creating occasions for both to reveal needed information. As Clayton Hamilton noted, Cayley also serves as *raisonneur*, a figure commonly appearing in plays by Dumas *fils*, functioning as mouthpiece for the author ("Introduction," xvii). In keeping with this stage tradition, Pinero puts worldly-wise advice into Cayley's mouth, such maxims as that "of all forms of innocence mere ignorance is the least admirable," and that even "an angel" must get her white robe "a little dusty at the hem" (*AWP1*, 109, 108). These traditional dramatic functions led some critics to dismiss Cayley, as they dismissed Ibsen's Christina Linden, as a theatrical stock type.[3] Yet, as Austin Quigley has observed, Cayley serves not simply as a traditional piece of expositional machinery or a repository for pragmatic sayings, but as a mouthpiece for Society and, presumably, those members of Society attending Pinero's play (*The Modern Stage and Other Worlds*, 75).

As in the previous chapter, I use the term "society" here in two senses: society (lowercase *s*), meaning the public or people in general, and Society (capital *S*), meaning the aristocratic social world, the network which Leonore Davidoff has described as "a system of quasi-kinship relationships," which offered the upper classes a rubric for "the evaluation and placing of newcomers" during the nineteenth and early twentieth centuries (*The Best Circles*, 15–17). Like Wilde, Pinero wrote largely for West End theaters such as St. James's, with titled *dramatis personae* and expensive costumes and scenery, catering to wealthy and aristocratic patrons as well as to prosperous middle-class viewers who idolized the aristocracy. These plays dealt with questions of marriage, gender, and sexual morality that drew discussion from many social levels of late-Victorian Britain. But the stakes and the framing of the discussion—the leisured lifestyles and above all the obsession with reputation and social acceptance—gave the plays' treatment of these issues a marked upper-class slant. Hence, the plays frequently conflate affluent Society with the broader community. It is often unclear to what extent Cayley and the *raisonneurs* of other plays are to be taken as speakers for humanity as a whole or for only an elite section of it.

Pinero calls attention to this ambiguity early in *The Second Mrs. Tanqueray* in a dialogue between Aubrey and Cayley. Aubrey, protesting against Cayley's tacit condemnation of Paula, concludes his protest with,

"Yours is the way of the world," drawing from Cayley the defensive response, "My dear Aubrey, I *live* in the world" (*AWP1*, 77). The world, as these men define it, is in fact a small upper-crust corner of the world, "our little parish of St. James's," as Aubrey retorts (*AWP1*, 77). As Weiss points out, Pinero uses Aubrey's reply to set a limit on the scope of Cayley's "world," rebuking Cayley's tendency to conflate "the world of St. James's" with "the world at large"—hence Cayley's authority as *raisonneur*, the play's chief maker of meaning, is undermined even in this early scene ("Our Little Parish of St. James's," 15). Yet, the reference to "St. James's" also connects Cayley more closely with the audience, or at least did so in the first performance—"St. James's," significantly, is the name not only of the fashionable London parish in which Aubrey and Cayley reside but also of the posh London theater in which George Alexander and Cyril Maude first spoke the lines. Thus, in the first production, the implied identification between Cayley and the audience was made explicit. In watching Cayley evaluate Aubrey and Paula's marriage by the standards of "St. James's," the play's viewers were watching themselves. The *raisonneur*, traditionally the author's mouthpiece, is here designated as the mouthpiece of the audience. The audience is left to infer from the play the extent to which those two perspectives might coincide or diverge.

Cayley is himself unmarried, a fact that Aubrey pointedly notes in the first scene. The same is true of most of the play's secondary characters: Ellean is single, Mrs. Cortelyon widowed. Their singleness offers the privilege of mobility. Ellean and Mrs. Cortelyon move easily from Surrey to Paris and back. Cayley can cover an even wider range, shifting from one domestic scene to another—the Tanquerays' country house, the yachts and flats of Paula's various former lovers, and Lady Orreyed's home in Bruton Street. He is equally welcome in all these settings. He can be in each space without being of it. This semi-nomadic domestic cosmopolitanism is a trait shared by other bachelors who serve as *raisonneurs* in Pinero's later plays, such as Hilary Jesson in *His House in Order* (1906) and Peter Mottram in *Mid-Channel* (1909)—men who, like Cayley, take it upon themselves to observe and improve their friends' troubled marriages, with varying degrees of success. Far from being an impediment to their understanding of married experience, their positions as unattached "spectators in life" are assumed to allow them knowledge unavailable to others (Cayley, for instance, enjoys continued access to the Tanqueray home when the married Jayne and Misquith must stay away to safeguard the harmony of their own domestic spaces). Their singleness is implied to be a neutral position, a performance-free ground from which to observe married (or supposedly married) associates.

The Tanqueray Dinner Theater

These married couples, in contrast to the privileged mobility of bachelor spectators, are confined to their own domestic spaces and often exhibit unease in the consciousness of being watched. This is evident in the first act of *The Second Mrs. Tanqueray* as Cayley asks Aubrey to "keep a stall" for him in the drama of his impending second marriage, and as Cayley's metaphor is reinforced throughout the play.

Aubrey's uneasiness dominates the play's first scene, in which, at a dinner in his flat, he tells of his upcoming wedding to a small group of friends and voices his worry regarding the probable effect of his marriage on their "hearty, unreserved, pre-nuptial friendships" (*AWP1*, 54). After a marriage, he warns them, "a damnable constraint sets in and acts like a wasting disease; and so, believe me, in nine cases out of ten a man's marriage severs for him more close ties than it forms.... [B]ut my marriage isn't even the conventional sort of marriage likely to satisfy society" (*AWP1*, 54). Intending to marry a former outcast, he anticipates censure from "the world" and attempts to circumvent it by removing himself and his wife from London. "I avoid mortification," he tells Cayley, "by shifting from one parish to another. I give up Pall Mall for the Surrey hills" (*AWP1*, 77). In essence, Aubrey wishes to live his married life isolated from critical spectators though he makes an exception for the sympathetic Cayley.

Yet, Aubrey's wish for an unobserved marriage exists alongside an opposing wish for open defiance and for public vindication of that defiance. He promises: "[I]n a few years, Cayley, if you've not quite forsaken me, I'll prove to you that it's possible to rear a life of happiness, of good repute, on a—miserable foundation" (*AWP1*, 78). Aubrey views his decision to marry Paula as, among other things, a social experiment. He aims to level the sexual double standard by allowing a promiscuous woman the same opportunities for social acceptance available to promiscuous men, including Aubrey himself and, the play implies, all men who have led "a man's life" (*AWP1*, 193). Paula, he tells Cayley, is one of the "women who have been roughly treated, and who dare to survive by borrowing a little of our [masculine] philosophy" (*AWP1*, 77). She deserves, he insists, to be valued on her individual merits, as men are, not automatically rejected because of her sexual past. Aubrey hopes to avoid criticism, but he is also eager for recognition—from Cayley, at least—for his marriage's anticipated success, which will justify the social risks he has taken.

Paula wishes differently: the presence of an audience is essential to her vision of married happiness. She wishes for a marriage neither of isolation nor of heroic defiance. She wants to be approved as a good woman in good Society. To be married, in her mind, is to entertain as a married couple, to perform one's marital status for guests. On the eve of the wedding, she describes to Aubrey a dream of a dinner party:

> I saw you at the end of a very long table, opposite me, and we exchanged sly glances now and again over the flowers. We were host and hostess, Aubrey, and had been married about five years.... And on each side of us was the nicest set imaginable—you know, dearest, the sort of men and women that can't be imitated.... But I haven't told you the best part of my dream.... Well, although we had been married only such a few years, I seemed to know by the look on their faces that none of our guests had ever heard anything—anything—anything peculiar about the fascinating hostess. (*AWP1*, 83)

She envisions a scene that combines respectability, affection, and social enjoyment. By serving as hostess to a company of genuine and "nice" people, she expects to confirm her status as a married woman. Yet, the dream oddly echoes what the audience knows of Paula's earlier promiscuous life. It is as a "hostess" that she has made Cayley's acquaintance, officiating at parties with her succession of domestic partners (*AWP1*, 76). By assisting in men's "cursed hospitality" with a politely fictitious "Mrs." affixed to her frequently changing surname, she has superficially acted as wife and in the process become known to her guests as a mistress, a morally questionable, "peculiar" woman (*AWP1*, 75). The party in her dream both re-enacts and reverses these earlier pseudo-marital spectacles, repudiating her false status as Mrs. Jarman, Mrs. Dartry, and so on and publicly announcing her legitimacy as Mrs. Tanqueray.

Paula's dinner party fantasy is grotesquely parodied in the third-act opening scene. All Aubrey's "nice" acquaintances—Misquith, Jayne, and their offstage wives, Mrs. Cortelyon, and even Ellean—have avoided the Tanquerays, knowing Paula's "peculiarity." Paula consequently seeks company in her own circle, inviting her friend Mabel Orreyed, another woman with a transgressive past who, like Paula, has married into high Society. Mabel and her drunken husband, Sir George, are the antithesis of the dinner guests in Paula's dream: far from being "the nicest set imaginable," "the sort of men and women that can't be imitated," they are reminders of her past, described as having nothing pleasant or authentic about them—"*a pretty, affected doll of a woman, with a mincing voice and flaxen hair*" and a man with "*a low forehead, a receding chin, a vacuous expression, and an ominous redness about the nose*" (*AWP1*, 125). The mood, as well as the guests, contrasts with Paula's dream. Coyly concealed tenderness is replaced by forced conviviality. Paula's insistence on inviting the Orreyeds has opened a fresh rift between herself and Aubrey, yet, ironically, the guests' presence is their chief inducement to conceal the rift. Mabel comments on this artificial civility, saying to Paula, "I fancied you and Aubrey were a little more friendly at dinner. You haven't made it up, have you?" Paula replies, "Oh, no. We speak before others, that's all" (*AWP1*, 126–127). Instead of "exchanging sly glances" to telegraph affection without the observation of third parties, they must try to converse in company to veil their hostility.

Pinero's plays, like Wilde's, frequently foreground the inherently theatrical nature of hospitality and social festivities, though the gatherings he depicts are often more intimate than Wilde's, less grandiose. Yet, Pinero's relatively simple social gatherings entail no less performance anxiety for the marital performers than Lady Windermere's crowded ballroom. In presenting a dinner party as a scene of marital tension, Pinero invokes a motif familiar in Victorian literature. Hospitality was an occasion not only for showing off a home's elegance and good taste but also for visibly displaying the host's conformity to ideals of domesticity and family comfort. Nineteenth-century manners guides, such as Agnes H. Morton's *Etiquette*, counseled readers that "The finest hospitality is that which welcomes you to the fireside and permits you to look upon the picture of a home life" and that "The guest should get a correct idea of the home atmosphere" (*Etiquette*, 58, 60–61). Such pieces of advice envisioned hospitality, especially at meals, as a spectacle in which guests evaluated hosts' lifestyles and family relationships.

The pressures faced by hosts and hostesses placing their homes, families, and marriages on display are memorably evoked in more than one piece of mid-Victorian fiction. One thinks of the artificial camaraderie of the Veneering parties and the cynical lovey-dovey displays of Alfred and Sophronia Lammle in *Our Mutual Friend* (1864). A more compact instance of this friction appears in the irony-laden festivity in George

Meredith's *Modern Love* (1862). One early stanza describes the unhappy couple presiding with forced cheerfulness at a dinner party:

> At dinner, she is hostess, I am host.
> Went the feast ever cheerfuller? She keeps
> The Topic over intellectual deeps
> In buoyancy afloat. They see no ghost.

***

> But here's the greater wonder; in that we,
> Enamour'd of our acting and our wits,
> Admire each other like true hypocrites.

***

> We waken envy of our happy lot.
> Fast, sweet, and golden, shows the marriage-knot.
> Dear guests, you now have seen Love's corpse-light shine. (*Modern Love*, stanza 17, lines 1–4, 9–11, 14–16)

The dinners in *The Second Mrs. Tanqueray*—Paula's hopeful dream and the later grim reality—carry pronounced echoes of Meredith's dinner scene, with its lively conversation, affectionate glances, and the festering but decorously masked bitterness that will ultimately drive the heroine (Meredith's as well as Pinero's) to suicide. Though neither Pinero nor Meredith commented on this resemblance, they may well have been conscious of it. Meredith was among the few acquaintances Pinero personally invited to the play's opening night, along with Edmund Gosse, Henry James, and publisher William Heinemann, "the few grown-up people whose word I care for," as Pinero called them (*Collected Letters*, 144).

The host and hostess performing their marriedness at dinner became a familiar trope in the New Drama plays that followed *The Second Mrs. Tanqueray*, often in scenes stiff with irony. Commenting on Henry Arthur Jones's Society comedies, William Archer joked about "Mr. Jones's famous panacea for all the ills of matrimonial life—a little dinner at the Savoy" (*The Old Drama and the New*, 298). Theophila Fraser, protagonist of Pinero's *Benefit of the Doubt* (1895), having lost her reputation by being sued as co-respondent in a friend's divorce case, determines to re-establish herself in Society by hosting a series of parties to "let 'em all see," as she explains to her husband, "that I'm a rattling good indoor, as well as outdoor, wife, and that you're frightfully devoted to me"—a plan her husband rebuffs as "play-acting" (*The Benefit of the Doubt*, 59–60). Shaw extracted humor from the dinner party scene in *You Never Can Tell* (1896) when Mr. Crampton unexpectedly meets his long-estranged wife and children at lunch and is asked to "take the head of the table" (*BH1*, 718). In examining the flaws of traditional marriage, dramatists repeatedly depicted couples hosting at meals and attempting (and generally failing) to give guests a favorable impression of their "home atmosphere."

In *The Second Mrs. Tanqueray*, the dream dinner and the actual dinner mark Paula and Aubrey's failure to secure a sympathetic marriage audience or avoid an unfriendly one. Consequently, their marriage is deteriorating long before the arrival of Paula's ex-lover Hugh Ardale, the coincidence that supplies the play's nominal climax.

Breaking Away from Melodrama

Paula's hopelessness, in fact, is sealed not so much by the entrance of Hugh as Ellean's fiancé, but by Ellean's assertion, in the wake of that discovery, that Paula's guilt is "in [her] face" (*AWP1*, 185). With this declaration, Ellean insists on Paula's inability to become or even appear a "good woman" (*AWP1*, 181). She likewise reaffirms the double standard that Paula and Aubrey have tried to disregard—that is, she denies Paula the forgiveness she has offered to Hugh Ardale for his "man's life" (*AWP1*, 186). Thus, by the measure of Paula's aims and Aubrey's, Ellean declares the marriage a failure.

Ellean's statement serves also to link Paula with the tradition of earlier Victorian melodrama, in which wickedness is assumed to be traceable in a character's physical appearance, in the burnt-cork complexion of the villain or the dark hair and expensive clothes of the villainess (Michael Booth, *English Melodrama*, 1965). Lady Audley, whose story was several times adapted for the stage, was shown in her Pre-Raphaelite portrait to have "a lurid lightness" in her complexion, a "strange, sinister light" in her eyes, a "hard and almost wicked look" in her mouth, and "the aspect of a beautiful fiend" (*Lady Audley's Secret*, 65). Villainesses in melodrama were most often cast in this same mold, blending seductress and demon. In *The Trumpet Call*, for instance, an 1891 Adelphi drama by Robert Buchanan and G. R. Sims, the gypsy temptress Astrea was described by *The Morning*

Post and *The Times* as "fierce, abandoned," "uncanny, necromantic" ("Adelphi Theatre," 6).

Paula's sexual guilt, declared to be "in [her] face," aligning her with the villainesses of melodrama, is thus designated as a quality whose visibility fixes it as the unalterable defining trait in her identity. It places her, in Ellean's judgment, on the wrong side of the sharp dividing line between virtue and sin—a line essential to melodrama and to respectable Victorian social norms. For Ellean, as for Adelphi audiences, as *The Times* expressed it, "there is only the grand distinction of the sheep and the goats, no hybrid specimens of humanity being acknowledged" ("Adelphi Theatre," 6). Ellean's harsh verdict might provoke playgoers to condemn Ellean, the Society she represents, and its unforgiving moral standards (Ellean herself ultimately arrives at this conclusion). But by invoking the earlier theatrical tradition, Pinero at once highlighted its absurdity and fused this older tradition onto a new one. Paula's face serves both as the melodramatic signifier of the transgressive taint that Society attributes to her and as a trigger for her more realistic (albeit exaggerated) anxieties about aging, losing her physical attractions, and forfeiting her husband's affection. Thus, Paula's despair and suicide, driven by Ellean's accusation, present an overwrought melodramatic ending propelled by a modern motive.

It is relevant to recall that Mrs. Patrick Campbell, before creating the role of Paula Tanqueray for George Alexander's company at St. James's Theatre, had been playing villainesses in Buchanan and Sims's melodramas at the Adelphi, among them Astrea in *The Trumpet Call* and Clarice Berton in *The Black Domino*. Seeing her in *The Black Domino*, St. James's designer Graham Robertson observed, "She did not look wicked—a startling innovation. She was almost painfully thin, with great eyes and slow, haunting utterance.... She played weakly, walking listlessly through the part" (*Time Was*, 248). He concluded that with her "interesting" appearance and unconventional acting style, Paula's role "would play itself" (*Time Was*, 248). Pinero, at first viewing, was less impressed by Campbell's departures from stock type and feared that her Adelphi experience would make her a bad fit for a genteel Society drama role. After seeing her in Buchanan and Sims's play, he wrote to George Alexander in language worthy of Henry Higgins, calculating his chances of successfully molding the actress who twenty years later would play Eliza Doolittle:

> Mrs. Patrick Campbell is playing in such a poor piece that it is difficult to form an estimate of her powers. She is however a very interesting actress, so

much makes itself apparent. Whether in a theatre such as yours, and under such good influences as we should hope to bring to bear upon her, she could rid herself of a certain artificiality of style, engendered doubtless by her present situation and surroundings, is a riddle which I cannot pretend to solve. (*Collected Letters*, 142)

Pinero was reluctant to associate Paula with the stereotype of the melodramatic villainess, either through Campbell's past roles or the acting style those roles had fostered. But the other actresses he had considered (among them Ibsen specialists Janet Achurch and Elizabeth Robins and established West End stars Olga Nethersole and Marion Terry) proved unfit or unavailable, and the wicked woman of the Adelphi was ultimately hired.

Whether or not the "good influences" of St. James's Theatre altered Campbell's acting style as Pinero wished, they did not imbue her with awe for her new manager or ensure harmony behind the scenes. The backstage cooperation between Campbell and Alexander reportedly grew every bit as tense as the onstage relationship of their characters. Doris Jones illustrated this dynamic with one telling morsel of theatrical gossip regarding the production of *The Masqueraders*, which followed *Mrs. Tanqueray* at St. James's the subsequent year:

> It is said that Sir George [Alexander] was not on speaking terms with his leading lady, so he wrote to her as follows, "Mr. George Alexander presents his compliments to Mrs. Patrick Campbell and he will be much obliged if she will refrain from laughing at him during the last act." I have been told that her reply was, "Mrs. Patrick Campbell presents her compliments to Mr. George Alexander. He is mistaken, she does not laugh at him during the last act. She waits until she gets home." (*Taking the Curtain Call*, 130)

Despite backstage personality clashes, onstage Campbell continued, as she had done in the Adelphi, to push against the mold of her stereotyped villainess character. In acting Paula's tantrums, for instance, she substituted the violent scripted stage directions with a restrained, understated displeasure, delicately dropping a single ornament to the ground when directed to knock down a shelf-full of them (Joel H. Kaplan, "Pineroticism and the Problem Play," 42). At the same time, Campbell declined to conform to the conventions of Society drama. When the script called for piano playing, instead of the waltzes that made up typical after-dinner drawing-room musical fare, the former Leipzig scholar cleanly executed a Bach invention for the left hand. This unexpected burst of baroque virtuosity, as Joel Kaplan reports, gave rise to speculation among reviewers regarding Paula's strangely scholarly antecedents ("Pineroticism and the Problem Play," 42). The piece also became something of a personal trademark for Campbell. A few years later, reviewing her performance in *Little Eyolf*, Shaw jokingly lamented that Ibsen's agonizing tragedy would be quite delightful if only the set could include a piano so that Campbell could find some occasion to interpolate "that study for the left hand we are all so fond of" (*TN2*, 272). Like the experimental casting choice that placed her in the role of Paula, Campbell's performance decisions connected Paula with the traditions of conventional melodrama and at the same time positioned her outside the confines of melodramatic stock characterization, shaping the role and herself into an individual character and an actress in her own right. Like Mrs. Patrick Campbell, Paula is typecast by her viewers as a "wicked woman," yet resists being contained by that type.

The success with which Campbell played against the grain of the villainous stock type would become central to several of her subsequent well-known characters. As Lady Macbeth she failed, by her own admission. After attempting the "Spirits of Evil" soliloquy in her first scene, she complained to Graham Robertson: "I can't do it. I feel all the time that the woman would not speak like that—she couldn't say such things—*I* shouldn't say such things" (*Time Was*, 251). Yet, she excelled at playing more complicated, humanized transgressive women such as Agnes in Pinero's *Notorious Mrs. Ebbsmith* (1895), with her severe costume and social reform aspirations, belying the image of the "beautiful temptress with peach-blossom cheeks and stained hair," and Lady Hamilton in Risden Home's historical drama *Nelson's Enchantress* (1897), who is portrayed as "respectable" and "lovable" despite being "notoriously a polyandrist" (*AWP1*, 224; *TN3*, 48).[4]

More Genre Trouble

Pinero's tendency to mix dramatic genres had drawn comment long before his experiments with melodramatic devices and casting in *Mrs. Tanqueray*. While still a young actor trying his hand at playwriting for Irving and the Bancrofts, he had earned reproof from Archer for "jumbling...farce and drama not only in the same play, but absolutely in the same scenes," and for "breaking the tension with an irrelevant grotesquery" (*About the Theatre*, 59–60). Referring to Pinero's *Low Water*, Archer explained that "the British public cannot stand the interruption of a scene of vital moment by the entrance of a coal-heaver to shoot a sack of coals into an ottoman; and in this the British public is quite right" (*About the Theatre*, 60). Despite Archer's rebuke, Pinero continued to test the tolerance of the British public in the matter of mingled genres, and in *The Second Mrs. Tanqueray*, the problem of dramatic genre and audience expectation becomes prominent as Paula's marriage spectators evaluate her in a variety of theatrical frameworks, passing judgments which, however superficial or erroneous, nevertheless come to define her.

While Ellean, Mrs. Cortelyon, and the absent friends and neighbors condemn Paula in melodramatic terms as "wicked" or a "mad-woman," Cayley Drummle the playgoer presents another theatrical lens through which to view Paula and her marriage (*AWP1*, 120, 57). On his belated arrival at Aubrey's bachelor dinner, immediately after Aubrey's announcement of his impending wedding, Cayley directs the talk toward another "horrible *mésalliance*," the elopement of the aristocratic Sir George Orreyed with the ill-reputed Mabel Hervey. He uses theatrical language to give a cynically comic description of the mistress-turned-bride:

> To do her justice, she is a type of a class which is immortal. Physically, by the strange caprice of creation, curiously beautiful; mentally, she lacks even the strength of deliberate viciousness. Paint her portrait, it would symbolize a creature perfectly patrician; lance a vein in her superbly-modeled arm, you would get the poorest *vin ordinaire*! Her affections, emotions, impulses, her very existence—a burlesque! Flaxen, five-and-twenty, and feebly frolicsome; anybody's, in less gentle society I should say everybody's, property! That, doctor, was Miss Hervey who is now Lady Orreyed. Dost thou like the picture? (*AWP1*, 61)

Mabel is the immediate subject of the description. Yet by its timing, closely following Aubrey's announcement of his own doubtful marriage, the description is made in his hearers' minds to encompass the entire "class" of unchaste women, particularly Paula. In comparing Mabel (and, by extension, Paula) to a "burlesque," Cayley alludes to a Victorian theatrical genre that specialized in irreverent parodies of highbrow theatrical forms such as Shakespeare and grand opera, as well as less prestigious ones such as sensation melodrama and blackface minstrelsy.[5] Replete with leggy costumes, gender-bending, and songs and dances set to every tune from operatic aria to minstrel melody, burlesque was considered a risqué genre (though far less raunchy than the associations the word now evokes). The comparison reinforces the sexual suggestions in Cayley's description, but the sexual implication is not its only significance. Mabel, like a burlesque performance, resembles something beautiful and admirable, but the resemblance is a cheap substitute for beauty, reducing the thing she imitates—be it love or life itself—to absurdity. She appears "patrician" and "immortal"—a counterfeit classical goddess. This vapid silliness is underscored even in Cayley's language. The thick-laid alliteration and concluding mock-Elizabethan flourish vaguely mimic the language of burlesque, even if he does not reproduce the couplets and strained puns typical of the genre.

When Mabel actually appears onstage in the third act, she seems to correspond to Cayley's "burlesque" description of cheap sex appeal and empty artificiality. The stage directions describe her as "*a pretty, affected doll of a woman*" (*AWP1*, 125). From her own speeches, she appears self-absorbed, very smug about her new aristocratic connections, and her aim in life is to persuade her tippling husband to buy her a diamond tiara (*AWP1*, 125). Framed differently, Pinero's portrayal of Mabel and her marriage with George Orreyed could have been made into an amusing puppet show or cartoon strip, Punch and Judy style, replete with the slapstick of smashed furniture, drunken stumbling, and alternating recriminations and caresses. Juxtaposed with Paula's depression, however, their silliness and pseudo-aristocratic self-contentment only compound the painfulness of the scene, presenting Paula and Aubrey with a mocking caricature of themselves as "the world" perceives them.

Even as Cayley gives his first description of Mabel in the first act, the association between Mabel and Paula in Aubrey's mind is evinced by his heightened discomfort, much as he protests against this association. He becomes, during their early months of married life, convinced that Paula, like Mabel, is unfit as a companion for Ellean, though he has earlier insisted to Cayley that Paula's "shades of goodness, intelligence, even nobility" set her apart from Mabel, despite the two women's similar backgrounds (*AWP1*, 77). Paula herself undercuts Aubrey's assertions of her superiority, keeping up her correspondence with the friend of her former life, calling her "kind-hearted," and declaring that "George Orreyed's wife is not a bit worse than yours" (*AWP1*, 94). During Mabel's visit, however, Paula's attitude toward her shifts. She confides to Cayley, "Somehow or another, I—I've outgrown these people. This woman—I used to think her 'jolly!'—sickens me" (*AWP1*, 135). She becomes disgusted by Mabel's insensitivity and smug shallowness. At the same time, she is miserably conscious of the resemblance that others (Cayley, Aubrey, Ellean) see between Mabel's character and her own. Cayley, in ridiculing Mabel (and by extension, Paula) as a "burlesque" of aristocracy and respectable femininity, has pronounced a judgment that proves self-fulfilling for Mabel and, however inaccurate for Paula, still inescapable.

Even when Cayley attempts to envision Paula and the Tanqueray marriage within a more benign dramatic framework—viewing it as a sentimental comedy in which he hopes for a "happy and comfortable" ending—his playgoer's perspective leads him into error and does damage (*AWP1*, 79). In the third act, in particular, when he counsels Paula to make up her quarrel with Aubrey, he envisions a romantic reconciliation:

> And this would have been such a night to have healed it! Moonlight, the stars, the scent of flowers; and yet enough darkness to enable a kind woman to rest her hand for an instant on the arm of a good fellow who loves her. Ah, ha! It's a wonderful power, dear Mrs. Aubrey, the power of an offended woman! Only realize it! Just that one touch—the mere tips of her fingers—and, for herself and another, she changes the color of the whole world. (*AWP1*, 133–134)

The saccharine clichés with which Cayley attempts to write a happy ending provoke Paula to compare him to "a very romantic old lady" (*AWP1*, 134). Yet, she does take his advice to return the letters she has hidden from Aubrey and to attempt a rapprochement.

From Cayley's viewpoint, this is essentially the end of the play. In these final scenes, there are two plays unfolding simultaneously: the tragedy of discovery that culminates in Paula's suicide and the gentle domestic comedy of Cayley's imagination. The next time he appears onstage, ignorant of Ellean's return, her romance with Hugh, and Hugh's past liaison with Paula, it is only to ask whether Paula and Aubrey are "good friends again," to be told, "quite, Cayley, quite," and to exit again, satisfied (*AWP1*, 171). When he returns for the last time, "*singing as he approaches the house,*" he anticipates only a romantic finale in which the restored harmony between Paula and Aubrey is rendered unexpectedly festive by the happy engagement of Ellean—both events that he, Cayley, has assisted, directly or indirectly (*AWP1*, 192). His cheerful expectations clash against the devastating facts with a darkly humorous absurdity, like the joyful shouts of the "saved" Torvald Helmer met by Nora's disillusioned silence. Aubrey, instead of thanking Cayley, reproaches him for arranging Ellean's removal, following his reproach with an explosive tirade against Hugh Ardale and men in general. Paula's suicide crushes Cayley's imagined finale with startling irrelevance, though it appears inevitable to audiences who have seen the Tanqueray marriage slowly deteriorate. Cayley's sentimental comedy view has proven as unsatisfactory in describing the facts as Ellean's melodramatic one. And it proves almost equally destructive. Paula's last words onstage are, "That's Cayley, coming back from the Warren. He doesn't know, evidently. I—I won't see him" (*AWP1*, 192). In her despair, Paula exits the room and exits life to escape Cayley, his singing, and the impending collision between his happy-ending fantasy and her disastrous reality. Cayley's optimistic spectatorship, like the unmerciful observation of Ellean, has "helped to kill her" (*AWP1*, 195).

Throughout the play, Ellean, Cayley, and the other onstage spectators, together with the spectators in the auditorium, become the arbiters for Aubrey's (and Pinero's) experiment in the sexually equal marriage, in which a woman's past is to be pardoned as freely as a man's customarily is. The experiment is declared a failure by the onstage viewers, and Paula suffers the usual fate of the woman with a past. The failure of the Tanqueray marriage reform takes on extra significance when compared with another experimental marriage that Pinero had dramatized a few years earlier in *The Profligate*, a play produced by John Hare at the Garrick Theatre in April 1889. Pinero described the play as a bold attempt "to test how far theatrical audiences were really prepared to accept serious drama without 'comic relief,'" and he pointedly noted that it was written a good two years before Ibsen's work made its first appearance in a professional English production (*The Profligate*, vi). The play depicts the reformed philanderer Dunstan Renshaw marrying the pure young Leslie Brudenell (who is unaware of her husband's sexual history). When the wife later discovers her husband's guilt, she separates from him, and he commits suicide. The fallen man thus receives the rejection and condemnation traditionally meted out to his female counterpart. Hare, however, requested an alternate ending to accommodate "the popular prejudice in favour of theatrical happiness in the last act of new plays" (*The Profligate*, vii). Pinero complied, though he reinstated the original tragic ending when the play was published by Heinemann two years later. The stage ending allowed the wife to arrive just in time to prevent the suicide and forgive the repentant husband, while in the printed ending she arrives a minute too late. The happy alternate ending gained widespread critical approval, confirming

Hare's intuition that where male transgressors were concerned, audiences preferred pardon to ostracism.

In *The Second Mrs. Tanqueray*, Pinero depicted an attempt to modify the double standard in the opposite direction: rather than subjecting a transgressive man to the same strict standards and punishments as a transgressive woman, Aubrey proposes to offer a woman the indulgence usually reserved for men. The marriage spectators, Ellean chief among them, reject such leniency, and even Aubrey's attitude toward Paula's past becomes less tolerant over the course of the play. Paula dies accordingly, and despite Ellean's remorse, neither George Alexander nor the critics demanded her resurrection. Thus, in both plays, public opinion was depicted as an ultimately impassable obstacle to any effort toward more equal sexual norms. The same is true in Pinero's later Society dramas, such as *The Gay Lord Quex* (1899) and *Mid-Channel* (1909), in both of which women are punished (or at least threatened with punishment) for their adulteries while men pass unscathed.

Conclusion

Nora's marriage is theatrical in that it is modeled around the conventions of traditional theatrical genres. The same is true in *The Second Mrs. Tanqueray*: marriages are defined by conventions of melodrama, burlesque, comedy, and tragedy, as well as by quasi-theatrical social performances such as divorce court speeches and dinner parties. But for Paula, a theatrical marriage means not simply an affinity with a particular genre, but most of all a marriage that is watched, presented to the "eyes of the world."

The concept of marriage as public, as enacted before an audience, did not originate with Pinero, Wilde, Ibsen, or the Victorians. The longstanding custom of including witnesses at a wedding service—those who, if they speak now and do not forever hold their peace, have the power to impede the marriage—serves as a built-in reminder that the marriage relationship is always under the eyes of society, subject to its approval. Yet, during the nineteenth century, this state of marriage under observation had become (like numerous other aspects of conventional marriage) a source of widely expressed unease in the works of social reformers, as well as in the fiction of Meredith, Dickens, and others. Writers of fiction and nonfiction feared that the marriage audience might be a coercive presence, requiring "proper" behavior regardless of inclination or authenticity.

Writers, such as Mona Caird, suggested the possibility of a more "private" form of marriage—that is, more individualized marriage contracts suited to the requirements of each couple, and a surrounding society that would hold back from close observation or criticism, respecting the rights of other couples to be married on their own terms ("Marriage," 198).

For Pinero, the ideas of a marriage performance and a marriage audience offered dramatic opportunities for psychological tension in scenes depicting anxious spouses questioning the opinions of their neighbors, as well as the curiosity and perplexity of those same neighbors. By commenting on current debates about sex, gender, marriage, and possible alternatives to marriage, he appealed to spectators interested in these discussions, eager for "up to date" entertainment. The idea of theatrical marriage also offered a convenient focal point for exploring his concerns with the relationships between old theater conventions and new ones, between the stage and the offstage world, as he made new uses of old theatrical devices. His marriage-spectator characters often fulfill the traditional dramatic functions of the confidant and the *raisonneur* in the well-made play. They assist with the exposition in the play's beginning, present the play's moral, or give the protagonists excuses to reveal needed information. Yet, Pinero expanded these characters beyond their expected mechanical functions. Through their observations and critiques of the protagonists and their marriages, they become identified with the audience, sharing in the satisfactions and frustrations of spectatorship. The influences these onstage viewers exert over the marriage spectacle are in many ways analogous to the influences of the audience over the plays and those who produced them. Pinero underscores this analogy with references to characters as "old-fashioned play-goers" and with the theatrical language in which marriage is often discussed in his plays. Like theatrical audiences, marriage audiences expect the spectacle and the people who present it to follow predetermined conventions—conventions of masculine authority and chivalry, female submission and chastity, and general harmony and easy resolution of all disputes. Wives and husbands who refuse to comply with these conventions risk misconstruction and consequent failure. The spectators have the last word, often literally as well as figuratively.

NOTES

1. Shaw's more acrid reviews of Pinero were carefully laced with disclaimers, as, for example, in his conclusion on *The Notorious Mrs. Ebbsmith*: "Many passages of the play, of course, have all the qualities which have gained Mr. Pinero his position as a dramatist; but I shall not dwell on them, as, to tell the truth, I disliked the play so much that nothing would induce me to say anything good of it" (*TN1*, 65).
2. See, for example, Susan L. Carlson, "Two Genres and Their Women: The Problem Play and the Comedy of Manners in the Edwardian Theatre"; Heather Anne Wozniak, "The Play with a Past: Arthur Wing Pinero's New Drama"; and Rudolf Weiss, "'Our Little Parish of St. James's': Centrality, Orthodoxy and Self-Reflexivity in the 1890s London Theatre."
3. For comments on the ways in which Mrs. Linden follows and diverges from the traditional confidant role in *A Doll's House*, see Chap. 2.
4. In "Lady Hamilton, *Nelson's Enchantress*, and the Creation of Pygmalion," Jesse Hellman gives a fascinating account of the production and reception of *Nelson's Enchantress*, discussing its importance in the relationship between Shaw and Campbell and suggesting Home's portrayal of Lady Hamilton as a possible prototype for Eliza Doolittle.
5. For details on burlesque conventions, as well as some samples of the genre, see Richard W. Schoch, *Victorian Theatrical Burlesques*.

REFERENCES

"Adelphi Theatre." *The Morning Post*, August 3, 1891a.
———." *The Times*, August 3, 1891b.
Archer, William. *About the Theatre*. London: Unwin, 1886.
———. *The Old Drama and the New*. Boston: Small, Maynard, & Co., 1923.
Booth, Michael. *English Melodrama*. London: Jenkins, 1965.
Braddon, Mary Elizabeth. *Lady Audley's Secret*. Edited by Pyckett Lyn. Oxford: Oxford University Press, 2012.
Caird, Mona. "Marriage." *The Westminster Review*, December 1888.
Carlson, Susan L. "Two Genres and Their Women: The Problem Play and the Comedy of Manners in the Edwardian Theatre." *The Midwest Quarterly* 24, no. 4 (1985): 413–24.
Davidoff, Leonore. *The Best Circles: Women and Society in Victorian England*. Totowa, NJ: Rowman & Littlefield, 1973.
Fyfe, Hamilton. *Sir Arthur Pinero's Plays and Players*. London: Ernest Benn, 1930.
Hamilton, Clayton. "Introduction." In *The Social Plays of Arthur Wing Pinero*, by Arthur Wing Pinero and edited by Clayton Hamilton, 3–36. New York: Dutton, 1917.

Hellman, Jesse. "Lady Hamilton, *Nelson's Enchantress*, and the Creation of Pygmalion." *SHAW: The Journal of Bernard Shaw Studies* 36, no. 2 (2015): 213–37.

Hutton, R. H. "Mr. George Meredith's 'Modern Love.'" In *Modern Love and the Poems of the English Roadside, with Poems and Ballads*, edited by Rebecca N. Mitchell and Criscillia Benford, 180–84. New Haven: Yale University Press, 2012.

Jones, Doris Arthur. *Taking the Curtain Call: The Life and Letters of Henry Arthur Jones*. New York: Macmillan, 1930.

Kaplan, Joel H. "Pineroticism and the Problem Play: Mrs. Tanqueray, Mrs. Ebbsmith, and 'Mrs. Pat.'" In *British Theatre in the 1890s*, edited by Richard Foulkes, 38–58. Cambridge: Cambridge University Press, 1992.

Meeuwis, Michael. "Representative Government: The 'Problem Play,' Quotidian Culture, and the Making of Social Liberalism." *ELH* 80, no. 4 (2013): 1093–120.

Meredith, George. *Modern Love*. In *Modern Love and the Poems of the English Roadside, with Poems and Ballads*, edited by Rebecca N. Mitchell and Criscillia Benford, 21–72. New Haven: Yale University Press, 2012.

Morton, Agnes H. *Etiquette: Good Manners for All People*. Philadelphia: Penn, 1892.

Nicoll, Allardyce. *British Drama*. New York: Crowell, 1925.

Pinero, Arthur Wing. *The Benefit of the Doubt*. Rahway, NJ: Mershon, 1895.

———. *The Collected Letters of Sir Arthur Pinero*. Edited by J. P. Wearing. Minneapolis: University of Minnesota Press, 1974.

———. *The Profligate*. London: Heinemann, 1891.

———. *The Social Plays of Arthur Wing Pinero*. Edited by Clayton Hamilton. 4 vols. New York: Dutton, 1917.

Quigley, Austin E. *The Modern Stage and Other Worlds*. New York: Methuen, 1985.

Robertson, Graham. *Time Was*. London: Quartet, 1981.

Schoch, Richard W. *Victorian Theatrical Burlesques*. Burlington, VT: Ashgate, 2003.

Shaw, Bernard. *Our Theatres in the Nineties*. 3 vols. London: Constable, 1932.

———. *The Bodley Head Bernard Shaw: Collected Plays with Their Prefaces*. Edited by Dan H. Laurence. 7 vols. London: The Bodley Head, 1970.

Weiss, Rudolf. "'Our Little Parish of St. James's': Centrality, Orthodoxy and Self-Reflexivity in the 1890s London Theatre." *Prague Journal of English Studies* 1, no. 1 (2012): 9–23.

Wozniak, Heather Anne. "The Play with a Past: Arthur Wing Pinero's New Drama." *Victorian Literature and Culture* 37, no. 2 (2009): 391–409.

CHAPTER 5

Henry Arthur Jones and the Business of Morality

In 1884, five years before *A Doll's House* made its professional English debut, *Breaking a Butterfly*, a play "founded on Ibsen's *Nora*" made its appearance at the Prince's Theatre. Henry Arthur Jones, who wrote the play in collaboration with Henry Herman, described it as an effort to turn the grim original into a "sympathetic play" (qtd. in Richard Cordell, *Henry Arthur Jones and the Modern Drama*, 52). William Archer, reviewing the play for *Theatre*, took it as an opportunity to debate on the tastes of British audiences and the merits of theatrical sympathy: "[I]n making their work sympathetic they [Herman and Jones] at once made it trivial. I am the last to blame them for doing so. Ibsen on the English stage is impossible. He must be trivialized" ("Breaking a Butterfly," 214). Jones countered that the fault of Ibsen's unpopularity in England lay with Ibsen, not the British public. He called Nora "the first of the tiresome hussies," and added that "*The Doll's House* should have ended with the husband helping himself to a whiskey-and-soda and saying, 'Thank God, she's gone'" (qtd. in Doris Jones, *Taking the Curtain Call*, 172).

A decade after *Breaking a Butterfly*, Jones was widely recognized, along with Pinero, as one of the leading dramatists of London's fashionable theaters, including St. James's, the Haymarket, and especially the Criterion. To Jones, Ibsen and his small circle of English enthusiasts were emblematic of "modern pessimistic realism, its littleness, its ugliness, its narrowness, its parochial aims" (*The Renascence of the English Drama*, ix). He was impatient with what he saw as Ibsen's didacticism and his fixation on the

© The Author(s) 2020
M. Christian, *Marriage and Late-Victorian Dramatists*, Bernard Shaw and His Contemporaries,
https://doi.org/10.1007/978-3-030-40639-4_5

103

unpleasant facts of life. He insisted that though drama should teach, "it should never teach directly and with a set purpose; if it does, it is meddlesome, intolerant, irritating, and tiresome. Briefly we may say, it should teach, but it should never preach" (*The Renascence of the English Drama*, 304–305). He reinforced this disavowal of pedantry in likening English drama to a "family friend," one who might congenially sympathize and wisely advise, but never be openly didactic (qtd. in Richard Cordell, *Henry Arthur Jones and the Modern Drama*, 59).

Yet with all his dislike of "pessimistic realism," he made a sharp distinction between "realism" and "truth"—between "small and arid facts" and "the great permanent realities of life" (*The Foundations of a National Drama*, 141). He argued that the art of playwriting required "the most severe, the most faithful, the most searching, the most *truthful* portraiture of modern life" (*The Renascence of the English Drama*, 88). Such truthful drama, he insisted, required dramatists to be more knowledgeable of science, religion, current events, and human lives. Plays must be respected, protected, and paid for as "a great national art and influence," and spectators, he argued, must know something of character development and plot construction, so as to come to the theater looking for artistry and ideas as well as fun (*The Renascence of the English Drama*, 23). He delivered lectures on playwriting and playgoing at the City of London College and elsewhere, and offered advice to novice playwrights. Shaw, beginning to write plays in the 1890s, more than once turned to Jones for guidance on royalty negotiations, apologetically explaining, "I have to ask you because you are the only person I know whose business faculty inspires me with the smallest confidence" (*CLS1* 420, 430). To Jones, the effort toward a more truthful theater was a multipronged campaign, entailing playwriting and publication, educating the public, and fostering support and organization within the playwriting community.

His insistence on theatrical "truth" and "reality" earned him the ridicule of Wilde, being sharply opposed to Wilde's artistic doctrines as set out in "The Decay of Lying." Among his own family and friends, Jones reportedly enjoyed quoting what he called Wilde's three rules for playwriting: "The first rule is not to write like Henry Arthur Jones, the second and third rules are the same!" (qtd. in Doris Jones, *Taking the Curtain Call*, 156).[1] Whether Wilde's so-called rules were Wilde's invention or Jones's, the sentiment behind them is consistent with the view Wilde expressed in an 1894 letter to actor-manager George Alexander, soon after Alexander had publicly praised Jones and Pinero for their contributions to English drama at a banquet in Birmingham. "I know and admire Pinero's work," Wilde wrote, "but who is Jones?...I have never heard of Jones. Have you?" (qtd. in Doris Jones, *Taking the Curtain Call*, 183). Shaw's assessment was more sympathetic. While he readily noted plot points and characters that struck him as illogical, he wrote in one review that "Mr Jones's plays are far more faulty than those of most of his competitors, exactly as a row of men is more faulty than a row of lampposts turned out by a first-rate firm" (*TN1*, 123).

Jones's concern for truth in playwriting led him, in many of his plays, to examine questions of human hypocrisy and concealment, as a brief survey of his play titles suggests—*Humbug* (1880), *The Masqueraders* (1894), *The Rogue's Comedy* (1896), *The Liars* (1897), *Whitewashing Julia* (1903), *The Hypocrites* (1906), *Dolly Reforming Herself* (1908), *We Can't be as Bad as All That* (1910), and *The Lie* (1914), to name a few. In many of these plays, issues of marriage, courtship, and sex offered an opportunity to explore the ideas of authenticity and façade, while at the same time attracting popular interest by discussing issues of current debate.

Like Pinero's and Wilde's works, Jones's plays often focus on marriages under the scrutiny of aristocratic Society—both the onstage fellow-characters and the upper-class spectators of St. James's, the Criterion, and Wyndham's Theatre. His plays, like theirs, frequently feature a bachelor *raisonneur* and a Greek chorus of partygoers who comment on the central couple. As in Pinero's plays, Jones's discussions on marriage, sex, and gender are generally resolved on the side of orthodoxy, whether through religious calls to virtue or pragmatic appeals to convenience. Yet these conventional resolutions seldom go entirely uncontested, either by performers, critics, or the characters themselves. Jones's plays thus offer insight not only on subtly shifting attitudes toward traditional marriage, authenticity, and performance but also on the tensions and negotiations between author, manager, actors, audiences, and critics that shaped performances in the fashionable London theaters of the 1890s.

DUTY AND ANDROMEDA

When *The Second Mrs. Tanqueray* concluded its long run at the St. James's Theatre in April 1894, it was succeeded by Jones's romance *The Masqueraders*, the first of several of Jones's plays to be produced by George Alexander. The play combines the melodramatic heroes, villains, and sensation scenes of Jones's early career with the leisurely drawing-room badinage expected in a fashionable Society play. The plot centers on a chivalrous astronomer, David Remon (played by Alexander), and his love for Dulcie Larondie (played by Mrs. Patrick Campbell), a well-born young woman whose poverty and orphanhood have forced her to take employment as a barmaid in a village inn. Dulcie initially dismisses the socially inept David and marries the wealthy baronet Sir Brice Skene (played by Herbert Waring) to escape the servitude of working for her living. Four years later, her husband, who has gambled away his property and become a confirmed drunkard, allows David the chance to win his wife and child in a card game. In a spectacular climax, David wins, declares Dulcie his wife, and settles her and her child in his observatory, out of Sir Brice's reach. However, rather than consummate their loving but unlawful union, David preserves Dulcie's purity by leaving her and setting out on an astronomical exploration in Africa.

The drama of Dulcie's marriage, like Lady Windermere's, unfolds amid a series of elegant social gatherings, surrounded by an assortment of fashionable, flippant aristocrats who observe the protagonists' love triangle as well as engaging in their own flirtations and intrigues. One partygoer, Montague Lushington, indulges in worldly witticisms throughout the play, announcing: "I find this world a remarkably comfortable and well-arranged place. I always do exactly as I like…. I am consistently selfish, and I find it pays; I credit everybody else with the same consistent selfishness, and I am never deceived in my estimate of character" (*MAS*, 60–61). The play invites the audience to take Lushington's cheerful cynicism as a general creed of the upper class. The shallowness, hypocrisy, and superficial respectability of these upper-class extras identify them early in the play as the "masqueraders" of the title. Early in the play, as David observes dancers at a ball, he muses: "They are only masquerading. Good God, I think we are all masquerading! Look at them! If you touched them with reality they would vanish" (*MAS*, 57).

The philosophy of the fashionable world, as expounded by Lushington, is most prominently on display in a sensational auction scene near the end of the first act. Dulcie, in the bar where she works, attempts to collect donations for the widow and orphans of a local man who has recently died in a riding accident. When one patron jokingly suggests that Dulcie raise the money by auctioning a kiss to the highest bidder, other men readily endorse the suggestion and open the bidding, ignoring Dulcie's protests. Lushington, as self-appointed auctioneer, justifies the sale by pointing out the ways in which sex is routinely commodified:

In an age when, as all good moralists lament, love is so often brought into the market, the marriage market—and other markets—and is sold to the highest bidder, it would, I am convinced, require a far more alarming outrage on propriety than that which we are now about to commit, to cause the now obsolete and unfashionable blush of shame to mount into the now obsolete and unfashionable cheek of modesty. (*MAS*, 30)

Lushington's cool rationalization of love in the market carries echoes of the famous slave auction tableau in Dion Boucicault's *The Octoroon* (1859), in which Zoe, the eponymous octoroon, stands atop the auction table as hero and villain fight to own her—an iconic image of masculine rivalry and female helplessness. Jones's melodrama presents a less violent version of the scene, in which the object up for auction is a single kiss. Nevertheless, the public sale graphically illustrates the vulnerability of Dulcie as a young, unmarried, moneyless woman, and the partygoers' indifference to her humiliation reveals an uglier side to their lighthearted *bons mots*.

Dulcie repeatedly refuses to participate in what she sees as prostitution, and, after Sir Brice outbids all competitors, she is only persuaded to accept his check for her charity when he adds to it a public marriage proposal. Sir Brice makes the proposal ostensibly to "save any further misconstruction," but in the context of the auction, it is an ambiguous offer (*MAS*, 34). It might be taken (as Dulcie evidently takes it) to legitimize the transaction and affirm her virtue. Yet, in the light of Lushington's earlier speech about the marriage market, the proposal might be seen as a continuation of the sexual bargaining, a simple raising of the price. Though Shaw did not comment on this scene, one can easily imagine him recalling the words he had penned for Kitty Warren a year before: "As if a marriage ceremony could make any difference in the right or wrong of the thing!" (*BH1*, 313). The auction's outcome, while purportedly certifying Dulcie's virtue and establishing her as a prominent hostess in the masquerading world she covets, ultimately leaves her as powerless as ever, if not more so.

The "masqueraders," led by Lushington, serve throughout the play as foils for the more earnest characters—in particular, for Dulcie's sister and confidant, Helen Larondie. A pious hospital nurse who preaches and practices duty, Helen insists that "the secret of living" is to "Forget yourself. Deny yourself. Renounce yourself" (*MAS*, 20). While Lushington and the other party guests comment on Dulcie and her marriage from a cynical, worldly-wise perspective, Helen presents a contrapuntal moral commentary. Early in the first act, as Dulcie fantasizes about making a wealthy marriage and encourages the attentions of Sir Brice Skene, Helen warns her, "He's not a good man" (*MAS*, 22–23). In subsequent acts, when Dulcie has disregarded her sister's advice and her husband has shown his true colors as a bankrupt bully, Helen reminds her of "The wife's duty" (*MAS*, 87). When Sir Brice, to feed his gambling addiction, orders his wife to wheedle money from her wealthy admirer even if she must offer sexual favors in return, Dulcie contemplates flight, but Helen continues to insist that Dulcie's duty is "To her husband to keep her vows. To herself to keep herself pure and stainless, because it is her glory.... And to society, to her nation, because no nation has ever survived whose women have been immoral" (*MAS*, 87–88). When, in the climactic card game, David claims Dulcie as his wife, Helen makes no effort to prevent her sister from accompanying him to his observatory. Yet even in the end, she urges David to leave Dulcie, to "keep her pure for her child" (*MAS*, 111). To this final plea, David's eccentric but loyal younger brother interjects, "That's God's voice speaking to you now, Davy" (*MAS*, 111). David yields, though he chastely promises to meet Dulcie in a future life in the far-off galaxy of Andromeda, where "All's real" (*MAS*, 113). Helen's deciding influence in the play's outcome, together with her sisterly devotion throughout the play, suggest that the playgoers, like David, are meant to accept her pronouncements on marriage and morality as authoritative.

Whether audiences did accept this authority is another question. The play had a successful run of 139 performances, and the fairy-tale aspects of plot and character were widely praised, as was Mrs. Patrick Campbell's acting. Archer, reviewing the play for *The World*, called the love story "infinitely pleasing" (*The Theatrical "World" of 1894*, 133). Ellen Terry, having read a copy of the script, sent Jones a glowing letter: "That girl!! Dulcie—she *lives*—her heartbreak is so true—her DEVILMENT so entrancing—enchanting—she's a Woman and a Fairy. She's a Witch—she's a Devil—an Angel—no, a Woman—and you're a *magic man*" (Qtd. in Doris Jones, *Taking the Curtain Call*, 125). Yet critics chafed at the moralizing conclusion. Archer confessed: "In my own unregenerate heart I hope, and even believe, that Dulcie and David ultimately foregather somewhere on this side of Andromeda" (*The Theatrical "World" of 1894*, 135). Shaw vehemently denounced Helen in a letter to Jones: "I believe you faked up that atrocious nurse for the express purpose of infuriating me.... Every one of that woman's allusions to duty elicited a howl of rage from me. She morally outrages my tenderest sensibilities" (*CLS1*, 443).

More broadly, Shaw disliked the grim moral perspective embodied in the contrast between Helen and the masquerading partygoers. He exclaimed, "Hang it all, Regent's Park, with all its drawbacks, is better than Andromeda. Why don't you chuck up these idiotic moral systems according to which human nature comes out base and filthy? It's the systems that are wrong and not we" (*CLS1*, 444).

The contrasting reactions the play provoked are perhaps not surprising, given the stark contrasts of the play itself, which juxtaposes fairy-tale romance, satiric comedy, and sermon-like moral exhortations. Fantasy, sentiment, irreverent humor, and earnest homily seem to compete for control of the play, without any one genre gaining a clear upper hand. Helen is presented, seemingly without irony, as a model of womanly goodness and selflessness, and her calls to duty ultimately determine the outcome of the play. Yet her authority is equivocal, given that, in the contest for viewers' interest and sympathy, the masquerading hedonists and the indefatigably devoted lover come out decidedly in front.

The tension is most pronounced in the third act, when the unmarried Helen lengthily outlines "the wife's duty" for her sister, reciting abstractions while saying nothing of the concrete circumstances that render Dulcie's marriage unbearable—her husband's alcoholism and gambling addiction, his threat to separate her from her child, his demand that she supply him with money even at the cost of prostituting herself. When challenged by Dulcie's questions regarding the husband's duty, Helen only responds, "I don't know whether it's a man's duty to be moral. I'm sure it's a woman's" (*MAS*, 88). Dulcie, maddened, launches into an anti-idealistic tirade that might have come from the mouth of Mrs. Alving, or from Shaw's *Quintessence*: "Moral! Moral!! Moral!!! Is there anything under God's sun so immoral, ah—guess it—guess it—to be married to a man one hates! And you go on plastering it and poulticing it and sugaring it over with 'moral' and 'ideal' and 'respectable,' and all those words that men use to cheat themselves with" (*MAS*, 88). The stage directions mark "*A long pause*" to follow Dulcie's speech, and Helen evidently has no answer ready (*MAS*, 88). Yet despite this seeming inadequacy of Helen's logic, her role as the play's ethical spokesperson is upheld in the play's conclusion.

This clash between Helen's moral authority and the never-fully-rebutted challenges to it reappears, with variations, in several of Jones's later plays. A married (or apparently married) couple faces trouble and is steered back into the path of respectability by an adviser figure (generally unmarried). Yet Jones modified his later *raisonneurs*: whereas Helen's moral voice is pitted both against the romantic longings of David and Dulcie and against the frivolity of the upper-class masqueraders, in his later plays, masquerade and morality are presented almost as synonymous. These later proponents of respectable marriage performance are generally male, hold prestigious titles, and occupy authoritative professional posts as lawyers, judges, or military officers. Though sometimes long-winded, these bachelor-spectators deliver their lectures with wit and good humor, appealing more to convenience than to virtue. Hence, rather than forcing instruction and amusement to compete, as *The Masqueraders* had done, Jones's later plays center both qualities in one character, supplementing moral and intellectual authority with that of patriarchy, law, and empire. Troubled marriages (or would-be marriages), together with the wise bachelor who sets them right, became signature features in some of the best-known of Jones's works, *The Case of Rebellious Susan* (1894), *The Liars* (1897), and *Mrs. Dane's Defence* (1900), plays written for Charles Wyndham, actor-manager at the Criterion, and later at his own namesake, Wyndham's Theatre.

THE INFALLIBLE BACHELOR

Charles Wyndham was an acclaimed gentlemanly comedian, popular with the aristocracy and some members of the royal family. In 1902, he would be knighted by Edward VII, the third British actor to be given that honor. In his younger years, he had specialized in humorous rake and trickster roles in plays such as *London Assurance*, *Wild Oats*, and *The Man With Three Wives*. Shaw wrote *The Philanderer*, and Wilde *The Importance of Being Earnest*, with him in mind, though he never acted in either play (George Rowell, "Criteria for Comedy," 36–37). He continued to play youthful comic or romantic characters such as Charles Surface in *The School for Scandal* well into his fifties, drawing from Henry Irving the mocking suggestion: "I say, Wyndham, why don't you do Little Lord Fauntleroy?" (Elizabeth Robins, *Both Sides*, 200).[2] Elizabeth Robins, newly arrived in England and just beginning to immerse herself in Ibsen, gave a similarly unflattering judgment: "I thought [Wyndham] too old and ravaged and rasping to play lovers; but secure in his own Theatre he was going on and on and on" (*Both Sides*, 200).

By the 1890s, however, as he approached sixty, Wyndham had transitioned toward a more respectable brand of comedy, taking roles that positioned him as the dignified and charming champion of patriarchal values. This shift enhanced both the respectability of his management and his popularity with upper-class audiences. Florence Teignmouth Shore, an early biographer, praised this persona of middle-aged gentlemanly comedian, declaring: "He has all the time such a twinkle in his eye, such humorous curves around his lips, and there is so much *savoir faire* and experience at the back of the twinkle, so much belief in and regard for human nature in the smile.... He is suave, persuasive, tender by turns; he has all the good qualities of the English gentleman on the stage" (*Sir Charles Wyndham*, 39). Shore, writing in 1908 as the women's suffrage movement gathered momentum, reported that

> He has a whimsical, half tender, wholly delightful way of scolding pretty women.... He always suggests such chivalry, such an almost old-fashioned courtesy and deference to women, that it is no wonder he is so popular with the sex, who while they loudly demand women's rights, mounting platforms and rostrums, are always susceptible to those delicate attentions which are not women's rights but their privileges. (*Sir Charles Wyndham*, 39)

With urbane charm, Wyndham retained popularity even among women's rights supporters who might well have chafed at hearing his characters proclaim that "this tiresome sexual business...was settled once for all in the Garden of Eden" (*HAJ2*, 350).

Jones's plays helped Wyndham to cultivate this persona of mature masculinity. Jones's *raisonneurs*, with their paternal didacticism tempered by wit and occasional sentiment, reinforced Wyndham's courtly image even as Wyndham's acting enabled some of the greatest successes of Jones's playwriting career.

About six months after the first production of *The Masqueraders*, *The Case of Rebellious Susan* opened under Wyndham's management at the Criterion Theatre on October 3, 1894. The play features Lady Susan Harabin, who, angered by her husband's infidelity, determines to "pay him back in his own coin," not to forgive him "till I have something to be forgiven on my side" (*HAJ2*, 276, 284). Susan's rebellion against Victorian sexual mores, however, proves even less successful than the Tanquerays' because Susan, like Paula and Aubrey, is ambivalent toward the fact that she is being watched. In the heat of her resentment, after her first discovery of her husband's guilt, she threatens to brave public opinion and even to court notoriety: "And in a few days all my friends will be saying, 'Look at poor dear Lady Sue!' They shan't say that. They shall say, 'Look at poor dear Jim Harabin!'" (*HAJ2*, 277). Months later, however, after she has succeeded in finding "a little romance" in Cairo with the young expatriate Lucien Edensor, she is much less indifferent to the prospect of exposure. She involves herself in a web of lies and evasions to conceal her flirtation from her friends, and declares to her lover, "Oh, I should kill myself if anyone knew!" (*HAJ2*, 308). Jones presents Susan's "rebelliousness" as a pose adopted by a fundamentally conventional woman. When her temper is piqued, she might set out to reform the world and walk out on her husband, Nora-like, but she loses her bravado when disgrace threatens.

This threat is pressed on her chiefly by her uncle, Sir Richard Kato, Q. C. (played by Wyndham), who assumes the role of adviser, mediator, and general spokesman for respectability (*HAJ2*, 276). As a veteran divorce court lawyer, he boasts: "I've never been *married*. But I've had twenty-five years' practice in the Divorce Court, and if I'm not qualified to give advice in a matter of this kind, I don't know any man in England who is" (*HAJ2*, 279). As he evaluates and monitors Susan's marital strife, he positions himself as a mouthpiece for Society and the law. Hence, as an audience to the marriage spectacle, he begins the play with far more official authority than Nurse Helen, Pinero's "old-fashioned playgoer" Cayley Drummle, or any of Wilde's watchful partygoers. Sir Richard's authority is most dramatically displayed in the play's second act, when Sir Richard, suspecting Susan of a flirtation, puts his courtroom skills to work and cross-examines his niece until the inconsistencies of her fabricated story become apparent, and she must either submit to his supervision or risk exposure. (Jones's later play, *Mrs. Dane's Defence*, contains a similar but far more intense cross-examination scene between a bachelor lawyer and a transgressive woman, which I will discuss later in the chapter.) The scene, putting Sir Richard in the spotlight in his capacity of lawyer, calls attention to the three-fold link that the play establishes between marriage, law court, and theater. Deftly exploiting his niece's terror at becoming "déclassé," Sir Richard persuades her first to abandon any further attempts at seeing Lucien, then to return to London under his chaperonage, and eventually to be reconciled to her husband, with promises of future faithfulness on both sides.

Sir Richard similarly serves as observer in the play's other unconventional marriage, that of his ward Elaine Shrimpton with the foppish Fergusson Pybus. Elaine, a specimen of the plentiful New Woman caricatures appearing in the wake of *A Doll's House*, mouths the New Woman's jargon even as she prepares to marry Fergusson, a caricature of the effeminate aesthete. Though neither knows anything of housekeeping, money, or simple dispute resolution, Elaine denounces Sir Richard's attempted dissuasions as "brute force" and righteously declares, "Fergusson has a career before him; I, too, have a career before me" (*HAJ2*, 294). Elaine and Fergusson serve as comic relief, full of lofty ideals that ultimately dissolve into wrangling about window blinds and broken mirrors, despite Sir Richard's efforts to soothe. Modern audiences would undoubtedly agree with William Archer's protest against this feminist straw-woman: "[Elaine] happens to be a fool and a vixen; but that is not the fault of her ideas—it is their misfortune" ("The Case of Rebellious Susan," 267). But the straw-woman tellingly illustrates the New Woman as Victorian conservatives envisioned her: strident, arrogant, proudly ignorant of all things domestic. She has all of Susan's shrewish impulsiveness with none of her underlying "womanly" traits—anxiety for reputation, desire for romance, emotional vulnerability. Hence, where Susan's inconsistency is depicted as excusable silliness, Elaine's consistency is irredeemably contemptible. When in the last act Elaine's political agitating get her into trouble with the police and she goes to prison "*in a glow of martyrdom*," the audience is evidently meant to agree with Sir Richard's conclusion that "women never will understand the Woman question" (*HAJ2*, 352).

THE LIMITS OF BACHELOR WISDOM

The play's uncomplimentary portrayal of its short-sighted "rebellious" women suggests that Sir Richard speaks for the author, and that the audience is intended to agree with his ultra-conservative doctrine that "sauce for the goose will never be sauce for the gander," and that "this tiresome sexual business...was settled once for all in the Garden of Eden" (*HAJ2*, 280, 350). But Jones persistently opposed the idea of thesis-driven or "doctrinaire" drama, particularly plays dealing with sex and gender. In a lecture a year before the premiere of *Susan*, he concluded that such argument-based plays are inherently unfair in their argument:

> We will suppose a doctrinaire dramatist who sets out to treat, say, of the equality of the sexes.... If he solves it according to his gallantry or prepossessions in favour of women, he has only to devise a story in which the women are palpably the intellectual and moral superiors of the men, and the thing is proved. But at once you say to him, "Of course, my dear fellow...You

have provided a solution to your problem, but your solution is utterly worthless, because you have arranged the world and your characters to your own liking." (*The Renascence of the English Drama*, 302)

Regarding his own dramatic methods, in contrast to the doctrinaire approach, Jones declared, "I didn't try to prove anything: I set myself to paint the thing as I saw it" (*The Renascence of the English Drama*, 303).

Jones's portrayals of Susan, Elaine, and Sir Richard appear, at first survey, directly opposite to these principles: while he scolded more feminist-leaning dramatists for weighting the scales in women's favor, he himself seems to have rigged the game in the opposite direction, discrediting gender equality by depicting rebellious women as the moral and intellectual inferiors of their male guardian. But Jones, in "paint[ing] the thing as [he] saw it," presented a more socially and psychologically nuanced picture of marriage and gender than appears in the play's outline. Several prominent elements of character and dialogue complicate a "straight" reading of the play's patriarchalism and undercut the authority of Sir Richard the bachelor-critic.

Jones, when publishing the play's text, included a preface, framed as a sarcastically polite dedicatory letter to "Mrs. Grundy," including a postscript in which he stated: "My comedy isn't a comedy at all. It's a tragedy dressed up as a comedy. But it is so far like life—you can shut your eyes, tuck your tongue in your cheek, and declare it is a comedy—or even a farce" (*The Renascence of the English Drama*, 330). The comment raises provocative questions regarding the play's apparent happy ending and the infallibility of Sir Richard, the ending's engineer. Is the play "tragic" because it depicts a woman rebelling against her wifely duties or because she lacks the courage to persist in rebelling against her unfaithful husband? Because Society's demands have forced a naturally sincere woman to practice the deceptions a secret liaison requires? Because she attempts to take a lover, or because her lover's affection proves even more shallow and fickle than her husband's, so that she is unable to find fulfillment with either? Is there an implied link between the "tragedy" and the "moral" the preface claims for the play—"That as women cannot retaliate openly, they *may* retaliate secretly—and *lie*" (*The Renascence of the English Drama*, 329)?

Whatever "tragedy" Jones alluded to, and whatever degree of irony or sincerity readers ought to ascribe to his remark, Jones's preface positioned *Rebellious Susan* as part of an ongoing conversation, aiming to stretch or redefine the traditional genre categories of tragedy and comedy. Traditional notions of tragedy, long associated in English playgoers' minds with Elizabethan costumes, royal protagonists, and blank verse, had been challenged by *A Doll's House* and Ibsen's subsequent plays, plays that claimed tragic horror and awe for the struggles and dilemmas of modern, ordinary people. Shaw wrote regarding this "modern" tragedy, "Shakespear had put ourselves on the stage but not our situations.... Ibsen supplies the want left by Shakespear. He gives us not only ourselves but ourselves in our own situations. The things that happen to his stage figures are things that happen to us" (*QI*, 218). Archer, reviewing Jones's *Breaking a Butterfly* in 1884, commented on what he saw as the unavoidable English trivialization of *A Doll's House*. He concluded: "[Ibsen's work] proved to me the possibility of modern tragedy in the deepest sense of the word; but it also proved the impossibility of modern tragedy on the English stage" ("Breaking a Butterfly," 72).

Jones, though dismissive of what he termed the "lobworm-symbolic school" of Ibsen and his followers, attentively studied the possibilities offered by old and the new approaches to tragedy (*The Renascence of the English Drama*, 326). He made a few practical experiments with tragic themes and scenes in his own plays, but found little audience demand in that direction, a fact for which he more than once expressed resentment. In Jones's plays, as in those of many nineteenth-century dramas, marriage was often a pivotal element in the distinction between a happy ending and an unhappy one: a happy ending was one in which the young lovers married, or in which the quarreling or separated spouses were reunited, while an unhappy one featured a separation, whether by death, divorce, or a woman's loss of virtue, which made her ineligible for marriage. Comedies and farces featured a happy ending, while a melodrama might end in either direction, as might a drama. This last category, "drama," Marjorie Northend has described as Victorian theater's nearest approximation to the tragic, a play of "serious content," but "lack[ing] the depth and dignity to merit the title of tragedy" ("Henry Arthur Jones and the Development of the Modern English Drama," 453). Jones attempted to create this tragic depth and dignity in some of his dramas, particularly in his blank-verse period play, *The Tempter* (1893), and his more contemporary piece, *Michael and his Lost Angel* (1896). Both plays, featuring conventional unhappy endings of sexual downfall leading to death, also presented psychologically nuanced (though not always consistent) characterization and posed serious questions about the roles of conscience and religious faith in modern life. Both pieces proved commercial failures, and scholars have generally classified them as dramatic failures as well.[3] Richard Cordell has argued that Jones failed at tragedy because "the grip of melodrama upon him was never sufficiently loosened" (*Henry Arthur Jones and the Modern Drama*, 74). Northend attributes the failure to Jones's inability to grasp the emotions of tragedy in the appropriate quality and intensity: "importance rather than greatness, self-pity rather than pity, worry rather than terror, are the qualities that make up his plays, and keep them smugly, comfortably below the level of tragedy" ("Henry Arthur Jones and the Development of the Modern English Drama," 455). Certainly, his early experience with melodrama may have caused him to rely heavily on fantastic settings, emotional excess, and forced events, undermining his efforts at serious drama, and it's hard to imagine a modern audience feeling much sympathy with either play. Nevertheless, according to his daughter Doris, *The Tempter* and *Michael* remained his favorites among his plays, which he regarded as his "children," "those over which he had taken the greatest trouble and which had been unfortunate" (*Taking the Curtain Call*, 156).

The Case of Rebellious Susan, written and produced between these two plays, bent the idea of tragedy in a different direction by applying the term to a play replete with witty badinage, nearly discovered flirtations, and fashionable leisured life, implying that these frivolous ingredients might be made into a medium for the same suffering and spiritual conflict presented in more somber-toned plays. More significantly, it labeled as "tragedy" a play whose conclusion, featuring the reconciliation of the estranged married couple, seemed better suited to the comic formula. *Rebellious Susan* displays a genre ambiguity similar to the ambiguity Susan Carlson notes in Jones's later play, *Mrs. Dane's Defence*. *Mrs. Dane's Defence*, Carlson argues, blends the conventions of the comedy of manners and the problem play. Carlson defines these genres as differing chiefly in their treatment of women: "[I]n comedies of manners, society is a school in which women learn about themselves and gain power; and in problem plays, this same society not only denies women power, but also destroys them" ("Two Genres and their Women," 414). Jones's earlier play, too, carries traits of both these genres. Susan is "schooled" over the course of the play, both by her uncle's homilies and by her experience in romantic intrigue, but the chief thing she learns is her powerlessness to seek romantic fulfillment outside her marriage and her seemingly small hope of improving her marriage's conditions.

Mary Moore, who played Susan in the first production at the Criterion Theatre, was impressed with Jones's idea of "tragedy dressed up as comedy," quoting the phrase in an interview with *The Penny Illustrated Paper* ("'Rebellious Susan' at Home," 226). She described Susan's character as an essentially serious one, a woman reproached by her husband for being "unromantic," yet unable to satisfy her own desire for romance either with her lover or with her husband. Moore called attention to a scene near the play's end, in which Susan and her husband agree to confess their past misconduct to each other, and Jim grows furiously jealous at Susan's narrative (a heavily edited one, which culminates with a kiss on the hand from an elderly musician). Moore identified this scene as one of subtle pathos and psychological realism: Susan is prepared to make a full, truthful confession to her husband, but first offers the hand-kissing episode as a "feeler" and is disgusted by her husband's overreaction. "She perceives," Moore explained, "that he has not soul enough to value the real generosity of her full confession, and resolves to be silent" ("'Rebellious Susan' at Home," 226). The scene, by Moore's interpretation, is essentially a tragic one, despite the bantering tone of the dialogue.

The play's comic disguise was evidently more effective as far as the audience was concerned, for more than one critic commented on the play's thorough lightheartedness, its complete absence of pathos or seriousness, in contrast with Ibsen or with Pinero's recent Society dramas. Archer, reviewing the play for *The World*, wrote: "At no point does Mr. Jones's play trend towards drama. Great problems, great passions, great sufferings, do not enter into its scheme" ("The Case of Rebellious Susan," 267). Another reviewer, writing for the *Yorkshire Herald* following an 1896 provincial production, remarked: "Only the lighter phase of the circumstances surrounding such relations between a married pair is touched upon. There is none of the deep laid tragedy of 'The Second Mrs. Tanqueray' or 'The Notorious Mrs. Ebbsmith'" ("The Case of Rebellious Susan," 5). Both reviewers, incidentally, gave an overall favorable verdict on the play, praising it as a "pure comedy" ("The Case of Rebellious Susan, 267). *Rebellious Susan*, Jones's preface implied, succeeded where his professedly tragic plays failed because here he "dressed up" the tragedy as comedy to gain the audience's approval.

Jones's comment on tragedy and comedy echoes a line in the play's dialogue, coming from the mouth of the young widow Inez Quesnel, Susan's friend and the object of Sir Richard's chaste and decorous adoration. Inez, like Sir Richard, observes and interprets Susan's marriage throughout the play. First played by the queenly Gertrude Kingston, for whom Shaw would later write *Great Catherine*,[4] Inez functions as a secondary *raisonneur* or *raisonneuse*, offering a feminine counterpoint to balance Sir Richard's self-assured commentaries. Inez's discussions with Sir Richard serve to point out the limitations of his infallible bachelor wisdom on women and on marital questions:

SIR RICHARD: After a life-time's practice in the Divorce Court I still feel myself like Newton, a mere child on the seashore, with all the boundless ocean of woman's mysterious nature stretching silent, and unnavigable, and unexplorable before me.
INEZ: Perhaps the Divorce Court isn't the best place to learn what unsuspected depths and treasures there are in woman's nature.... Yes, treasures of faithfulness, treasures of devotion, of self-sacrifice, of courage, of comradeship, of loyalty. And above all, treasures of deceit—loving, honourable deceit, and secrecy and treachery.
SIR RICHARD: I had already suspected there might be an occasional jewel of that sort in the dark, unfathomed caves.
INEZ: You're laughing at me. You men never will see anything but a comedy in it. So we have to dress up our tragedy as a comedy just to save ourselves from being ridiculous and boring you.... That's our real modern tragedy—we laugh at the tragedy of our own lives! (*HAJ2*, 303–304)

In Inez's assessment, the difference between tragedy and comedy is likened to the difference between masculine and feminine perspective, between women's characters and actions and men's comprehension of them. Women, in her analogy, are the performers of a play, men the audience or critics whom they are obliged to please. While Sir Richard might be sardonic or indulgently amused at Susan's affection for Lucien Edensor and her anxious concealment of it, for Inez (and for Susan herself) these experiences bring pain that is all the more lasting for being necessarily hidden or made light of. By taking Inez's theatrical language on the misunderstanding between the sexes and using her comment in the preface to define the play itself, Jones lends extra weight to her feminine perspective on Susan's marriage and on marriage in general and subtly contests Sir Richard's supremacy as bachelor-spectator. From the gently persuasive Inez, Gertrude Kingston would later move on, as an active suffragist and actor-manager of the Little Theatre at the Adelphi, to more outspoken feminist repertoire such as *Lysistrata* and Cicely Hamilton's *Just to Get Married*.

Inez serves to counterbalance Sir Richard in action as well as in dialogue, particularly in his interventions in Susan's business. Her companionship with Susan in Egypt offers a milder alternative to Sir Richard's avuncular supervision. Her matronly presence checks excess, but she remains sympathetically oblivious to Susan's attachment to Lucien, acting on her friendly philosophy of *"Honi soit qui mal y pense"* (*HAJ2*, 363). Later, when Sir Richard questions Inez regarding this attachment, she deflects his inquiries with the assurance: "You needn't trouble about Sue. We women know the value of appearances. We are awful cowards, and have terrible leanings towards respectability. Sue won't shatter Mr. Harabin's family gods…or burst up Mr. Harabin's family boiler with any new-fangled explosive. And so long as Mr. Harabin's family boiler remains intact, why should you meddle with Sue?" (*HAJ2*, 341). Like Sir Richard, Inez recognizes Susan's essential conventionality and her anxiety regarding public opinion. But rather than using this bias to coerce her, Inez trusts it as a check in itself, sufficient to keep Susan from scandal. Inez does not resist Sir Richard's conclusions regarding the need to follow social conventions (she joins the general family chorus of protest when Susan announces her intention of leaving her husband), but she questions his infallibility as marital drama critic.

Morality and the Box Office

Charles Wyndham, in producing *Rebellious Susan*, was anxious that the play should support the respectable and aristocratic ethos he had built for the Criterion Theatre—and also, George Rowell suggests, anxious that it should help to efface the less respectable image associated with the risqué repertoire of his earlier career ("Criteria for Comedy," 25–28). Consequently, he was reluctant to produce a play in which the heroine possibly (though not certainly) commits adultery and is allowed to pass undiscovered and unpunished. While rehearsing the play, he repeatedly urged Jones to revise his script to correct what he, Wyndham, considered its immoral tendencies. In particular, he demanded that Jones alter the dialogue to assure the audience of Susan's chastity (technical chastity, at least), eliminating the suspicious line "I should kill myself if anyone knew." When Jones refused, insisting that this ambiguity was needed to promote discussion, Wyndham persisted. He objected on moral grounds and commercial as well. Shocked by the idea of female adultery, he also argued that Susan's doubtful conduct would damage ticket sales. Six weeks before the play opened, he wrote to Jones:

> I stand as bewildered to-day as ever at finding an author, a clean-living, clear-minded man, hoping to extract laughter from an audience on the score of a woman's impurity.... I am equally astounded at a practical long-experienced dramatic author believing that he will induce married men to bring their wives to a theatre to learn the lesson that their wives can descend to such nastiness, as giving themselves up for one evening of adulterous pleasure and then return safely to their husbands' arms, provided they are clever enough, low enough, and dishonest enough to avoid being found out. Finally I am puzzled to wonderment as to the source from which he expects to draw his audience, since it is evident to me that married men will not bring their wives and mothers will not bring their daughters.... I am not speaking as a moralist, I am simply voicing the public instinct. (qtd. in Doris Jones, *Taking the Curtain Call*, 134–135)

Wyndham, like Sir Richard Kato, spoke as a shrewd man of the world and as a self-appointed patriarch defending purity and virtue.

On receiving Wyndham's letter, Jones vented his disgust in his snide prefatory letter to "Mrs. Grundy," which was published with the play's text:

> Perhaps you will say that my comedy is quite unlike life. I am aware that I have no warrant in the actual facts of the world around me for placing on the English stage an instance of English conjugal infidelity. There is, I believe, madam, a great deal of this kind of immorality in France, but you will rejoice to hear that a very careful and searching inquiry has not resulted in establishing any well-authenticated case in English life. And even had the inquiry revealed a quite opposite state of things, I am sure you will agree with me that it would be much better to make up our minds once for all that the facts are wrong and stick to that.... So, my dear madam, I have to own frankly that I have not the slightest justification in fact for laying the scene of my comedy in England, and I am again justly open to the charge, so often made against me, of being quite false to life as my countrymen see it. (*The Renascence of the English Drama*, 328)

Representing English life—in particular, marriage and gender relations—authentically was central to Jones's projects of reforming theater and educating audiences, and ambiguous appearances and the possibility of guilt were, he implied, often part of real life. To Jones, Wyndham's concerns seemed simply a servile willingness to cater to Victorian prudery even at the cost of suppressing fact and truth. In ironically invoking the muse of English manners and morals, he voiced his annoyance both at Wyndham and at his audience.

Jones remained adamant in his refusal to alter the play's dialogue, despite the united protests of Wyndham's business instincts and his Victorian morality. Wyndham, in turn, instructed Mary Moore to omit the line "I would kill myself if anyone knew" in performance.[5] Copies of Jones's (unedited) dramatic text, however, cued attentive first-nighters in regarding the omitted line. Susan, in short, was represented as chaste on stage, unchaste on page.

The discrepancy between text and performance not only called attention to the ambiguity of Susan's conduct but also made public the tug-of-war between author and manager that the question had provoked. The *Sporting Times* reviewer gleefully reported: "Mr. Wyndham argues the debated point from the stage point of view, i.e., the omitted line point; Mr. Jones argues it from the author's point of view, i.e., the full text of the printed book. Mr. Wyndham says 'No;' Mr. Jones says 'Yes'" ("Things Theatrical," 3). Reviewers were divided in their assessment of Susan's behavior, and of the play's conclusion—*The Era* supposed the play's "moral" to be that "resistance is hopeless," while *The Bury and Norwich Post* read the play as saying that "it is quite justifiable for a wronged wife to be revenged" ("The Case of Rebellious Susan," 11; "'The Case of Rebellious Susan' at the Criterion Theatre," 7). Most, however, simply returned a verdict of "not proven" on the morality question and praised this unsolved riddle as a shrewd business ploy. *Hearth and Home* commented: "That money will roll into [Wyndham's] coffers is a foregone conclusion. Society will rush *en masse* to pronounce Lady Sue guilty or not guilty" ("At the Play," 811).

Wyndham's worries that risky ambiguity would be bad for the box office proved unfounded, for the play had a solid run of 164 performances (Doris Jones, *Taking the Curtain Call*, 137). Wyndham and Jones, despite their fierce and well-publicized dispute, were evidently satisfied with this result. Wyndham revived the play seven years later, by which time the once-controversial piece appeared "strangely antiquated," "too obviously

Victorian," as the *Times* reviewer remarked ("Wyndham's Theatre," 3). Moreover, the success of *Rebellious Susan* set the pattern for Jones's and Wyndham's subsequent joint productions and for the characters Wyndham would play in them. *The Liars* (1897) and *Mrs. Dane's Defence* (1900) proved to be among the greatest successes for both author and actor-manager.

Despite Jones's seeming triumph over Mrs. Grundy, he was evidently unwilling to risk another clash with Wyndham, for in the later plays he wrote for Wyndham at the Criterion and later at Wyndham's Theatre, he eschewed any suggestion of moral ambiguity like Susan's. In *The Liars* (1897) and *Mrs. Dane's Defence* (1900), the action was again led by the clever middle-aged bachelor played by Wyndham, who again served as spokesman for conventional morality, steering his protégés away from the wrong partners and toward the right ones. There was no more doubt about innocence and guilt. Lady Jessica was kept carefully within the pale, however near the edge she strayed, and Mrs. Dane, having gone over the edge, was duly ostracized. Yet these plays, like *Susan*, pushed back against the traditional marriage and morality championed by Wyndham's *raisonneurs* in a variety of subtle ways—hardly a violent upending of the social order, but enough to make one question whether Jones had really, as George Rowell has argued, "embraced Victorian convention with the fervor of a convert" ("Wyndham of Wyndham's," 205).

Wyndham, in the characters of Colonel Sir Christopher Deering and the judge Sir Daniel Carteret, again spoke with authority not only as man and head of family but also as representative of the law, the military, the state, and the empire (Jones's preferred method of breaking off unsuitable matches was to send love-struck young men to some colonial location for military service or some vaguely defined empire-building "duty"). Like Sir Richard Kato, these later *raisonneurs* demonstrated the impracticality of attempts at unconventional marriage or pseudo-marriage, often gaining leverage from the couple's fear—the woman's fear especially—of the unfriendly "eyes of the world." Sir Christopher, for example, in the closing scene of *The Liars*, arrests the elopement of his friend Falkner with the married Lady Jessica with a lengthy lecture:

> Now! I've nothing to say in the abstract against running away with another man's wife! There may be planets where it is not only the highest ideal morality, but where it has the further advantage of being a practical way of carrying on society. But it has this one fatal defect in our country—it won't

work! You know what we English are, Ned. We're not a bit better than our neighbors, but, thank God! We do pretend we are, and we do make it hot for anybody who disturbs that holy pretence.... You know it's not an original experiment you're making. It has been tried before. Have you ever known it to be successful? Lady Jessica, think of the brave pioneers who have gone before you in this enterprise. They've all perished, and their bones whiten the anti-matrimonial shore. (*HAJ3*, 172)

Sir Christopher goes on to enumerate the social suicides of past "pioneers," insisting that whatever unpleasantness marriage may involve, even marriage with Lady Jessica's bad-tempered husband, any unconventional alternative to marriage is likely to be still more uncomfortable. The speech reads like a paraphrase of Wyndham's own strictures on *Susan*, with its synthesis of righteousness and pragmatism. Yet there is an element of parody in Jones's paraphrase, with Sir Christopher's repeated and humorously exaggerated admissions of hypocrisy. He does not "defend the prejudices of Mayfair as if they were cosmic truths," in Joel Kaplan's phrase ("Henry Arthur Jones and the Lime-lit Imagination," 116). He defends them as what they are: the prejudices of Mayfair. Lady Jessica's rejection of marriage, like Jones's play, is doomed to failure if the spectators are displeased. Lady Jessica (being a Mayfair citizen) ultimately succumbs to this logic, the elopement is averted, and again the play concludes with a happy ending in which husband and wife patch up their differences with a good dinner. Yet Jones repeatedly insists, through the mouth of Sir Christopher (and the mouth of Wyndham), that this correct conclusion is not given in the service of "ideal morality," but only to keep up a "holy pretence."

Sir Daniel Carteret, the *raisonneur* of *Mrs. Dane's Defence*, is even more inflexible in his insistence on social orthodoxy. Though he has sown his share of wild oats, he stands as a judge in every sense of the word over his son's transgressive fiancée as he unveils her past sins and declares that "whatever I've done, whatever I've been myself, I'm quite resolved my son shan't marry another man's mistress" (*HAJ3*, 261). But as masculine orthodoxy gains vigor in this play, so does the feminine resistance that quietly undermines or openly opposes it. As Rowell has pointed out, Jones placed considerable emphasis on Mrs. Dane's attractive qualities. She is gentle and dignified, in contrast with the shrewishness or flightiness of earlier transgressive women such as Dulcie, Elaine, Susan, and Jessica. She sincerely loves Sir Daniel's son, and she has done wrong only in having been seduced while very young and having told necessary lies to conceal this lapse from her unforgiving neighbors ("Charles Wyndham and Mrs. Dane's Defence," 303). Lena Ashwell, in playing the role at Wyndham's Theatre, rose from relative obscurity to stardom. Jones later said, "God made Lena Ashwell for Mrs. Dane, just as he made Mrs. Pat Campbell for Mrs. Tanqueray" (qtd. in Doris Jones, *Taking the Curtain Call*, 177). Ashwell, nevertheless, like Campbell, resisted being lastingly defined by the character with which others most identified her. Within the following decade, she would display her versatility and physical prowess as Lina Szczepanowska in the premiere of Shaw's *Misalliance*, as well as becoming actor-manager at the Kingsway Theatre and a prominent member of the Actresses' Franchise League (AFL).

Several reporters commented on the sympathy Mrs. Dane seemed to engender from the audience. The tense cross-examination in the third act, in which Sir Daniel gradually pries from Mrs. Dane the truth about her past and identity, culminating in the judicial declaration, "Woman, you are lying!", received noisy applause—"You could lean up against it," Wyndham later said (qtd. in Doris Jones, *Taking the Curtain Call*, 176). Yet, judging by reviewers' remarks, more than half the applause and nearly all the sympathy fell to the share of Mrs. Dane and Ashwell. Reviews praised Wyndham's acting as a matter of course, but implied, if they did not frankly state, that this was really Ashwell's play, a vehicle for the consummate emotional actress. *The Country Gentleman* was typical in announcing that "the triumph of the play is Miss Ashwell's acting in the third act" ("Mrs. Dane's Defence," 1288). J. T. Grein, founder of the Independent Theatre Society, which had pioneered in producing Ibsen's *Ghosts* and Shaw's *Widowers' Houses* a few years earlier, noted Ashwell's predominance with evident surprise, saying: "[Jones's] sole idea was to write an entertaining play with a great part for Mr. Wyndham and a good one for a woman. This he has done, and, as it happens, it is the woman who gets the great part, and the actor obtains merely second best" ("Mrs. Dane's Defence," 247). Grein also described at some length the sympathy Ashwell called forth during the interrogation scene:

> Question upon question racked the unhappy woman.... It was as if the garotte closed round her neck, tighter and tighter and tighter.... I felt the moral torture so intensely, the cunningly devised phrases of the author, the insinuating force of Wyndham's dulcet manner, of his screwing, digging, exploding voice, the terrible mortified face of Miss Ashwell—all that

concentration of influence to destroy the new life of a woman!—it made me almost implore aloud for mercy. It was painful, physically as well as mentally. Yet I do not complain, for authors and actors between them had but reproduced an episode of real life, and, in placing it before us, they had, if anything, softened its awful veracity. ("Mrs. Dane's Defence," 245)

The scene is one of excitement, and also of intense discomfort. Grein, with his violent imagery, labeled Sir Daniel a pitiless "torturer" and identified himself with the woman's suffering, feeling her pain. Yet he also recognized the scene as an indictment of the rigid Society who filled the auditorium seats and who had come to be entertained by this "torture," since the scene was presenting "real life," and Mrs. Dane's suffering mirrored that of real women who came into conflict with Society's laws.

These laws, as advocated by Sir Daniel, are further questioned by the convincing arguments of Lady Eastney, Sir Daniel's neighbor and love-interest. Like Inez Quesnel in *Rebellious Susan*, Lady Eastney is a winsome and intelligent widow who proves an intellectual match, as well as a romantic one, for the *raisonneur*, and who offers an often-skeptical feminine perspective on the morality he champions. Acted by Mary Moore, the wayward Lady Susan of a few years before, Lady Eastney combines Inez's arch sagacity with a more mature, moderate degree of Lady Susan's indignation at injustice. As Sir Daniel condemns Mrs. Dane for her past scandal, Lady Eastney takes up her defense: "Oh, aren't you Pharisees and tyrants, all of you? And don't you make cowards and hypocrites of all of us? Don't you lead us into sin and then condemn us for it? Aren't you first our partners and then our judges?" (*HAJ3*, 260). Lady Eastney's protest is rendered especially pointed by Sir Daniel's own past, which, as he has informed her in an earlier scene, has included an attempted (though unsuccessful) elopement with a married woman. Faced with Lady Eastney's appeal to justice, Sir Daniel can only reiterate his insistence on the value of appearances, his demand that "at any rate the outside of the platter must be clean" (*HAJ3*, 260).

As Susan Carlson observes, the element of rebellion that Jones introduces into the play through Lady Eastney is tempered by her position as an insider of the social system, by the fact that it is only as an approved adherent to Society's rules that she can protest against those rules: "Not only has Lady Eastney accepted the existence of the double standard, but she has also learned to use it to her advantage.... By remaining in the system and playing by the rules, she gains the chance to triumph, she gains the opportunity to condemn the double standard and its disastrous effect on Mrs. Dane" ("Two Genres and Their Women," 416). Carlson concludes that although Lady Eastney suggests an alternative to Sir Daniel's rigidly gendered moral code, "We are not to accept her answers.... She is to act as a palliative to lure those of us who agree with her into accepting Sir Daniel's very different conclusions" ("Two Genres and their Women," 416). In the play's end, the heated moral debate subsides into playful flirtation, and Lady Eastney agrees to marry Sir Daniel, hypocrisy notwithstanding. Morality is upheld, fallen Mrs. Dane expelled, and Sir Daniel has his way.

Yet Lady Eastney's resistance to the double standard remains unsubdued to the last moments of the play: knowing the truth of the accusations against Mrs. Dane, she, nevertheless (in the face of Sir Daniel's opposition), coerces and manipulates Mrs. Bulsom-Porter, the troublemaking neighbor who has spread those accusations, into signing a formal (and untruthful) denial and apology for her story. Mrs. Dane must, at Sir Daniel's demand, leave the community, but Lady Eastney determines that she will settle in her next neighborhood "without a stain on her character" (*HAJ3*, 262). At parting with Mrs. Dane, moreover, Lady Eastney promises, "If you call, I shall be at home" (*HAJ3*, 272). That is, according to the terms of Victorian upper-class visiting culture, she promises to acknowledge Mrs. Dane's acquaintance, not to "cut" her as a moral outcast. The idea of being "at home" is given special emphasis a few lines later, at the end of the play. As Lady Eastney leaves Sir Daniel's house to go to her own, Sir Daniel urges her, "Say that you are at home now," and she assents with, "I am at home now" (*HAJ3*, 273). Sir Daniel's last repetition of his oft-repeated marriage proposal, and Lady Eastney's final acceptance, echo her promise of continued friendship with Mrs. Dane. If ever Mrs. Dane does return to Sunningwater, and if Lady Eastney keeps her promise of being "at home," she will be "at home" in Sir Daniel's library. The placement of Lady Eastney's line, as well as its content, seems subtly symbolic. In the previous plays Jones wrote for Wyndham, the last line had always been spoken by Wyndham's character. In this way, the plays had cemented the bachelor-spectators' authority over the marriages they observed, as well as reinforcing the theatrical predominance of the actor-manager. Here, however, Lady Eastney the *raisonneuse* literally has the last word. Thus, even as Sir Daniel upholds patriarchal morality, the future of that morality seems in question, for its chief dissenter prepares to make herself "at home" in his house.

LAST ACT

Richard Cordell has regretted the play's last act, suggesting that Jones wrote it in response to a misguided "marketing impulse"—that after the trauma of Mrs. Dane's humiliation, he supposed the audience to need a little middle-aged romance to sugarcoat their last impressions of the play (*Henry Arthur Jones and the Modern Drama*, 164). If this was Jones's aim, then it evidently met with limited success, for the closing conversation between Lady Eastney and Sir Daniel held little interest for most first-night reviewers. Like the discussion scene of *A Doll's House*, it taxed the audience's attention just when they thought the play ought to be over. Critics almost unanimously condemned the play's fourth act as superfluous. After the exhilarating agony of the cross-examination scene, they argued, once the imposter had been unmasked, little remained to be done. *Punch* suggested that the act was simply a consolation prize for Mary Moore, the longtime leading lady cast in a supporting role, allowing her a brief moment in the spotlight ("A Woman with a Queer Past and a Great Future," 290). J. T. Grein, reviewing the play from his Independent Theatre perspective, complained: "Mr. Jones...evidently does not place great reliance on our intelligence.... For, really, it was not at all necessary to create an anti-climax by clenching the long pending engagement between the judge and the charming Lady Eastney.... We are not so dense as all that, and it worries us to have our noses bumped on the obvious" ("Mrs. Dane's Defence," 246).

The *Times* reviewer, however, suggested a different function for the play's last act. He was intrigued by the moral debate that accompanied the romantic denouement, supposing it to be an attempt, though perhaps an incomplete one, to include thoughtful inquiry and discussion as a part of the play. He was inclined, moreover, to join in the debate. Examining the logic of one of Sir Daniel's harangues to his son Lionel, he commented: "Mr. Justice Carteret evidently carries the audience with him when he tells his son that domestic peace can never be founded upon a faulty past. Yet, we suspect, much might be urged upon the other side. There is the famous 'wild oats' theory, for instance, so commonly accepted for bridegrooms, which might, once in a way, be tried, perhaps, in the case of a bride" ("Wyndham's Theatre," 3). The reviewer evidently wished that Jones had allowed Lionel, Mrs. Dane, and Lady Eastney to argue back more vigorously rather than allowing Sir Daniel to win the argument with so vague a conclusion as: "The rules of the game are severe. If you don't like them, leave them alone. They will never be changed" (*HAJ3*, 260). Even so, the reviewer implies, by compelling Sir Daniel to justify himself and allowing his interlocutors to respond (however unsatisfyingly), Jones was attempting the discussion scene which Shaw considered essential to the New Drama. He was appropriating a method common to Ibsen and Shaw in order to arrive at a rather more conservative, un-Ibsen-like conclusion.

In the end, the reviewer grudgingly excused the curtailment of the argument by conceding that "it would be vain to expect so audacious an experiment at Wyndham's Theatre" ("Wyndham's Theatre," 3). Jones's Sir Daniel had declared that "The rules of the game...will never be changed," and Wyndham had, for years past, made a career of upholding the rules of marriage and the rules of dramatic convention. The experiment of the "wild-oats" bride had, of course, been tried seven years before with Paula Tanqueray as guinea pig, and her marriage had failed through the disapproving spectators in London and Surrey and the demands of the St. James's Theatre audiences. The *Times* reviewer concluded that audiences in Sunningwater and Wyndham's Theatre were likely to be equally uncooperative regarding any "irregular" departures from conventional marriage. Sir Daniel, hypocrisy notwithstanding, was still held to be the spokesman for Jones, Wyndham, and Society.

NOTES

1. Wilde's supposed advice was to gather extra irony when Jones's longest-running play, *The Liars*, was premiered five months after Wilde's release from prison. According to Doris Jones, rumor attributed the play to Wilde, who was surmised to have borrowed Jones's name to avoid the scandal attached to his own.
2. According to Robins, the exchange between Irving and Wyndham took place at a dinner party, and was later repeated to her by Herbert Beerbohm Tree.
3. *Michael*, however, did find a champion in Shaw, who blamed the play's failure on manager Johnston Forbes-Robertson and the cast, opining that "the English stage got a good play, and was completely and ignominiously beaten by it" (*TN2*, 20).
4. In the preface to *Great Catherine*, Shaw recounted: "I once recommended Miss Kingston professionally to play queens. Now in the modern drama there were no queens for her to play; and as to the older literature of our stage, did it not provoke the veteran actress in Sir Arthur Pinero's Trelawney of the Wells to declare that, as parts, queens are not worth a tinker's oath?

Miss Kingston's comment on my suggestion, though more elegantly worded, was to the same effect; and it ended in my having to make good my advice by writing Great Catherine. History provided no other queen capable of standing up to our joint talents" (*BH4*, 899–900).
5. Interestingly, Moore was much less insistent than Wyndham regarding Susan's chastity. In an interview soon after opening night, she remarked, "Mine is rather a naughty part perhaps." Her interviewer challenged this imputation, offering as acquitting evidence Lucien's line, "People can never know what never took place." Unpersuaded, Moore answered: "So you, like most of the men, are of the opinion that that remark whitewashes Lady Susan's reputation. We women, and I suspect the author too, read a subtler meaning in that phrase" ("'Rebellious Susan' at Home," 226.).

References

"A Woman with a Queer Past and a Great Future." *Punch*, October 24, 1900.
Archer, William. "Breaking a Butterfly." *The Theatre: A Monthly Review of the Drama, Music, and the Fine Arts*, June 1884.
———. "The Case or Rebellious Susan." In *Victorian Dramatic Criticism*, edited by George Rowell, 267–70. London: Methuen, 1971.
———. *The Theatrical "World" of 1894*. London: Walter Scott, 1895.
"At the Play." *Hearth and Home*, October 18, 1894.
Boucicault, Dion. *The Octoroon; or, Life in Louisiana*. In *Early American Drama*, edited by Jeffrey H. Richards, 444–94. New York: Penguin, 1997.
Carlson, Susan L. "Two Genres and Their Women: The Problem Play and the Comedy of Manners in the Edwardian Theatre." *The Midwest Quarterly* 24, no. 4 (1985): 413–24.
Cordell, Richard. *Henry Arthur Jones and the Modern Drama*. Port Washington, NY: Kennikat, 1968.
Grein, J. T. "Mrs. Dane's Defence." In *Victorian Dramatic Criticism*, edited by George Rowell, 244–46. London: Methuen, 1971.
Jones, Doris Arthur. *Taking the Curtain Call: The Life and Letters of Henry Arthur Jones*. New York: Macmillan, 1930.
Jones, Henry Arthur. *Representative Plays by Henry Arthur Jones*. Edited by Clayton Hamilton. 4 vols. Boston: Little, Brown, & Co, 1925.
———. *The Foundations of a National Drama*. New York: George H. Doran, 1913.
———. *The Masqueraders*. London: Macmillan, 1899.
———. *The Renascence of the English Drama*. London: Macmillan, 1895.
Kaplan, Joel H. "Henry Arthur Jones and the Lime-Lit Imagination." *Nineteenth-Century Theatre* 15, no. 2 (1987): 115–41.
"Mrs. Dane's Defence." *The Country Gentleman*, October 13, 1900.

Northend, Marjorie. "Henry Arthur Jones and the Development of the Modern English Drama." *The Review of English Studies* 18 (October 1942): 448–63.
"'Rebellious Susan' at Home." *The Penny Illustrated Paper and Illustrated Times*, October 13, 1894.
Robins, Elizabeth. *Both Sides of the Curtain*. London: Heinemann, 1940.
Rowell, George. "Charles Wyndham in Mrs. Dane's Defence." In *When They Weren't Doing Shakespeare*, edited by Judith L. Fisher and Stephen Watt, 299–311. Athens, GA: University of Georgia Press, 1989.
———. "Criteria for Comedy: Charles Wyndham at the Criterion Theatre." In *British Theatre in the 1890s*, edited by Richard Foulkes, 10–23. Cambridge: Cambridge University Press, 1992.
———. "Wyndham of Wyndham's." In *The Theatrical Manager in England and America*, edited by Joseph W. Donohue, 189–214. Princeton: Princeton University Press, 1971.
Shaw, Bernard. *Bernard Shaw: Collected Letters, 1874–1897*. Edited by Dan H. Laurence. Vol. 1. 3 vols. New York: Viking, 1965.
———. *Our Theatres in the Nineties*. 3 vols. London: Constable, 1932.
———. *The Bodley Head Bernard Shaw: Collected Plays with Their Prefaces*. Edited by Dan H. Laurence. 7 vols. London: The Bodley Head, 1970.
———. *The Quintessence of Ibsenism*. In *Shaw and Ibsen: Bernard Shaw's The Quintessence of Ibsenism and Related Writings*, edited by J. L. Wisenthal, 97–237. Toronto: University of Toronto Press, 1958.
Shore, Florence Teignmouth. *Sir Charles Wyndham*. London: John Lane, 1908.
"The Case of Rebellious Susan." *The Era*, October 6, 1894.
———." *The Yorkshire Herald and the York Herald*, February 25, 1896.
"'The Case of Rebellious Susan' at the Criterion Theatre." *The Bury and Norwich Post, and Suffolk Standard*, November 6, 1894.
"Things Theatrical." *The Sporting Times*, October 13, 1894.
"Wyndham's Theatre." *The Times*, October 10, 1900.
———." *The Times*, May 17, 1901.

CHAPTER 6

Shaw's Marriage Sermons

Toward the close of Shaw's 1890 Ibsen sequel "Still After the Doll's House," the middle-aged Nora recalls the twenty years since her departure from the Helmer household, remarking, "I have peeped into a good many doll's houses; and I have seen that the dolls are not all female" ("Still After the Doll's House," 135). She points to the newly respectable Nils Krogstad, now a mayor and bank director married to Christina Linden, as an example, ridiculing him as his wife's "puppet" ("Still After the Doll's House, 135). Shaw's Nora suggests that as Torvald Helmer once directed the dressing-up and dancing of his Doll-wife, Christina now makes her husband dress and behave as befits a pillar of society.

Joan Templeton has suggested that "Still After the Doll's House"—an argumentative, dialogue-driven short story and "a sequel to a sequel to a play"—might have been one of the factors that convinced Shaw, after several unsuccessful efforts at novel writing, that "perhaps his real talent lay in writing plays" (*Shaw's Ibsen*, 28). In exercising his new-found "real talent" a few years later, Shaw would elaborate on this reverse-gendering of Ibsen's characters in his second "Pleasant Play," *Candida* (1894), which

---

An early version of this chapter was published in 2015 in *SHAW: The Journal of Bernard Shaw Studies* under the title "Not a Play": Redefining Theater and Reforming Marriage in *Candida*." The material is republished here with the permission of Penn State University Press.

© The Author(s) 2020
M. Christian, *Marriage and Late-Victorian Dramatists*, Bernard Shaw and His Contemporaries,
https://doi.org/10.1007/978-3-030-40639-4_6

he described as "a counterblast to Ibsen's Doll's House, showing that in the real typical doll's house it is the man who is the doll" (*BH1*, 603). In *Candida*, Shaw presented the idea of the male "puppet" in greater detail. He depicted another theatrical marriage, in which two men, a husband and a would-be interloper, use familiar stage scenes and character types to compete for a wife's attention and affection.

In *Bernard Shaw's Marriages and Misalliances*, Leonard Conolly and Jennifer Buckley have suggested that *Candida*, along with the other "Pleasant Plays," marks a turning point in Shaw's attitude toward marriage. His *Plays Unpleasant*, Conolly argues, is chiefly concerned with debunking the pious and romantic hypocrisies of conventional marriage, demystifying "the mystical union that is betwixt Christ and his Church" and laying bare the mercenary interests and animal sex instincts which Shaw presents in these plays as marriage's only true motives ("The 'Mystical Union' De-Mystified," 25). Buckley, in her chapter on *Plays Pleasant*, shows Shaw's critique taking a more constructive direction, portraying characters' marriages as "pragmatic partnerships" into which men and women enter, not necessarily discarding affection or desire, but rejecting religious and sentimental idealism and frankly acknowledging the social and ideological compromises their partnerships will require ("The Pragmatic Partnerships of *Plays Pleasant*," 53). *Candida* illustrates a fair number of marital compromises and lampoons both the ideals of romance and domesticity and some of the theatrical genres most closely associated with these ideals. Yet on the idea of performance itself, *Candida* gives an odd sense of ambivalence—like Nora's discussion scene, the play's conclusion seems to reject religious and romantic idealism only to set up a new ideal, an unperformed, authentic "real self."

Significantly, both men who pursue Candida are presented as men with a gift for public performance, and both are associated throughout the play with familiar stock-types of late nineteenth-century theater. James Morrell, her husband, is a popular Christian Socialist minister whose masterful choice of words and energetic delivery make his preaching entertaining and charismatic, "as good as a play," as his wife says (*BH1*, 562). Eugene Marchbanks, the teenage family friend, is a sensitive poet, self-consciously "*uncommon*" and even "*unearthly*" (*BH1*, 535). Throughout the play, Shaw plays with the conventions of these two theatrical types, stage minister and stage poet, as well as with the related performance genres of religious homiletics and poetry reading. The different kinds of performances are examined and evaluated in terms of both their general theatrical effectiveness and the ways in which they might shape attitudes toward marriage, sex, and love.

THE PREACHER, ON STAGE AND IN THE PULPIT

As a stage minister, James has easily identifiable antecedents. As a figure in drama and literature, the clergyman had been recognizable at least since Molière's time—a figure marked by ostentatious moralizing or spiritual earnestness, often an object of admiration and desire, and sometimes unscrupulous about cultivating and exploiting this admiration. Tartuffe had his Victorian counterparts in such characters as Aminadab Sleek in Morris Barnett's comedy *The Serious Family* (1849). A few decades later, W. S. Gilbert (reportedly an admirer of Barnett's comedy) jokingly revived the image of the irresistible "saintly youth" mobbed by female admirers in the popular ballad of the "Pale Young Curate" (Carolyn Williams, *Gilbert and Sullivan: Gender, Genre, Parody*, 154; W. S. Gilbert, *The Sorcerer*, 51). More recently, and more immediately of interest in Shaw's circle, English productions of *Ghosts* and *Rosmersholm* had presented Ibsen's contrasting tragic treatment of the idealistic and admonitory minister and his influence over feminine hearts and consciences. Henry Arthur Jones, since his melodramatic beginnings in the 1880s, had presented variations on this same motif in plays such as *Saints and Sinners* (1884) and *Judah* (1890). Shortly after Shaw completed *Candida*, Jones drew accusations of blasphemy from some reviewers by depicting a church service onstage in his tragedy *Michael and his Lost Angel* (1896), a play for which Shaw was a lone defender.[1]

James Morrell, though the antithesis of Sleek in his likable sincerity and jovial generosity, and a cheerful contrast to the grim solemnity of Ibsen's Manders, has the stage clergyman's propensity for moralizing (as his name implies). His charismatic zeal shades into pomposity. In his early expositional dialogues, he finds frequent occasions to exhort his listeners to cultivate charity, diligence, and honesty, even in minor disputes over work schedules and lecture invitations. The stage directions suggest that the delivery, as well as the content of his words, is that of a man accustomed to an audience. He speaks to his secretary "*with a sadness which is a luxury to a man whose voice expresses it so finely*" and to his father-in-law "*in [a] tone of quiet conviction*" which "*becomes formidable.*" Without a pulpit available for pounding, he "*strikes the back of the chair for greater emphasis*" (*BH1*, 519, 530). He likewise possesses the stage clergyman's knack for drawing male followers and female adorers, though he seems in general to use this fascination unconsciously. His curate, Lexy Mill, regards him with "*doglike devotion*" (*BH1*, 520). He has unknowingly ensnared the heart of his secretary, Prossy Garnett. By Eugene's report, he can easily intoxicate his male listeners with enthusiasm, and, by Candida's account, numerous female parishioners share "Prossy's complaint" (*BH1*, 563).

Shaw had extensive experience not only with stage ministers but also with the Christian Socialist ministers with whom he made acquaintance as a Fabian lecturer, and these were the men he claimed as the chief models for James, including the "Flaming" Charles Fleming Williams, literary historian Stopford Brooke, and his own fellow Fabians Henry Cary Shuttleworth and Stewart Duckworth Headlam (*BH1*, 602). This last associate is an especially interesting figure, considered as a model for James's pulpit performance, for Headlam, as Richard Foulkes has pointed out, had connections with theater as well as church. In 1879, he had organized the Church and Stage Guild, an association of clergy and theatrical professionals who met to foster solidarity between the two institutions, affirm the spiritual value of theatrical workers as creators of beauty, and warn against the dangers of the clergy's indiscriminate condemnation of the performing arts (*Church and Stage in Victorian England*, 170).

Shaw himself addressed the Guild in an 1889 lecture titled "Acting, by One who does Not Believe in It," in which he commended Headlam for acknowledging (despite the opposition of theatrical critics) "that the world behind the footlights was a real world, peopled with men and women, instead of with despicable puppets" (*Platform and Pulpit*, 20–21). Shaw shared Headlam's belief that religion and theater had each lost much by their long-standing segregation, and that each would gain by accepting the other as an ally. Shaw saw church services, and sermons in particular, as inherently theatrical, just as he recognized a fundamentally religious element in the act of theatrical performance, referring to his plays as "stage sermons" (*BH1*, 234).[2] Thus, to call a sermon "as good as a play," as Candida calls James's, might be taken as a term not necessarily of ridicule, but of genuine praise.

Yet Shaw argued that pulpit performances that were too boisterously theatrical risked losing their edifying spiritual power, becoming simply laughable. This is implied, for instance, in his 1888 letter to the editor of the *Star*, describing a sermon by the Bishop of Rochester. Assuming the cockney persona of "Jem Nicholls," Shaw likened the meeting to a music hall in which "the boys sung a sam like mad" in noisy competition with the organ, to a prizefight in which the bishop violently "give it" to various authority figures, and to a variety entertainment in which listeners declared that "It was a treat to hear him give everybody a setting down all round" (*CLS1*, 199–200). "Jem Nicholls" finished his letter by declaring: "I must say I never see a man come more up to my notion of a Bishop as him. I wish I was one" (*CLS1*, 200–201). Shaw suggested that the popular preacher, like a theatrical star, gains a celebrity status, inviting viewers to imaginatively identify with him, perhaps at the expense of spiritual or intellectual enrichment. Theater and religion, he concluded, could both at their best be vital revealers of reality, but at their worst were merely "refuge from real life" (*Platform and Pulpit*, 19).

In *Candida*, James's sermons seem to have something of this showy frivolity, appealing to his congregation more as entertainment than spiritual benefit. When Candida declares his energetic preaching to be "as good as a play," she means that his congregation regard it as a pleasurable "rest and diversion" (*BH1*, 562). The capitalist businessmen, by her account, enjoy Christian Socialist preaching by way of variety, so as to "go back fresh and make money harder than ever" in the coming week (*BH1*, 562). They apparently view James as "Jem Nicholls" viewed the Bishop of Rochester, as "a treat." The sort of "play" to which Candida likens James's preaching, in short, is the sort that Shaw was readiest to attack, created by artists who are "keeping up a Fool's Paradise in order to save themselves the trouble of making the real world any better" (*Platform and Pulpit*, 20).

Eugene dismisses James's dramatic homiletics even more bluntly, invoking the Old Testament narrative of King David, who "danced before the Lord" in a scanty linen garment. The allusion carries a sexual overtone, for Eugene also mentions David's wife Michal, who, in the biblical account, scolded her husband for having "uncovered himself today in the eyes of the handmaids of his servants" (2 Samuel 6:13, 20, King James Version). Eugene explicitly links James's religious fervor both with disorderly public display and with erotic suggestion. Eugene is hardly an unbiased commentator, yet to James, at least for the moment, this taunt appears accurate enough to infuriate and to lastingly unsettle.

Eugene's equation of moral exhortation, public spectacle, and carnal desire becomes especially telling when James is preaching about his wife, or to her. When he describes his marriage, it is almost always in religious language, pointing to conjugal love as the starting point for his Christian Socialist aspiration toward the "Kingdom of Heaven on earth" (*BH1*, 521, 542). James equates happy marriage not only with spiritual rightness but also with intellectual superiority, proudly declaring: "Larochefoucauld said that there are convenient marriages but no delightful ones. You don't know the comfort of seeing through and through a thundering liar and rotten cynic like that fellow" (*BH1*, 539). Describing his marriage, he frequently uses the words "sacred" and "noble." James appears at times to view his relationship with Candida almost as a theatrical performance in itself, or as an extension of a sermon. He makes this perspective most explicit in inviting Eugene to lunch after Candida's return from her holiday, explaining, "In a happy marriage like ours, there is something very sacred in the wife's return to her home.... I'm very fond of you, my boy; and I should like you to see for yourself what a happy thing it is to be married as I am" (*BH1*, 539). The importance of Eugene's presence is emphasized by the fact that Candida would evidently prefer him to be absent, having warned him to decline any invitations James might offer. While she wishes to keep their scenes of marital intimacy private, James is eager for an approving and sympathetic spectator. He envisions Candida's return both as a tender reunion with the woman he loves and as an edifying and pleasurable spectacle for Eugene, his select audience of one.

His tendency to conflate the homiletic and the personal is, if anything, even more pronounced when he speaks directly to Candida. Eugene accuses him of deliberately preaching to her in order to fascinate and woo her, of using the oratorical ability that has proven so crush-inducing for Prossy and the other smitten women in his congregation—a kind of clerical lovemaking. Eugene asks, "Do you think a woman's soul can live on your talent for preaching?" (*BH1*, 543). He later adds, "You can't make a woman like Candida love you by merely buttoning your collar at the back instead of the front" (*BH1*, 577). To be married to James, Eugene suggests, is simply to be a perpetual captive audience to his sermonizing. "Captive" is not too strong a word, for he announces: "I'll fight your ideas. I'll rescue her from her slavery to them" (*BH1*, 545). Exaggerated as Eugene's taunt is, James seems to admit a few degrees of truth in the implied equation of preaching and love, for he retorts: "When Candida promised to marry me...my collar was buttoned behind instead of in front.... It was there [in the pulpit] that I earned my golden moment, and my right, in that moment, to ask her to love me" (*BH1*, 577–578). Deliberate or not, James's intimate moments with Candida are certainly marked by his preacherly vocabulary and manner—and, though his parishioners might be impressed, Candida is not. When James expresses confidence in her "goodness and purity," she objects: "What a nasty, uncomfortable thing to say to me. Oh, you are a clergyman, James: a thorough clergyman" (*BH1*, 564). In Candida's eyes, James's status and persona as a minister—the very qualities that attracted the admirers of Gilbert's "Pale Young Curate"—degenerate into simple pedantry and narcissism when brought to bear on questions of marriage and affection. James is at once reiterating conventional assumptions about marriage and chastity that Candida does not share and associating his feelings for her with his pulpit performances, both of which displease her. She is, as the delivery notes explain, "*offended by his yielding to his orator's instinct and treating her as if she were the audience at the Guild of St Matthew*" (*BH1*, 587). As Eugene has observed, Candida does not wish her husband to treat her as a one-woman congregation.

Poetic Attitudes

Eugene is less perceptive, however, regarding his own rhetoric and persona. Like his rival, Eugene is a close cousin to a familiar theatrical stock-type, the stage poet. During the previous decade, this theatrical type had become particularly recognizable as the Aesthetic movement gathered attention, both admiring and contemptuous. In F. C. Burnand's comedy *The Colonel* (1881), in the cartoon sketches of George du Maurier, and, most famously, in Gilbert and Sullivan's comic opera *Patience* (1883), poets were held up to ridicule for their opaque vocabularies, disdain for ordinary pleasures and activities, admiration for all things medieval, and unconventional dress and mannerisms. In *Patience,* Gilbert summed up these poetic oddities in the song of the "fleshly poet" Reginald Bunthorne:

> If you're anxious for to shine in the high Aesthetic line
> As a man of culture rare,
> You must get up all the germs of the transcendental terms
> And plant them everywhere.

> * * *
> And everyone will say
> As you walk your mystic way,

'If this young man expresses himself in terms too deep for me,
Why, what a very singularly deep young man
This deep young man must be!' (*Patience*, 293)

The poet, in Gilbert's assessment, is above all a manipulative showman who craves female attention, and his picturesque costume and archaic speech are masks cynically assumed. "In short," Bunthorne sings, "my mediævalism's affectation / Born of a morbid love of admiration" (*Patience*, 293).

Shaw's early descriptions endow Eugene with several of these stereotypically poetic and Aesthetic traits. He is "a strange, shy youth of eighteen, slight, effeminate, with a delicate childish voice, and a hunted tormented expression and shrinking manner," with unkempt, "anarchic" clothes (*BH1*, 534). He is painfully inept with commonplace technology and social exchanges. His paroxysms of "horror" at the mention of lamp-filling, boot-blacking, and onion-slicing have more than a touch of Gilbert's aesthetic caricatures. Like Bunthorne declaiming "O Hollow! Hollow! Hollow!," Eugene indulges in "the wail of the poet's heart on discovering that everything is commonplace" (*Patience*, 287).

In some of these traits, as Carolyn Williams has observed, the traditional stage stock-types of poet and clergyman overlap, both commonly exhibiting supposed spirituality or unworldliness, both eager for feminine attention, both possessing manners so mild as to be unmanly. The poet and parson were commonly used to retell a familiar narrative of poetic or clerical effeminacy in competition with conventional masculinity—with the latter generally emerging triumphant. Gilbert and Burnand essentially used the poet as a substitute for the stage clergyman to capitalize on the aesthetic craze of the early 1880s. The poet, they suggested, was just like the minister, only more so.[3] Shaw highlights this trend by placing the two types side by side. The spiritual sensitivity of the cleric is pressed into the stereotypically masculine role when juxtaposed with the romantic effeminacy of the poet. Shaw takes pains in his initial descriptions to set up James, with his "*robust*" physique and "*athletic*" voice, as a sharp contrast to Eugene's "*childish*" fragility (*BH1*, 517, 534).

As Martin Meisel has argued, in presenting this drama of competing masculinities, Shaw also drew on the tradition of domestic comedy, in which a wife is tempted away from her prosaic husband by a glamorous but unscrupulous admirer (*Shaw and the Nineteenth-Century Theater*,

226–229).[4] In these plays, such as Tom Taylor's *Still Waters Run Deep* (1855) and *Victims* (1857), the would-be adulterer charms the woman with romantic affectations, sham artistic pretensions, or dashing boasts of duels and foreign travel, convincing her that he is the soul mate who can satisfy the romantic yearnings that her husband has failed to appreciate or fulfill. Eugene, in his pursuit of the married Candida, takes the position of the dashing interloper. In declaring his superior understanding of another man's wife, he is identified early in the play with the theatrical tradition of the cynical poseur striking aesthetic "attitudes" to impress women. A Victorian audience, familiar with the domestic comedy scenario, would thus be prepared to see Eugene bested by the common sense or masculine solidity of the husband.

For all this carefully arranged opposition between the unconventional poet and the manly man, the two rivals are ironically similar in their assumptions about Candida. Eugene is contemptuously aware of the trite unsatisfactoriness of James's homiletics as a means of lovemaking. But in deriding the "metaphors" and "mere rhetoric" with which James attempts to feed his wife's "great soul," he does not notice that his own rhetoric is, for the most part, equally trite (*BH1*, 543).[5] In worshipping Candida as the "Virgin Mother" and an "angel" with a "wreath of stars" and "lilies in her hand," he is doing little more than mouthing the jargon of the Pre-Raphaelites (*BH1*, 579). As Walter King has noted, no less than James, Eugene is "in love with words" ("The Rhetoric of *Candida*," 75). He rightly divines that James's understanding of Candida is limited by his doctrine-bound assumptions on gender relations and by his habit of seeing all events as possible material for a sermon, but does not realize that in describing Candida in poetic language and protesting against her household chores as a violation of his idealized vision, he is limiting his own view of her in exactly the same way.

However flawed Eugene's poetry and his assumptions about Candida might be, he is not simply a caricature to be ridiculed, like Gilbert's Bunthorne.[6] Eugene does not adopt the aesthetic pose cynically, but shows himself painfully sincere. The earnestness of his artistic aspiration contrasts vividly with the "aesthetic sham" of Bunthorne and his hypocritical literary ancestors. Eugene's horror of onions and his inability to write with a typewriter might provoke laughter. But his material ignorance and his sometimes-trite poetic maunderings are intermingled with flashes of keen psychological intuition, sudden moments of insight into the minds of Prossy, James, and Candida, and ultimately his own mind as well. This emotional knowledge prevents audiences from dismissing him, as they readily dismiss Bunthorne and his disciples, as merely ridiculous. Indeed, in his initial description of Eugene, Shaw turns the critical gaze from the poet to the poet's observers: "*He is so uncommon as to be almost unearthly; and to prosaic people there is something noxious in this unearthliness, just as to poetic people there is something angelic about it*" (*BH1*, 535). In *Patience*, Gilbert raises laughter at the expense of gullible female poet-worshippers and invites operagoers to identify with the sensible characters who see through the sham. But Shaw suggests that dismissal of the poet, as well as worship, is a response that requires questioning, and that both reactions might reveal more about the observer than they do about the poet.

Another Masquerade

Shaw began writing *Candida* a few months after reading Henry Arthur Jones's romantic drama *The Masqueraders*, another play preoccupied with questions of disguises and authenticity (see previous chapter). Shaw had exhorted Jones to "chuck up these idiotic moral systems according to which human nature comes out base and filthy" (*CLS1*, 444). His second pleasant play might be viewed as, among other things, an effort to combine precept with example, repurposing many of the scenes and plot motifs from Jones's play to show what they might look like without Jones's conventional "moral systems." Both plots center on a romantic triangle between a wife, a husband, and an imaginative, romantic-minded admirer. But the dynamics of the Morrell-Marchbanks rivalry are less clear-cut, without an obvious hero or villain, without an abusive husband or a heroine in need of rescue. By dismantling the melodramatic good-and-evil binary that classes Jones's two leading men, Shaw created a lower-stakes setting in which the questions of marriage commitment, romantic love, and gender relations could be more thoughtfully explored.

In the husband, James Morrell, Shaw created an opposite to Jones's bully, Sir Brice Skene. The gambling drunkard is replaced by an affectionate, steady, Helmer-like model of masculine virtues, and those virtues are themselves re-evaluated in the course of the play (perhaps not by coincidence, one of the actors Shaw early considered for the role was Herbert Waring, who had played both Torvald and Sir Brice[7]). Shaw made James the play's spokesman for conventional morality, much as the confidant Helen Larondie serves in *The Masqueraders*—the character of whom Shaw wrote, "Every one of that woman's allusions to duty elicited a howl of rage from me" (*CLS1*, 443). Some of James's speeches, in fact, seem close paraphrases of Helen's infuriating exhortations. Helen, for example, tells the romantic hero, David Remon: "We are all soldiers on this earth, bound to be loyal to every one of our comrades, bound to obey the great rules of life, whether they are easy or hard" (*MAS*, 110). This military metaphor is echoed in *Candida* when James admonishes Eugene: "Even at home, we sit as if in camp, encompassed by a hostile army of doubts. Will you play the traitor and let them in on me?" (*BH1*, 543). As Dulcie desperately seeks an escape from her abusive husband, Helen insists that it is a wife's duty "to keep herself pure and stainless, because [purity] is her glory" (*MAS*, 87). James, similarly, exasperates his wife by praising her "goodness and purity" (*BH1*, 564, 565). Jones gave Helen the last word in the duty debate, allowing her to speak with "God's voice" (*MAS*, 111). Ideologically, *Candida* begins where *The Masqueraders* leaves off: the moral claims with which Helen concludes one play hold center stage at the beginning of the other, in the person of Reverend James, only to be eroded by Eugene's skepticism and Candida's affectionate ridicule.

Eugene, the "*strange, shy youth*," likewise has much in common with the chivalrous and socially awkward David (*BH1*, 534). For Eugene's physical appearance, Shaw may well have drawn from Jones's description of David's younger brother Eddie, who serves mostly as a go-between in his brother's romance, and who is characterized as "*a delicate boy of about twenty, highly refined, overstrung, unbalanced*" (*MAS*, 5). Shaw, preparing to produce *Candida*, asked Jones for casting suggestions for Eugene, and Jones immediately recommended H. V. Esmond, who had played Eddie (Doris Jones, *Taking the Curtain Call*, 172). Shaw enthusiastically agreed to the suggestion, calling Esmond "the only possible man for it," though this engagement eventually fell through (*CLS1*, 630). Eugene, like David, claims ownership of another man's wife, declaring his determination to "rescue" her. Yet his declarations, like James's platitudes, are undercut by being removed from their melodramatic context. Candida, neither destitute nor battered, has none of Dulcie's need of rescue, and Eugene's promises consequently fall flat as yet one more piece of sensational posturing.

The Real Self and the Preaching Match

Though Eugene initially inhabits the roles of stage poet, rescuer, and seducer unconsciously, Candida makes him aware of the theatrical conventions within which he acts. She makes his association with the domestic comedy seducer explicit when they are left alone together, teasingly observing, "I'm sure you feel a great grown-up wicked deceiver. Quite proud of yourself, arnt you?" (*BH1*, 574). When it is pointed out to him, Eugene is intrigued and perhaps even aroused by his new role, and attempts to experiment with it. Kneeling beside her chair with "*his blood beginning to stir*," he asks, "May I say some wicked things to you?" (*BH1*, 574). Now that he has seen the possibility of acting a seduction scene, he appears pleased at the prospect.

Candida, however, deflates his eagerness, calling it "a mere attitude—a gallant attitude, or a wicked attitude, or even a poetic attitude" (*BH1*, 574). Eugene's poetic behavior to Candida, like James's preacherly behavior, is "as good as a play," and she will accept neither a seduction drama nor a morality play as the template for her relations with men. As she has earlier done with James, she deprecates Eugene's theatrical pose and calls for what she considers a more authentic relationship: "[Y]ou may say anything you really and truly feel. Anything at all, no matter what it is...so long as it is your real self that speaks.... Now say whatever you want to" (*BH1*, 574). Though postmodern performance theorists might critique Candida's invitation for its suggestion of a performance-free ontological state for pure, role-less "real selves," it brings Eugene a vital piece of self-knowledge. In removing the poetic and adulterous parameters of the situation, her speech forces him to think outside his habitual vocabulary of words and ideas and to discover that "all the words I know belong to some attitude or other" (*BH1*, 574). Having made this discovery, he abruptly loses interest in seduction. When Candida asks him, "Do you want anything more?"—that is, does he want sex?—he answers, "No" (*BH1*, 575). Now, the authentic speech act of calling Candida by her name—addressing her "real self"—is enough to satisfy him, and he declares, "I have come into heaven, where want is unknown" (*BH1*, 575). He becomes aware that in breaking the conventions of Victorian morality, he has been merely enacting the theatrical conventions of the poetic stage-seducer. He discovers also that his poetic "attitude" (pose), however sincerely adopted, has shaped his attitude (way of thinking) toward Candida, leading him to mistakes not unlike James's.

The parallel that Eugene discovers here between his error and James's is underscored in this scene by the parallel occupations of the two men. Act III opens with the two rivals desperately and simultaneously showing off their rhetorical talents—"having a preaching match," as Eugene later says (*BH1*, 581). James is offstage, lecturing to the Guild of St. Matthew, giving, as he and his listeners later recount, the best lecture of his life. Eugene, meanwhile, is awkwardly giving a private poetry reading with Candida as an oblivious and irreverent audience. Meanwhile, both men wait anxiously as their respective claims to Candida hang in the balance. Eugene, having received Candida's admonition on authenticity and "attitudes," comprehends the likeness of their two positions. He explains this likeness as he summarizes the events of the evening to James: "I have been making a fool of myself in private whilst you have been making a fool of yourself in public.... I have been playing the Good Man. Just like you" (*BH1*, 576). If the role of the stage-seducer is an "attitude"—poetic, gallant, or wicked—then, Eugene concludes, the role of the "Good Man" (the clergyman or the non-seducer) is equally artificial, another pose to be assumed. He attempts to follow up his epiphany by discovering James's "real self," as distinct from the social role and pulpit performance of the clergyman. "The man I want to meet," he declares, "is the man that Candida married.... I do not mean the Reverend James Mavor Morrell, moralist and windbag. I mean the real man that the Reverend James must have hidden somewhere inside his black coat: the man that Candida loved" (*BH1*, 577).

Up to this point, the play has parodied several dramatic forms and social performances, including the domestic comedy triangle, the seduction scene, religious homiletics, and poetry reading. Each of these forms, Shaw suggests, has been found wanting as a pattern for a play and, besides, has helped to shape problematic popular attitudes toward marriage and gender roles, whether through moral tenets, romantic imagery, or emotional display. The last brief play-within-the-play, the auction scene in which Candida demands that each man make a bid to determine whom she should belong to, is both the most sensational and the most disturbing in its implications for the marriage relationship. Here again, Shaw draws from Jones's *Masqueraders*, as well as from Boucicault's *Octoroon* and a long line of performance history (see previous chapter). In placing herself "up for auction," Candida renders literal the common nineteenth-century accusation against marriage—that it entails the ownership of a woman by a man—and implies that sensational theatrical spectacles have helped to naturalize and perpetuate the assumptions that permit this injustice.

Candida, of course, is no helpless Zoe or Dulcie Larondie, but puts herself up for sale only after having made it clear in Ibsenite fashion that "she belongs to herself" (*BH1*, 590). She sarcastically addresses James and Eugene as "my lords and masters," again implying a link between marriage and the slave market, but with a skepticism that distances her from the process, rendering her a spectator to the men's active performance. James and Eugene, thus rebuked and challenged, are invited to take the role of buyers and to try for the woman's favor with one final rhetorical display. This "preaching match" in miniature allows Candida (and the audience) to see how the two men have responded to her critiques on their performance and their behavior to her. Eugene no longer attempts to woo her with idylls of boats or angels, but offers only his "weakness," "desolation," and "heart's need"—a move that Candida praises as a "good bid," seeing that he has profited from her lesson on "real selves" (*BH1*, 591).

James shows her influence in another way. Even now, he cannot present himself except with carefully measured cadences that announce his masculine "strength," "honesty," "industry," and "authority" (*BH1*, 591). Yet in the midst of his declaration of strength, he breaks down and becomes a "wounded animal" (*BH1*, 590). He chokes out, "I can't speak"—for James, there could be no more abject admission of defeat (*BH1*, 590). In his moment of distress, losing his hold on his preacherly role, he reveals the "real self" detached from this role. As actor Charles Charrington prepared for the role of James Morrell, Shaw explained to him that this crucial moment shows the irresistibly handsome preacher "making [himself] diabolically ugly (by indulging in *genuine* emotion)" (*CLS1*, 612).

SIT AND TALK: THE NEW DRAMA

Candida signals a definitive end to oratory by inviting James and Eugene to "sit and talk comfortably over it like three friends" (*BH1*, 591). The line markedly echoes the closing scene of *A Doll's House*, with Nora's call to discussion. Shaw follows Ibsen's example in using this discussion to delay the play's ending after the main plot has been resolved, to stretch the audience's patience, requiring them not only to view the play's events but also to consider why those events have taken place. Candida sets aside the emotional intensity of the auction scene and the love triangle, the moral and romantic diction of the sermons and sonnets that have dominated the play hitherto, and talks.

"Talk," throughout the play, seems a distinctly feminine word.[8] Candida frequently uses "talk" to refer to her own words, as opposed to the "speak," "preach," "words," "sermon," "lecture," "poetry," and "conversation" that designate the men's communication. She repeatedly interrupts the men's writing or reading with coaxing requests to "come and talk" and insistences that "I must be talked to" (*BH1*, 562). James and Eugene underscore the idea of "talk" as Candida's province by their persistent resistance to her invitations: "No: I mustn't talk," Eugene protests, while James replies, "I cant talk. I can only preach" (*BH1*, 573, 567). Candida's "talk," in contrast to the oratorical flourishes that she has rebuked as showy or artificial, blends emotional intimacy with utilitarian literalness, with attention divided between chopped onions and fractured relationships. She calls attention to the simplicity and even ineptitude of her own speech compared with her husband's. When repeating the phrases of James's bid—"his strength for my defence! his industry for my livelihood!"—she breaks off, adding apologetically, "Ah, I am mixing up your beautiful cadences and spoiling them, am I not, darling?" (*BH1*, 593). Candida's final invitation to "talk" allows the men and the audience, after two and a half acts of competing masculine rhetorics, to hear a sustained sample of this plain, relatively untheatrical speech.

Once Candida has issued this invitation, she, like Nora, does most of the talking. In marked contrast to Nora, however, Candida chiefly speaks not of herself, but of the two men: first Eugene as the lonely misfit, then James as a "strong and clever and happy" man who must be sheltered by female relatives from anything that threatens his strength, cleverness, or happiness (*BH1*, 592–593). In initiating this discussion, she marks a decisive change of direction: hitherto, much of the play's action has consisted of the two men speaking about her. Now, she talks about them, showing that she understands them better than they understand her. Their conceptions of her have been inflected by religion, romanticism, and the dramatic genre-bound assumptions of the seducer and the socially correct husband—generalized phrases about a "good woman" and "happy marriage," or else biblically inspired ornamental images of a "flaming sword" and feet "beautiful upon the mountains" (*BH1*, 559). The concrete facts of Candida's domestic life, if the men mention them at all, have been quickly shied away from as "rough" or "coarse-grained" (*BH1*, 557). Concrete facts, however, are the essence of Candida's retelling of their narratives:

Eugene's school miseries and family conflicts, James's cricket victories and money difficulties, and the unpoetical age difference that she asks Eugene to make into a "little poem" (*BH1*, 594). Most of her information she has heard from them or gained from observation, and they acknowledge it as accurate. Her speech is presented as an unmasking of her own "real self" and those of the two men, a behind-the-scenes glimpse of the poet and the pulpit performance, an exercise in the authenticity which—as she and Shaw both imply—is essential both to good marriage and to good plays.

Candida's final decision reverses Nora's declaration of independence: Candida, when offered an opportunity to leave the doll's house, chooses to stay with her doll-husband. The one who exits through the slamming door is Eugene, the rejected lover. This is, in one sense, a fairly conventional domestic comedy's ending: to preserve morality, the illicit interloper is expelled and the married couple is reconciled. Shaw, however, subverts this conclusion, as he later explained to James Huneker: Eugene is not ousted as a home-wrecker, but rather flees from the comfortable home, regarding it as a "greasy fool's paradise" (*Iconoclasts: A Book of Dramatists*, 255). For the reconciled James and Candida, the play's conclusion is almost a typical happy ending. Yet Shaw calls the dramatic convention of the "happy ending" into question. The rejected Eugene is placed at an advantage, since, as Candida observes, "He has learned to live without happiness" (*BH1*, 593). Through Eugene, Shaw follows Gilbert's example in caricaturing poetic idealizations of women, but he ultimately dignifies the figure of the poet. Early in the play, Eugene has provoked laughs by recoiling in horror from Candida's onions and scrubbing-brush, clinging to his reverential vision of Candida as a pure spirit or angel. In the end, however, Eugene repudiates domestic love not because he is unprepared for its smelly realities, but because his poetic vocation is to him a "nobler" reality. The last stage direction—"*They [Candida and James] embrace; but they do not know the secret of the poet's heart*" (*BH1*, 594)— leaves a mystery hanging to the play's ending, much as "the miracle of miracles" that can create a true marriage gives Nora's departure the air of an unanswered question.

With this unsettled, questioning conclusion, Shaw, like Ibsen, resisted the easy, predetermined resolution of conventional theatrical genres. By imitating the structure of *A Doll's House*, beginning with a conventional well-made play and ending with a discussion of the play's action, Shaw prepared the way for his later plays, in which discussion would take an increasing share of the stage time, sometimes to the near-exclusion of any plot. Even in this early play, the brief space accorded to the discussion seemed disproportionate to some of Shaw's associates. Years later, Shaw recalled Ellen Terry protesting, after having seen Janet Achurch in a touring performance in Eastbourne, that "it was utterly impossible for a stage heroine to say calmly, just when the audience was feeling for its hats and caps, 'Let us sit and talk comfortably over it like three friends'" (*BH1*, 600). Actor-manager Richard Mansfield, who had arranged the play's abortive 1895 production in New York with himself as Eugene, expressed himself even more vehemently in a letter to Shaw as he abandoned the project: "*Candida*...is not a play.... Here are three long acts of talk—talk—talk" (*CLS1*, 523).[9] Like its Ibsen counterpart, Shaw's discussion scene and long conversations challenged the habits of actors and playgoers, disrupting their understanding of what a play ought to be.

Ten years after writing *Candida*, Shaw concluded his short story "The Theatre of the Future" with an imaginary advertisement that might be taken as a sly commentary on *Candida*, Mansfield's complaints, and theatrical marriages generally:

> The manager of the C.F.A [Cash For Admission] Theatre regrets to have to announce that his attempt to procure a new play introducing a married woman in love with her own husband, and without a past, has been wholly unsuccessful. An appeal to our leading dramatic authors to write to such a play has elicited a unanimous refusal to compromise their professional reputation by dealing with an abnormal situation and catering for morbid tastes. ("The Theatre of the Future," 79)

Shaw himself had endeavored to depict "a married woman in love with her own husband, and without a past," seeing dramatic potential in this seemingly mundane premise. The resistance the play met with from producers and spectators alike (even as dramatists such as Pinero and Jones gained resounding applause for their fashionable dramas of women endeavoring to conceal their scandalous pasts and their extramarital attachments) shows how violently this innovation flouted dramatic custom.

STAGING MARRIAGE AND DIVORCE

Mansfield's complaint, that *Candida* was "not a play," but only "talk—talk—talk," was repeated by many critics regarding Shaw's subsequent plays over the following years. Shaw took these complaints as proof of his early assertion that discussion—as introduced in the final acts of *Candida* and *A Doll's House*—was a defining technical innovation of New Drama. In 1913, in his expanded edition of *The Quintessence of Ibsenism*, he reported, "we now have plays, including some of my own, which begin with discussion and end with action, and others in which the discussion interpenetrates the action from beginning to end" (*QI* 213).

Though commercial actor-managers were reluctant to stage conversational plays of this kind, smaller, more experimental theater organizations such as the Independent Theatre and the Stage Society offered spaces to test some of his early plays. Later, from 1904 to 1907, the Vedrenne-Barker management at the Royal Court Theatre would offer a venue for many of his works. Replacing the star actor system and high-budget costumes and scenery of the West End with ensemble acting and bare-bones sets, Vedrenne and Barker's emphasis on plays' dialogue and characters perfectly suited Shaw's dramatic discussions.

One of his most proudly and self-consciously discussion-based plays was *Getting Married* (1908). Produced under the Vedrenne-Barker management at the Haymarket (shortly after the conclusion of their final season at the Court), it was subtitled "A Disquisitory Play." In an article for *The Daily Telegraph*, written a few days before the play's premiere on May 12, 1908, he described the play as his "revenge on the critics," a play in which "There will be nothing but talk, talk, talk, talk, talk—Shaw talk" (*BH3*, 665). As an established dramatist, Shaw had less need to classify his plays within the conventional categories of comedy, history, farce, or melodrama, as he had earlier in his career. He could present the Shavian discussion play unapologetically as a genre in itself.

If British drama at the turn of the twentieth century frequently treated marriage as inherently theatrical, *Getting Married* might be seen as one extended play within the play—or as an elaborate backstage spectacle. As Peter Gahan has noted, the play foregrounds costumes, especially uniforms for those in official roles: the General, the Bishop, the Alderman, the Lady Mayoress, and the Beadle ("Marriage and Mating," 106). Meanwhile, Edith, the bride, enters gownless and unveiled, in "*dressing-jacket and petticoat*," standing as "a sartorial question mark over the dramatic action" ("Marriage and Mating," 106). The play is set in the kitchen, while the primary spaces of the wedding's action—the church and the dining room where the wedding breakfast will be held—are offstage, only given brief occasional mentions. Shaw described it as "a perfect Greek play with the unities of time and space strictly preserved," and he likewise followed the ancient Greek convention of allowing the definitive action (in this case, the wedding ceremony) to happen offstage, with the event afterwards reported by messengers (*BH3*, 663). The belated wedding is doubly offstage in that it takes place only when nearly all the spectators have left the church. Throughout the play, participants set the stage for the wedding performance and then wonder if the show will go on or not—a sort of matrimonial forerunner to Michael Frayn's *Noises Off.*

The play centers on the preparations for one offstage marital spectacle. Yet, early in the action, Shaw draws attention to the aftermath of another, a far less respectable performance, the divorce of Reginald and Leo Bridgenorth. The event is first described by the most traditional-minded characters in the play, the General and the Bishop's wife, who present it as a melodrama of domestic abuse and abject shame. The General exclaims: "Bridgenorth of Bridgenorth! To beat his wife and go off with a low woman and be divorced for it in the face of all England!" (*BH3*, 563–564). Reginald, in the General's telling, is simply a brutal husband, Leo a helpless victim.

When Reginald and Leo appear onstage, however, the story appears more farce than melodrama as the divorcees reveal how thoroughly scripted and staged their separation was. Reginald grumbles:

> I had to go out and dig the flower bed all over with my own hands to soften it. I had to pick all the stones out of it. And then she complained that I hadnt done it properly, because she got a worm down her neck. I had to go to Brighton with a poor creature who took a fancy to me on the way down, and got conscientious scruples about committing perjury after dinner.... How would y o u like to go into a hotel before all the waiters and people with—with t h a t on your arm?...And then I'm held up in the public court for cruelty and adultery. (*BH3*, 568–569)

Shaw used the Bridgenorth divorce as a dramatic underscoring for one of the recurring claims of his lengthy preface, the need for no-fault divorce as a precondition for functional marriage laws. Through Reginald and Leo, Shaw presented a *reductio ad absurdum* of the narrowly defined conditions that circumscribed the availability of divorce in Edwardian England (the requirement either of a husband's adultery compounded by desertion or cruelty or of a wife's simple adultery). Many couples, facing these conditions, attempted to circumvent them by some private agreement. Allen Horstman has reported that in the decades following the passing of the

Matrimonial Causes Act in 1857, about five percent of English divorce suits were denied on the ground of collusion after having been investigated by the Queen's Proctor (*Victorian Divorce*, 102). Such collusion most often consisted in the suppression of evidence of mutual infidelity or in the respondent's non-contest of a thinly evidenced accusation of adultery (*Victorian Divorce*, 101). Such cases ended with the would-be divorcees, whether both adulterous or both faithful, being condemned, in Shaw's phrase, "to perpetual wedlock" (*BH3*, 543). He protested against this policy both through the comic predicament of Leo and Reginald and through his recommendations for divorce reform in the conclusion of the preface: "Make divorce as easy, as cheap, and as private as marriage," "Grant divorce at the request of either party," and "Make it impossible for marriage to be used as a punishment as it is at present" (*BH3*, 542–543).

With the melodrama-farce of Leo and Reginald's divorce, *Getting Married* echoes the real-life divorce court dramas that had become a much-discussed entertainment genre in the second half of the nineteenth century, transforming actual marital conflicts into sensational theatrical acts. Horstman reports that after 1857, divorce cases became "a popular spectator sport" that allowed observers to gratify both their salacious curiosity and their sense of respectable superiority (*Victorian Divorce*, 87). Listeners competed for opportunities to hear the particulars of adultery, incest, or violence. Those who did not come in person could read newspaper narratives, and newspaper editors relied on racy reports to boost their sales. The detailed news reports of divorce trials provoked numerous letters of complaint from subscribers who protested against the "loathsome details" dwelt on in court reports and the need to "keep the daily papers out of their daughters' hands," comparing the corrupting influence of newspapers with that of the theater ("An Old Woman Without a Past," 11). Queen Victoria complained that "None of the worst French novels…can be as bad" (qtd. in Horstman, *Victorian Divorce*, 86). William Gladstone, Thomas Huxley, and Cardinal Manning, among hundreds of others, signed petitions to the Lord Chancellor calling for restrictions on divorce court publicity (*Victorian Divorce*, 99). Shaw added his voice to this chorus of protest in his preface to *Getting Married*. He declared that he looked forward to a time when "there will be no more reports of divorce cases, no more letters read with an indelicacy that makes every sensitive person shudder and recoil as from a profanation, no more washing of household linen, dirty or clean, in public" (*BH3*, 518). He opposed such reports not only because of their luridness but also for the same reason many moralists, even opponents of divorce, supported them: the detailed exposures of misconduct that were demanded as grounds for divorce were "the only means the public now has of ascertaining that every possible effort has been made to keep the couple united against their wills" (*BH3*, 518). With greater privacy in the divorce process, he argued, would come easier divorces and, ultimately, better marriages.

The Reginald/Leo/Sinjon love triangle was, among other things, a farcical reenactment of the domestic interloper scenario presented in *Candida*. Whereas the earlier play shows an older husband and a younger family friend pursuing the love of one wife, the later play shows one wife struggling to keep possession of a younger family friend and her older husband. Leo, described in the stage directions as "*a born fusser about herself and everybody else for whom she feels responsible*," might be taken as a not-very-successful imitator of Candida, the able housewife (*BH3*, 566). The husband, Reginald, "*a muddled, rebellious, hasty, untidy, forgetful, always late sort of man*," is like James in "*very evidently need[ing] the care of a capable woman*," but unlike him in having "*never been lucky or attractive enough to get it*" (*BH3*, 564). Sinjon, smartly dressed, intellectually conceited, and indecisive in his dealings with women, is the opposite of the shy, unworldly, but ultimately self-knowing Eugene.

Shaw explicitly invited comparisons between the two plays in his preface to *Getting Married*. He alluded to *Candida* as an illustration of the "sentimental basis" of monogamy, the idea that the role of a spouse within a marriage is a "place that is large enough for one only" (*BH3*, 511, 514). He held up James's demand that Candida choose between him and Eugene as "What an honorable and sensible man does when his household is invaded" (*BH3*, 514). Whereas Eugene, James, and Candida all take for granted Shaw's assertion that "nobody has room in his or her life for more than one such relationship [marriage partner] at a time," this claim is questioned early in *Getting Married* (*BH3*, 511–512). Leo protests: "Oh, how silly the law is! Why cant I marry them both?...I should like to marry a lot of men. I should like to have Rejjy for every day, and Sinjon for concerts and theatres and going out in the evenings, and some great austere saint for about once a year at the end of the season, and some perfectly blithering idiot of a boy to be quite wicked with" (*BH3*, 572). Her polyandrous aspiration is mainly played for laughs. When she attempts to sketch it in practical terms, the plan falls to pieces. Her proudly unconventional rejection of monogamy is undercut by her unwillingness to share either husband with another woman. On being told that the "alliance" contract can accommodate "any number of ladies or gentlemen," she protests: "Not any number of ladies. Only one lady" (*BH3*, 607). Hence, when Mrs. George Collins becomes a second lady in Sinjon's affection, Leo abandons her double marriage scheme and returns to Reginald, offering, like *Candida*, a telling illustration of Shaw's defense of monogamy. And like Candida, Leo ultimately chooses the man she believes to need her more.

Leo's attempt at polyandry is one of several unconventional unions that are negotiated in the "alliance" contract scene in an effort to correct what various characters see as the injustices of English marriage law. Edith objects to the lack of pay for the wifely work of housekeeping and childbearing, and to marriage's lifelong commitment, which would remain binding even if her husband commits a crime. Her fiancé, Cecil, fears being bankrupted by libel lawsuits resulting from Edith's inflammatory public speeches. Lesbia, a self-declared old maid, wants children but dislikes the prospect of giving a husband unlimited access to her living space and her body. All attempt to create contracts that offer the desirable features of marriage without the disadvantages, though the attempts founder on details such as the duration of the agreement and the custody of children. The negotiation ends more or less where Shaw's preface does—with the conclusion: "You can make divorce reasonable and decent: that is all" (*BH3*, 619).

Marriage and Fellowship

The contract discussion scene is presided over by two clergymen who, as in *Candida*, are used as spokesmen for the church's perspective (or rather, its several perspectives) regarding marriage. In *Candida*, Shaw had used the Reverend James Morrell to express the Christian Socialist conviction that union with "a good woman" is a foretaste of "the Kingdom of Heaven...on earth" (*BH1*, 521). The Bishop Alfred Bridgenorth, though, like James, a comfortably married man, is less optimistic. Having (like Shaw) authored a treatise on marriage, he is convinced by his study of ancient Rome that the marriage institution in England is on the point of dying out due to lack of easily accessible divorce. His pronouncements seem to take more from Shavian doctrine than the Church of England, frequently echoing ideas from the dramatist's preface. Where James praises feminine "goodness and purity," the Bishop defends his sister-in-law's desire for two husbands on the ground that "many very interesting men have been polygamists" (*BH3*, 575). He plays devil's advocate, figuratively and literally, repeating the refrain, "You must give the devil fair play" (*BH3*, 597).

James's long-held confidence in Christian marriage, along with the Bishop's ambivalence, is flatly contradicted by the other cleric in *Getting Married*, Father Anthony Soames, the chaplain-solicitor. Anthony, whose chosen name reflects his embrace of celibacy and asceticism, asserts that the Christian church "was founded to put an end to marriage and to put an end to property" and therefore advises his married or engaged listeners to take "the Christian vows of celibacy and poverty" (*BH3*, 610). When his hearers ask, "how could the world go on?", he responds: "Do your duty and see. Doing your duty is your business: keeping the world going is in higher hands" (*BH3*, 610). For audience members who tended (like James Morrell) to conflate marriage with Christianity and moral goodness, Shaw used the early church's emphasis on celibacy to undercut this assumption. He likewise used Anthony's refusal of romance and domesticity—like those of Lesbia Grantham, Vivie Warren, Richard Dudgeon, and his other "Puritan" heroes—to counter the excessive sentimentality of Victorian theater. *Getting Married* ends, like *Mrs. Warren's Profession*, with a lone celibate character on the stage, "*writing tranquilly*" (*BH3*, 662). Singleness, the play suggests, is as worthy of dramatization as romance.

The final preacher, of sorts, to appear onstage is Mrs. George Collins—not an officially ordained member of the clergy, yet presented as a spiritual authority of another kind. She is first presented to the audience by other characters' descriptions as a serial philanderess and a clairvoyant, and as "Incognita Appasionata," the mysterious writer of love letters to the Bishop (*BH3*, 555, 578). Her doctrine of marriage is presented late in the play, when she demonstrates her clairvoyant ability. Her visionary trance-born speech is a protest against the law's relentless coupling of sex with marriage:

> When you loved me I gave you the whole sun and stars to play with. I gave you eternity in a single moment, strength of the mountains in one clasp of your arms, and the volume of all the seas in one impulse of your souls. A moment only; but was it not enough? Were you not paid then for all the rest of your struggle on earth? Must I mend your clothes and sweep your floors as well? Was it not enough? I paid the price without bargaining: I bore the children without flinching: was that a reason for heaping fresh burdens on

me? I carried the child in my arms: must I carry the father too? When I opened the gates of paradise, were you blind? Was it nothing to you? When all the stars sang in your ears and all the winds swept you into the heart of heaven, were you deaf? were you dull? was I no more to you than a bone to a dog? Was it not enough? We spent eternity together; and you ask me for a little lifetime more. We possessed all the universe together; and you ask me to give you my scanty wages as well. I have given you the greatest of all things; and you ask me to give you little things. I gave you your own soul: you ask for my body as a plaything. (*BH3*, 645)

This prophetic oration, while describing sexual ecstasy in metaphors and parallelisms reminiscent of the Psalms and the book of Job, denounces the conditions that law and custom attach to sex. Mrs. George's marriage sermon might be taken as a feminine corollary to Don Juan's complaint in the Hell scene of *Man and Superman*. Don Juan, as a man, resents women's insistence on "honourable" conditions for sex, including marital property settlements and financial support, lifelong companionship, and perpetual monogamy—conditions which he declares to by "exorbitant and inhuman" and utterly irrelevant to his simple desire to receive and give sexual gratification (*BH2*, 676). Mrs. George, in a similar vein, speaks against the demands that man-made rules heap upon women within marriage. These declamations give dramatic emphasis to Shaw's contentions about "the impersonality of sex" in his preface to *Getting Married*: "to make marriage an open trade in it [sex] as it is at present, with money, board and lodging, personal slavery, vows of eternal exclusive personal sentimentalities and the rest of it as the price, is neither virtuous, dignified, nor decent" (*BH3*, 498).

These diverse preachers have one idea in common, one that, on the surface, seems to have little connection with marriage. Through Anthony, the Bishop, and Mrs. George, Shaw foregrounded what he took to be the central message both of Christ and of socialism, which he later articulated in the preface to *Misalliance*: the teaching that all humans are "members one of another"[10] (*BH4*, 74). This concept of spiritual and social equality going hand in hand—an idea antithetical to the stratified social and economic system Shaw deplored in England—is a thread that repeatedly resurfaces throughout the play as a secondary theme. Tellingly, this idea is introduced in the first few minutes of *Candida*, when James goes out of his way to serve the working-class Hoxton anarchists on the ground that he and they "have the same father—in Heaven" (*BH1*, 519). In *Getting*

Married, Anthony echoes this idea, speaking of the "communion of saints" and "Christian fellowship" as the rightful basis of social organization (*BH3*, 619, 661). The Bishop speaks of the Anglican baptismal service as "a terribly democratic thing," conferring on infants of every social class a "high and awful" rank as soldier and servant of God (*BH3*, 586). Mrs. George points to this message from the Bishop—the message that all humans "come from the same workshop"—as the basis of her clairvoyant power, her capacity to speak for "the whole human race" (*BH3*, 640, 555). She tells the Bishop, "It was from you that I first learnt to respect myself" (*BH3*, 640). In her trance, she declares: "When you spoke to my soul years ago from your pulpit, you opened the doors of my salvation to me; and now they stand open forever.... I do for men what you did for me" (*BH3*, 646). Like Major Barbara, Mrs. George defines salvation less in terms of orthodox Christian doctrine than in terms of self-respect, courage, a sense of purpose, and a recognition of shared humanity.

This lesson of human kinship is most vividly driven home by the portrayal of Sinjon Hotchkiss, the self-proclaimed arch-snob who refuses as a soldier to obey the orders of an ungentlemanly officer, recoils from being introduced to a grocer, and insults the coal merchant's wife with whom, much to his own horror, he ultimately finds himself in love. From his first appearance onstage, he scoffs at the doctrine of spiritual or social equality. His infatuation with Mrs. George, who is at once a vulgar woman, a social inferior, and an apostle of this democratic teaching, is a stroke of poetic justice that links the secondary theme of equality with the play's primary emphasis on marriage. As Sinjon and Mrs. George discuss their proposed relationship, she schools him in courtesy, instructing him to "amuse George" and "be a perfect gentleman" (*BH3*, 629). He ends by resolving to apologize to past victims of his snobbery, declaring himself converted to a belief in equality on the ground that "The coal merchant and I are in love with the same woman. That settles the question for me for ever" (*BH3*, 657). Having reached an understanding, the couple-for-the-moment exits from the kitchen to the dining room, leaving the theatrical audience for an offstage audience of wedding guests.

Throughout the play, characters have argued over the best methods to "make marriage reasonable and decent" (*BH3*, 619). Though no settled answer is reached, Shaw suggests through his three stage preachers that an acceptance of human equality—through socialism, Christian fellowship, or both—must be a necessary precursor to any such reason and decency.

Conclusion

In *Getting Married*, Shaw built on the questions he had raised about marriage and theater in *Candida* and other early plays. He also presented a more theory-based version of the marital alterations that Jones and Pinero had depicted a decade earlier. Whereas Paula Tanqueray, Lady Susan Harabin, and Lady Jessica Nepean rush impulsively into experiments with revised sexual mores, Sinjon, Mrs. George, and the various branches of the Bridgenorth clan first attempt to map out blueprints for their unconventional unions. In his preface to *Getting Married*, Shaw explicitly criticized anti-matrimonial rebellions of the kind depicted in earlier plays. He ridiculed people who aimed at "reforming our marriage institutions by private enterprise and personal righteousness" (*BH3*, 453). In a language reminiscent of Jones's bachelor *raisonneurs*, he pointed out the danger of attempting to defy law and public opinion:

> Now most laws are, and all laws ought to be, stronger than the strongest individual. Certainly the marriage law is. The only people who successfully evade it are those who actually avail themselves of its shelter by pretending to be married when they are not, and by Bohemians who have no position to lose and no career to be closed. In every other case violation of the marriage laws means either downright ruin or such inconvenience and disablement as a prudent man or woman would marry ten times over rather than face. (*BH3*, 453–454)

Jones and Pinero depicted marital or quasi-marital experiments breaking down due to irresolute participants or intrusive spectators. Shaw's contract-makers, in the end, fare little better.

Certainly, viewed from the standpoint of traditional theater, blueprints make much less rousing entertainment than many experiments. Shaw acknowledged this, warning reviewers beforehand: "The characters will seem to the wretched critics to be simply a row of Shaws, all arguing with one another on totally uninteresting subjects.... The whole thing will be hideous, indescribable—an eternity of brain-racking dullness" (*BH3*, 665). In placing at the center of his play an argument over a contract that is never fully drawn up, he reused and built on the structure he had earlier noted in Ibsen's plays and his own. In *A Doll's House* and *Candida*, the injunction to "sit down and talk" was viewed by many as a jarring deviation from dramatic custom; in *Getting Married*, characters do little else. *Getting Married* represented, among other things, a conclusion to a suggestion Shaw had posed in *Candida*: that more discussion might mean better theater—and better marriage.

Notes

1. Shaw did, however, attack the performance of actor-manager Johnston Forbes-Robertson, saying, "He made the mistake—common in an irreligious age—of conceiving of a religious man as a lugubrious one" (*TN2*, 20). He countered the charge of blasphemy by asserting: "The real objection to Mr Jones's play is the objection to Michael's treatment of religion as co-extensive with life: that is, as genuinely catholic. To the man who regards it as only a watertight Sunday compartment of social observance, such a view is not only inconvenient but positively terrifying" (*TN2*, 23).
2. See also *The Quintessence of Ibsenism* and preface to *Major Barbara*.
3. Williams has pointed out that Burnand's *Colonel* is in essence a re-working of Barnett's *Serious Family*, substituting sham poets for the unscrupulous cleric, and that Gilbert did the same in basing *Patience* on "The Rival Curates," one of his earlier Bab Ballads written for *Fun* magazine (154–155).
4. Meisel notes that Shaw also plays with this scenario in *How he Lied to her Husband* and inverts it in *The Doctor's Dilemma*, making the artist the husband and the prosaic professional man the would-be lover.
5. Walter King makes this point in "The Rhetoric of *Candida*," describing Eugene's poetry as "a pouring out of tired romantic phrases sodden with the diluted Platonism one would expect in a gifted child growing up in an age when Yeats himself was wallowing in romantic mishmash" ("The Rhetoric of *Candida*," 75).
6. Even before *Candida*, Shaw's humor had been compared to Gilbert's, to Shaw's annoyance. Both William Archer and A. B. Walkley, reviewing *Arms and the Man*, likened it to Gilbert's fairy play *The Palace of Truth* (1870), in that both plays provoked laughter at the expense of characters who failed to live up to their extravagant declarations of love, patriotism, or bravery. Shaw, however, insisted to Archer that his brand of social critique was essentially different from Gilbert's: Gilbert, a "paradoxically humorous cynic," sneered at humanity for failing to reach ideals that Gilbert implicitly approved; Shaw, by contrast, found fault with the ideals themselves and proposed an alternative, namely "the practical life & morals of the efficient, realistic man" (*CLS1*, 427).
7. Shaw expressed reservations regarding Charles Charrington, who insistently put himself forward to play James opposite his wife's Candida. Recalling Charrington's *Doll's House* performance, Shaw told him: "The Doll's House was all right when you played Rank the Unfortunate. It was

all wrong when you played Helmer the Smug & Self Satisfied.... Waring …will not exactly fail: he will only underplay; and all the papers will treat him with great politeness. You will either fail or succeed; and if you fail, the result will be damnation" (*CLS1*, 612). Waring, however, proved either uninterested or unavailable, and Charrington took the role in the 1897 provincial tour as well as the 1900 London production.
8. Prossy, like Candida, also uses the word "talk" frequently, but less often as an invitation and more often as a complaint or a criticism.
9. Mansfield's dislike of the play's verbosity and its lack of conventional heroics may be part of the reason why the production was abandoned in the rehearsal stage, though financial disagreements between Achurch and Mansfield were the more immediate cause.
10. Shaw drew a sharp distinction between this concept of Christian fellowship and the tenets he abhorred in mainstream Christianity—in particular, the doctrines of Christ's vicarious suffering and atonement for human sin—which he critiqued at length in the prefaces to *Major Barbara* and *Androcles and the Lion*, among other places.

References

"An Old Woman Without a Past." *The Times*, December 11, 1894.
Buckley, Jennifer. "The Pragmatic Partnerships of *Plays Pleasant*." In *Bernard Shaw's Marriages and Misalliances*, edited by Robert A. Gaines, 39–56. New York: Palgrave Macmillan, 2017.
Conolly, L. W. "The 'Mystical Union' De-Mystified: Marriages in *Plays Unpleasant*." In *Bernard Shaw's Marriages and Misalliances*, edited by Robert A. Gaines, 21–38. New York: Palgrave Macmillan, 2017.
Foulkes, Richard. *Church and Stage in Victorian England*. Cambridge: Cambridge University Press, 1997.
Gahan, Peter. "Marriage and Mating in the Plays of Bernard Shaw and Granville Barker, 1908–1911." In *Bernard Shaw's Marriages and Misalliances*, edited by Robert A. Gaines, 105–24. New York: Palgrave Macmillan, 2017.
Gilbert, W. S. *Patience: Or, Bunthorne's Bride*. In *The Complete Annotated Gilbert and Sullivan*, edited by Ian Bradley, 265–354. Oxford: Oxford University Press, 1996a.
———. *The Sorcerer*. In *The Complete Annotated Gilbert and Sullivan*, edited by Ian Bradley, 41–112. Oxford: Oxford University Press, 1996b.
Horstman, Allen. *Victorian Divorce*. New York: St. Martin's, 1985.
Huneker, James. *Iconoclasts: A Book of Dramatists*. New York: Charles Scribner's Sons, 1907.
Jones, Doris Arthur. *Taking the Curtain Call: The Life and Letters of Henry Arthur Jones*. New York: Macmillan, 1930.

Jones, Henry Arthur. *The Masqueraders*. London: Macmillan, 1899.
King, Walter. "The Rhetoric of Candida." *Modern Drama* 2, no. 2 (1959): 71–83.
Meisel, Martin. *Shaw and the Nineteenth-Century Theater*. Princeton: Princeton University Press, 1963.
Shaw, Bernard. *Bernard Shaw: Collected Letters, 1874–1897*. Edited by Dan H. Laurence. Vol. 1. 3 vols. New York: Viking, 1965.
———. *Our Theatres in the Nineties*. 3 vols. London: Constable, 1932.
———. *Platform and Pulpit*. Edited by Dan H. Laurence. New York: Hill & Wang, 1961.
———. "Still After the Doll's House." In *The Works of Bernard Shaw*, vol. 6, 125–37. London: Constable, 1931.
———. *The Bodley Head Bernard Shaw: Collected Plays with Their Prefaces*. Edited by Dan H. Laurence. 7 vols. London: The Bodley Head, 1970.
———. *The Quintessence of Ibsenism*. In *Shaw and Ibsen: Bernard Shaw's The Quintessence of Ibsenism and Related Writings*, edited by J. L. Wisenthal, 97–237. Toronto: University of Toronto Press, 1958.
———. "The Theatre of the Future." In *Short Stories, Scraps and Shavings*, 55–84. London: Constable, 1934.
Templeton, Joan. *Shaw's Ibsen: A Re-Appraisal*. New York: Palgrave Macmillan, 2018.
Williams, Carolyn. *Gilbert and Sullivan: Gender, Genre, Parody*. New York: Columbia University Press, 2010.

CHAPTER 7

A Woman's Play: Elizabeth Robins and Suffrage Drama

Elizabeth Robins, describing her early encounters with Ibsen's works, recalled her youthful enthusiasm for plays that seemed "alive," "less like a play than like a personal meeting" (*Ibsen and the Actress*, 31). While many of Ibsen's admirers and attackers took his name as a synonym for women's rights, social critique, propaganda, and general didacticism, Robins had, at least initially, little interest in reading his plays from a political angle. Her first attention was not directed at the oppressive social conditions imposed on Ibsen's heroines within their marriages—that is, their economic dependence, the objectifying and infantilizing attitudes of their husbands and other men, and the lack of education that made them vulnerable to financial or sexual blackmail. Rather, it was in the drama of human life and the acting opportunities they offered. Recounting her experience viewing *A Doll's House* and producing *Hedda Gabler*, she wrote, "If we had been thinking politically, concerning ourselves about the emancipation of women, we would not have given the Ibsen plays the particular kind of whole-hearted, enchanted devotion we did give. We were actresses—actresses who wouldn't for a kingdom be anything else…. How were we to find fault with a state of society that had given us Nora and Hedda and Thea?" (*Ibsen and the Actress*, 31–32). She asserted that Ibsen had understood "the general bearing of Hedda's story" all along, though she had not (*Ibsen and the Actress*, 31). In retrospect, nearly forty years after the event, Robins admitted her early lack of political engagement with the plays in an almost apologetic tone, as if this were a myopia to be excused

© The Author(s) 2020
M. Christian, *Marriage and Late-Victorian Dramatists*, Bernard Shaw and His Contemporaries,
https://doi.org/10.1007/978-3-030-40639-4_7

on the score of her naïve ardor, before she was old enough to understand the plays better. She hastened to add, "We got over that" (*Ibsen and the Actress*, 31).

As a young actress, Robins looked on Ibsen's dramatic realism and women's political situation as separate issues, the former fascinating and the latter irrelevant. In her later work, she came to see these two issues as one. She viewed writing and acting, mirroring life in print and on stage, as political acts in themselves, especially where representation of women was concerned. Disgusted by the "chocolate-box 'type[s]'" of women created by many male authors, she exhorted fellow writers and suffragists not to discard the ideas of romance and marriage in their narratives of women, but to expand their stories to include other roles as well: "[T]here she stands—the Real Girl!—waiting for you to do her justice…. The Great Adventure is before her. Your Great Adventure is to report her faithfully…. Sweethearts and wives—yes, and other things besides: leaders, discoverers, militants, fighting every form of wrong" (*Way Stations*, 236). Thus, Robins argued, women writers, artists, and actresses had unique contributions to make to the feminist cause.

By the time Robins penned her own play *Votes for Women!* sixteen years after her *Hedda* production, her views on women's rights had taken definite shape, and so had her estimation of the possible uses of theater in pursuit of those rights. In Hedda, she said, as in Nora and some of his other heroines, Ibsen had shown a woman as "a bundle of unused possibilities" (*Ibsen and the Actress*, 18). In *Votes for Women!* Robins openly posed the questions that had been implicit in Ibsen's plays: Why are the possibilities of women such as Hedda allowed to go unused? And what might such women accomplish by putting their energies to work? In effect, Robins followed up and extended Ibsen's critique of marriage: where Ibsen had exposed marriage's failure to offer wives such as Nora and Hedda a constructive outlet for their energies and imaginations, Robins presented political action as one such outlet.

Robins's play presents suffrage activism as an alternative to marriage. This is not to say that marriage and suffrage activism are presented as mutually exclusive or even necessarily inimical, but that for Robins's heroine, Vida Levering, the cause of women's rights absorbs her thoughts and energies much as romantic desires or marital duties were assumed to absorb the thoughts of romantic stage heroines and women in general—her life is *about* women's rights, just as the life of the stereotypical Victorian "womanly woman" was supposed to be *about* marriage and motherhood.

Marriage, the play suggests, is an important fact of human society, but not the one essential fact. The inequities associated with the marriage institution—the sexual double standard, the economic dependence of married women, the lack of education that leaves women few options outside marriage—are simply a few of the countless manifestations of "the greatest evil in the world...the helplessness of women" (*VW*, 38). The suffrage cause and the central characters' conversion to it provide the structuring framework of the play, much as the mid-Victorian comedies of Robertson and Tom Taylor were structured around courtships or marital quarrels.

Like Ibsen, Shaw, Wilde, Jones, and Pinero, Robins adapted conventions and character types from several performance genres, employing what Sheila Stowell terms "a grab-bag of conventions recycled for feminist ends" (*A Stage of their Own*, 2). The first act's setting and subject matter resemble those of Jones's and Pinero's Society dramas. The third is a series of Ibsen-like discussions in which the principal characters explain their motives and perspectives. Between them, in the second act, Robins shifted the focus to the performance of political oratory, re-creating an open-air suffrage meeting with four speakers using actual suffrage speeches. While the early scenes of the play show women in the normative feminine roles of wives, sweethearts, hostesses, and chaperones, the second act shows women—old and young, rich and poor, married and single—as articulate orators and political activists. The principal characters include a woman with a past, her seducer, and a youthful ingénue, yet these melodramatic stock-types ultimately transfer their attention, and that of the audience, away from the preoccupations of courtship, pregnancy, romance, and sexual stigma and toward broader questions of women's rights.

Hedda Gabler and the New Woman Onstage

Born in Louisville, by her mid-twenties, Robins was an experienced actress. She had played, by her own estimation, nearly 300 roles, touring North America extensively first with James O'Neill (father of Eugene) and later with leading US Shakespeareans Lawrence Barrett and Edwin Booth. In the summer of 1888, during what was intended as a brief visit in England, she was introduced to Oscar Wilde and Herbert Beerbohm Tree, both of whom urged her to remain in England to make an attempt in the London theater. This encouragement so strongly impressed her that she would later credit Wilde as "the man who, all unconsciously, was to give me

England for my home" (*Both Sides of the Curtain*, 9).[1] Nevertheless, the months of networking that followed led to few results beyond understudy appointments in plays such as Pinero's *The Profligate* and an adaptation of *Little Lord Fauntleroy*. Robins became disenchanted with the seemingly universal disdain toward women in the theatrical profession. Professional theatrical companies were nearly all controlled by male actors who had gained enough capital to set themselves up as actor-managers, and women were cast at actor-managers' discretion, often valued more for looks than skill. The once-venerated Henry Irving disgusted her by declaring: "Women have an easy road to travel on the stage. They have but to *appear* and their sweet feminine charm wins the battle" (*Both Sides of the Curtain*, 241). Years later, in her feminist treatise *Ancilla's Share*, she would denounce this superficial attitude toward female performers, which caused even the most acclaimed actresses and musicians "to be everywhere ranked with the harlot" (*Ancilla's Share*, 129). Such women, she wrote, were "often paid well as the harlot is, paid and dismissed; and never at any time to be taken seriously" (*Ancilla's Share*, 129).

When Robins first encountered Ibsen's work on June 18, 1889, seeing *A Doll's House* at the Novelty Theatre, her initial response was favorable but brief. Her diary entry that evening merely called it a "Remarkable play" (qtd. in Angela John," *Elizabeth Robins: Staging a Life*, 53). Nearly forty years later, as part of an Ibsen Centenary lecture series organized by the British Drama League, Robins recounted her early impressions at greater length. Her admiration, by her account, had little to do with the play's subject matter, at least at first. Rather, she was amazed by the "unstagey" acting, a contrast to opulent West End productions. Achurch's Nora, she reported, "must have been one of the earliest exceptions…to the rule that an actress invariably comes on in new clothes, unless she is playing a beggar. This Nora, with her home-made fur cap on her fair hair, wore the clothes of Ibsen's Nora, almost shabby, with a touch of prettiness" (*Ibsen and the Actress*, 10). Robins admired Achurch's refusal to privilege fashion over character as she played the middle-class housewife who had for years pinched her dress allowance to repay a secret debt. Though the simple costumes and the "poverty-struck setting" might have had much to do with the labels of "suburban" and "provincial" with which hostile critics frequently derided Ibsen's plays, Robins declared it "the most satisfyingly *done* modern play I had ever seen" (*Ibsen and the Actress*, 13).

If, as Robins claimed, the first explicit lessons she learned from Ibsen "had nothing to do with the New Woman" and "everything to do with...the art of acting," her later work producing and acting in his plays showed her how closely related these two fields were (*Ibsen and the Actress*, 32–33). Her first Ibsen characters were relatively minor ones—Martha Bernick in an 1889 performance of *The Pillars of Society* and Christina Linden in a matinée revival of *A Doll's House* in January 1891—but she recalled them as more intellectually demanding than any of her previous roles. "In mere length," she wrote, "Mrs Linden is a small part, but it was for me a great experience. I despair of giving an idea of what that little part meant, not only of vivid pleasure in working at and playing, but of—what I cannot find any other word for than—self-respect. Ibsen was justifying what some of us, with very little encouragement, had blindly believed about the profession of acting" (*Ibsen and the Actress*, 14–15). She described Martha Bernick as "a woman of thirty or so, painted in neutral tones," yet she "was something alive, that called to me" (*Both Sides of the Curtain*, 208). By giving her interpretive work to do, these supporting roles made her a partner in the creative process. In the conclusion of *Ibsen and the Actress*, she explained what she considered Ibsen's unique contribution to the work of actors—and of actresses:

> More than anybody who ever wrote for the stage, Ibsen could, and usually did, collaborate with his actors. I do not mean that he ever consulted one of them; the collaboration was a subtler thing than that. Ibsen was by training so intensely *un homme du théâtre* that, to an extent I know in no other dramatist, he saw where he could leave some of his greatest effects to be made by the actor, and so left them. It was as if he knew that only so could he get his effects—that is, by standing aside and watching his spell work not only through the actor, but by the actor as fellow-creator. ... All that he seemed to require of the actor was that he should not be too conceited, or too hopelessly divorced from naturalness to be fit to collaborate with such a playwright. (*Ibsen and the Actress*, 52–53)

The intelligent participation that Ibsen's characters required, the care with which the dramatist developed the individuality even of minor characters, and the "self-respect" that resulted from working on such a project—all these factors reinforced Robins's discontent with the "hack-work" of actresses in mainstream theaters, offered her an unprecedented degree of professional autonomy, and led her to reflect on how theater might further be used to empower actresses and women in general.

Her enthusiasm for *Hedda Gabler* placed her in still more active collaboration with the dramatist. In particular, her determination to produce the play forced her to confront the actor-manager system that dominated the London theatrical establishment and the marginalization of women that it caused. That is to say, established actor-managers typically refused any play that lacked a strong leading role for themselves, and actresses, even the most successful, generally had little say in the selection of plays, roles, or performance styles. Robins later recalled in her autobiography that "[n]ot even actresses who by some fluke had proved their powers—had any choice as to what they should act. Not Ellen Terry herself, adorable and invaluable as she was, had any choice of parts, nor choice of how the parts chosen for her should be played" (*Both Sides of the Curtain*, 250). These actor-managers, Robins reported, greeted *Hedda* with a chorus of "But this is a woman's play" and "There's no part for *me*!" (*Ibsen and the Actress*, 16).

To produce the play, Robins and her friend and compatriot Marion Lea were ultimately obliged to become actor-managers themselves, overseeing the finances, casting, text preparation, and staging throughout the production process. Female actor-managers were not unprecedented in Victorian London, managing independently or, more often, in partnership with their husbands. Some, such as Madame Vestris, Marie Wilton, and Madge Kendal, had achieved considerable popularity and financial success. But they were unusual. The management venture of Robins and Lea, two young single actresses little known in London, was considered a novelty, condescendingly characterized by one reviewer as "Two plucky little American girls" (qtd. in Angela John, *Elizabeth Robins: Staging a Life*, 63). Shaw, writing a few years later, described their enterprise more seriously, as a sign of the times. Along with Janet Achurch, Florence Farr, and the few other women who undertook Ibsen productions, Robins and Lea demonstrated that "[W]e are on the verge of something like a struggle between the sexes for the dominion of the London theatres" ("Preface" in *The Theatrical "World" of 1894*, xxix).

The two borrowed the necessary £300, offering jewelry and other valuables as security. They negotiated the fine-tuning of the text with publisher William Heinemann and translators Edmund Gosse and William Archer, making a speakable English script without sacrificing fidelity to Ibsen's original. They maneuvered within a complicated set of copyright restrictions, mediating between the two feuding translators, carefully keeping Gosse in the dark regarding Archer's involvement in the project, conducting what Robins called "secret diplomacy worthy of a major political crisis" (qtd. in Angela John, *Elizabeth Robins: Staging a Life*, 57).[2] They leased the Vaudeville Theatre, assembled a cast, rehearsed painstakingly, and oversaw a production run of ten matinées followed by a month of evening performances, covering costs and bringing in an additional £281—impressive results for so experimental a venture. Robins and Lea's success with *Hedda* set a precedent for other actresses such as Lena Ashwell, Gertrude Kingston, and Edith Craig's Pioneer Players, who in the next two decades would undertake theatrical management with more overtly political aims. In producing *Hedda* and, later on, other Ibsen plays, Robins learned the practice of independence before she began to take interest in the theory of feminism.

The character of Hedda, no less than the production experience, influenced her so profoundly that she wrote years later, "I came to think of my early life as divisible into two parts: 'before or after Hedda'" (qtd. in Angela John, *Elizabeth Robins: Staging a Life*, 55). Hedda, she argued, was an outstanding acting opportunity not in spite of her "corrosive" qualities—"her unashamed selfishness; her scorn of so-called womanly qualities; above all, her strong need to put some meaning into her life, even at the cost of borrowing it, or stealing the meaning out of someone else's"—but because of them (*Ibsen and the Actress*, 21). "I was under no temptation," she wrote, "to make her what is conventionally known as 'sympathetic'" (*Ibsen and the Actress*, 20). Rather, she recognized Hedda as a tragic figure because, though surrounded by admiration and elegance, "she knew there was joy in life that she hadn't been able to grasp, and that marriage only emphasized what she was missing" (*Ibsen and the Actress*, 20).

In retrospect, in the context of her wider political knowledge, Robins noted the social significance of Hedda's character, identifying her troubles as those typically experienced by leisure-class women in the late nineteenth century: "Hedda...was a good many of us...educated to fear life; too much opportunity to develop her weakness; no opportunity to develop her best powers" (*Ibsen and the Actress*, 18–19). Like Nora, Hedda questioned the conventional Victorian wisdom of the universal "natural" womanly vocation of wifehood, child-rearing, and general caregiving—a dissent which made her appear deranged and even monstrous to many viewers. Clement Scott, struggling to reconcile his horror of Hedda with his fascination with Robins's acting, ascribed to the actress an almost demonic power. Hedda, he insisted, was a "repulsive...creature," "an unwomanly woman," "a sublimated sinner," "a savage," yet Robins had "made vice attractive by her art," "almost ennobled crime," and "stopped [his] shudder" ("Hedda Gabler," 227). Robins countered his litany of epithets with: "Mr Clement Scott understand Hedda—any man except that wizard Ibsen understand her? Of course not. That was the tremendous part of it. How should men understand Hedda on the stage when they didn't understand her in the persons of their wives, their daughters, their woman friends?" (*Ibsen and the Actress*, 18). The play, Robins claimed, realistically represented many married women's experience, but was not accepted as realistic by men because women's experiences of helplessness and sexual threat "appear so unreal to decent men as to appear as melodrama" (*Ibsen and the Actress*, 30). In Robins's reading, Ibsen's play claimed that the economic coercion and sexual threat that many men associated with sensational theatrical spectacles were the routine realities of many women's lives. In expressing their disgust with Hedda, male spectators refused to acknowledge this claim.

Two years later, Robins used her own first play, *Alan's Wife*, to present another slant on Ibsen's critique of common assumptions about the "womanly" roles of wife and mother. In doing so, her play, like *Hedda*, unsettled many viewers. Adapted from a short story by Swedish author Elin Ameen, Robins anonymously co-authored the play with her friend Florence Bell, a prosperous Middleborough industrialist's wife. The play was produced in May 1893 in two matinées at Terry's Theatre, under the management of J. T. Grein's Independent Theatre Society.

The play's protagonist, Jean Creyke, whom Robins played in the Independent Theatre performance, is portrayed early in the play as Hedda's antithesis, a devoted wife and thoroughly domestic woman. The contrast between Jean's marriage and Hedda's is drawn in the first scene. The play appears to reinforce the gender norms *Hedda Gabler* categorically rejects. Unlike the bookish, boyish George Tesman whom Hedda despises, Jean's husband is a robust laborer, uneducated, but described as "brave and strong," "a Hercules" (*AW*, 9, 14). When Jean's mother (rather tactlessly) reminds her that she would have preferred a more learned son-in-law, Jean responds: "We can't all marry scholars, Mother dear—some of us prefer marrying men instead" (*AW*, 7). Jean's admiration of her husband's muscular masculinity is expressed in busy domestic activity. At the start of the scene, she is preparing "a dinner fit for a king," and her mother remarks, "Yes, it's always Alan's dinner, or Alan's tea, or Alan's supper, or Alan's pipe. There isn't another man in the North gets waited on as he does" (*AW*, 5). Alan appears to be the one person Jean respects as a superior. She says, "I want a husband...who is my master as well as other folks'" (*AW*, 9). Robins and Bell present a woman who is strong-willed like Ibsen's heroines, who yet willingly yields her independence to a man whose strength exceeds hers. These sympathetic portrayals of traditional masculinity and femininity—the anti-Hedda mated with the anti-Tesman, the loving and domestic woman who not only submits but delights to submit to the man she calls "master"—seem tailored for conservative audiences who had been offended by *A Doll's House*, *Ghosts*, and *Hedda Gabler*.

Yet after Alan's death, Alan's womanly wife commits a more violent action than any done by Nora, Hedda, or any of Ibsen's selfish, "unsexed" heroines, smothering her crippled baby in his cradle. And this decision, Jean claims, does not signal a rejection of her wifely and motherly duty, but is a direct expression of her love for both husband and child. Before Alan's death, she anticipates motherhood as passionately as Hedda dreads it because the baby, in her vision, will grow to be a second Alan, a copy of his father's strength, capability, and good looks. By the second scene, however, this dream has been shattered first by the sudden death of Alan the father in a mining accident, and then by the birth of Alan the son, who, far from being a sturdy copy of his father, is born disabled (as a result, it is implied, of the pregnant Jean's shock at seeing her husband's mangled corpse on the stretcher).[3] Jean, at this double loss, concludes that she must kill the child in order to save it from a lifetime of suffering and to allow it a life of health and strength in Heaven (like Ameen's original heroine and also like Thomas Hardy's Tess, she is anxious to baptize the infant before he dies).[4] The play presents a variation of Ibsen's iconoclasm: while several of Ibsen's protagonists reject traditional ideals of marriage and motherhood, Robins and Bell suggest that a woman may have sincere marital and maternal affection and, not in spite of this affection but because of it, be capable of actions as shocking as those of any iconoclast. Jean, unlike Nora, does not repudiate the moral standard by which she is judged but instead invokes it to explain her actions as she prepares for the gallows: "I've had courage just once in my life—just once in my life I've been strong and kind—and it was the night I killed my child!...I had to do what I did, and they have to take my life for it. I showed him the only true mercy, and that is what the law shows me!" (*AW*, 47–48).

The play's conclusion affirmed traditional values of motherly duty and marital affection, values which Ibsen's plays had been fiercely condemned for questioning. But the grim and violent re-definition of these duties—suggesting that motherly duty, under some extreme circumstances, might include infanticide—shocked many in the audience even more than Ibsen's iconoclasm. Like *A Doll's House*, *Candida*, and other works of Ibsen and Shaw, *Alan's Wife* challenged conventional categories of drama and art. The *Morning Post* critic declared it to be "not really a play, but a tragic episode of an extremely painful kind" ("Terry's Theatre," 3). Other reviewers put it still more strongly: "not in any sense a work of art," "simply a blood-curdling, heart-breaking series of miserable incidents…a dramatised police case, a playhouse shocker" ("At the Play," 822; "Feathers from the Wings," 225). Others were equally eloquent in the play's defense. The London correspondent of the *Derby Daily Telegraph* reported that "'Alan's Wife' is a bit of human life transferred bodily to the stage. It may not be art, but it sweeps over one's emotions like a tempest" ("Our London Letter," 2). Grein, in his introduction to the published playtext, scoffed at the charge of artlessness, insisting that "to deny that *Alan's Wife*, with its directness, its exquisite writing, its soul-stirring power, is a work of art, is simply anathematising tragedy altogether" ("Introduction" to *Alan's Wife*, viii). Archer, in a second introduction, took the controversy as he had taken past disputes over Ibsen: as an opportunity to argue for "the artist's right to 'see life steadily and see it whole'" ("Introduction" to *Alan's Wife*, xvi). Robins and Bell joined with Grein, Shaw, and Archer in unsettling received definitions of drama, stretching the boundaries of dramatic structure, technique, and subject matter. At the same time, their play reinforced the public's tendency to associate New Drama with tragedy or "unpleasant" plays.

The Masquerade of Playwriting

In producing *Hedda Gabler* and subsequent Ibsen plays, Robins claimed an authority not available to actresses working under male actor-managers in mainstream theaters, an authority to select the plays, roles, and styles in which she would perform. In writing *Alan's Wife*, she went still further in actively creating the spectacle for the stage, including the role in which she herself would act. Yet the step toward independence was taken in secret, for Robins and Bell, like numerous female writers and especially dramatists of the period, wrote and published the play anonymously, concealing their authorship even from close friends and associates. Even Grein and Archer, in their introductions to the published play, claimed ignorance regarding the dramatist's identity, though their lengthy comments on the secrecy on which Robins insisted (in her supposed capacity of liaison between author and editors) might be a hint that they suspected or guessed. Grein concluded, "I cannot but express my regret that I am not able to divulge the name of the author, which, in deference to my solemn promise to Miss Robins, I have not even endeavored to ascertain" ("Introduction" to *Alan's Wife*, viii).

Anonymity worked to Robins's professional advantage in several ways. For many viewers, the mystery of the author's identity added to the play' fascination. The *Edinburgh Evening News* reported (probably hyperbolically) that "a hundred names have been suggested in connection with it," including Thomas Hardy, novelist and journalist Lucy Clifford, and Frederick Wedmore, a theater critic for *The Academy* who had warmly praised recent productions of Ibsen's plays ("To-day's London Letter," 3). The controversial content of *Alan's Wife* probably also had much to do with Robins and Bell's decision to withhold their names.[5] Robins's acting in the play reinforced the reputation she had gained in her Ibsen performances, as a "powerful" actress who "to some extent redeemed the horror of the story" ("Terry's Theatre," 3). Anonymous authorship allowed her to take credit for the redemption even as she avoided blame for the horror.

Perhaps even more importantly, anonymity allowed the play to avoid the dismissive and patronizing reception often accorded to female dramatists and female writers in general. Regarding women dramatists throughout the Victorian period, Kerry Powell argues: "Masculinity...was counted as a qualification for writing plays, and as an attribute of the theatre as an institution.... The ideal play would therefore be written for, as well as by, men" (*Women and Victorian Theatre*, 83). Powell's explanation helps to account for Robins's preference for anonymity, as well as for the intensely negative press for *Alan's Wife*, *Hedda Gabler*, and other plays that focused on women's experiences. Both Grein and Archer, in their introductions for *Alan's Wife*, consistently described the author as male, whether ignorantly or disingenuously. Grein called the play "one of the truest tragedies ever written by a modern Englishman" ("Introduction" to *Alan's Wife*, viii). Reviewers tended to follow suit; with the exception of Clifford, most of the "hundred names" suggested as possible authors were names of men. Robins took advantage of this supposed male identity to ensure that the play was taken seriously as she took the traditionally masculine role of dramatist. She did the same in the fiction she published during the 1890s under the pseudonym of C. E. Raimond, including *George Mandeville's Husband* (1894), a caricature of the mannish woman writer and her meek, domesticated husband. The expediency of Robins's anonymous authorship and assumed masculine identity was confirmed later in the decade as her other plays, such as *The Mirkwater* and *The Silver Lotus* (also "women's plays," and this time written and submitted under her own name), were rejected by mainstream actor-managers and set aside unacted and unpublished.

Yet Robins was troubled by the irony inherent in this gender masquerade, her discovery that to find a voice as a writer, a woman was often obliged to take, or seem to take, the identity of a man, leaving her feminine perspective as silent as ever. Years later, in *Way Stations*, her chronicle of the suffrage movement, she described the dilemma of the woman writer:

> What she is really doing is her level best to play the man's game, and seeing how nearly like him she can do it. So conscious is she it is his game she is trying her hand at, that she is prone to borrow his very name to set upon her title-page. She does so, not only that she may get courage from it to talk deep and go a-swashbuckling now and then, but for the purpose of reassuring the man. Here is something quite in your line, she implies; for lo! My name is "George." (*Way Stations*, 6)

To correct this gender bias in literature, especially in playwriting, was for Robins an essential component of theatrical reform. If actresses were to have opportunities to act in lifelike and memorable roles, woman dramatists must be encouraged to write such plays, and to write in their own voices, *as* women. As the women's suffrage movement gained prominence at the turn of the century, years after her early playwriting ventures, Robins saw female authorship as both a strategy for gaining the vote and an important end in itself. She served as the first president for the Women Writers' Suffrage League (WWSL), an organization formed by Cicely Hamilton and Bessie Hatton in 1908 to support women's suffrage by "the methods proper to writers—the use of the pen" (*Way Stations*, 106). In a speech delivered at a WWSL reception in May 1909, she told league members, "It is the business (the business as well as the high privilege) of men and women writers to correct the false ideas about women which many writers of the past have fostered" (*Way Stations* 110).

Her early experience in playwriting enabled Robins to examine critiques of marriage and conventional femininity from an angle different from that of Ibsen's plays even as it increased her agency in shaping the theatrical spectacle and her own role in it. Yet it also caused her to see more clearly the limits of that agency and the need for collective action on the part of actresses and women writers.

Persons, Principles, and Political Drama

Only one of Robins's plays, *Votes for Women!*, was publicly staged under her own name, more than a decade after her early Ibsen productions. Having been commissioned in 1906 to write a play for newly established actor-manager Gertrude Kingston, Robins took as her topic the unfolding real-life drama of the women's suffrage movement. Yet it is unclear whether the project, at its outset, was intended as suffragist propaganda, or even as a sympathetic portrayal of the struggle. Robins was initially, as she later phrased it in *Collier's Weekly*, "an ignorant opponent of Woman Suffrage." She recounted, "my head [was] full of masculine criticism as to woman's limitations, her well-known inability to stick to the point, her poverty in logic and in humour, and the impossibility, in any case, of her coping with the mob" (*Way Stations*, 38). She had several prominent and committed "antis" among her close friends, including her erstwhile literary collaborator Florence Bell. Another friend, liberal MP Sir Edward Grey, was frequently singled out for harsh public criticism from suffrage leaders.

She was gradually won over, however, despite conflicting personal loyalties, by her indignation at the unjust law enforcement and inaccurate press representation meted out to protesters, and by the earnestness and logic of speakers she went to hear in open-air meetings, though she gave several differing accounts as to how and when she began to support the movement. She credited a Trafalgar Square Meeting on October 1, 1906, and a protest at the House of Commons later that month as the most direct causes of her conversion. But as Angela John points out, Robins had already been carrying on research for *Votes for Women!* (or *The Friend of Woman*, as it was initially titled) at least since July of that year, and had met with Emmeline Pankhurst to discuss the play on 16 September (*Elizabeth Robins: Staging a Life*, 144–146). By early November, she was showing rough drafts of the script to Henry James and other friends—drafts containing a few minor characters and some lines of dialogue that were later altered, but with the plot and principal characters more or less as they would finally appear onstage. It seems likely that Robins was first intrigued by the dramatic potential of the women's suffrage campaign and gradually, in the course of her research, became impressed by the justice of its aims. Once converted, Robins gave her wholehearted commitment to the cause, speaking in support of militant tactics and offering Backsettown Farm, her home in rural Sussex, as a refuge where activists worn out by imprisonment and hunger strikes could recover health. In September 1907, she joined the governing committee of the militant Women's Social and Political Union (WSPU), and the following year helped to found the Women Writer's Suffrage League and the AFL. Robins described *Votes for Women!* to Millicent Fawcett, head of the nonmilitant National Union of Women's Suffrage Societies (NUWSS), as "the first thing I shall have written under the pressure of strong moral convictions" (qtd. in Angela John, *Elizabeth Robins: Staging a Life*, 147). The final play took an unapologetically propagandist tone, subtitled in the playbill as "A Dramatic Tract in Three Acts." Having first taken the suffragettes as convenient material for a topical play, Robins came to regard the stage as a useful vehicle for presenting the suffrage message.

The play was staged in May 1907 at the Royal Court Theatre under the Vedrenne-Barker management (see previous chapter).[6] Under Harley Granville-Barker's leadership since 1904, the company at the Court had become an important player in the New Drama movement. They specialized in plays by emerging dramatists such as Shaw, Galsworthy, and Granville-Barker himself and built on the work of earlier experimental groups such as Grein's Independent Theatre, the Stage Society, and Robins's own Ibsen productions with Marion Lea. Like many of the Court productions, *Votes for Women!* looked both backward and forward, dramatically as well as politically, blending seduction melodrama, drawing-room comedy, political documentary spectacle, and the drama of ideas. Through this deliberate and somewhat messy blend of genres, Robins attempted, as Laura A. Winkiel has phrased it, "to represent the roles of women in an unstable, rapidly changing society in which conventional forms of representation could no longer serve" ("A Suffrage Burlesque," 573).[7] More important for my argument, the hybrid structure of *Votes for Women!* also returned to the critiques against traditional marriage and traditional theater that *A Doll's House* had pressed on the attention of London critics and playgoers more than a decade before, and the attack on romantic domesticity that Robins herself had brought forward in *Hedda Gabler*. It followed up the various attempts of Wilde, Shaw, Jones, and Pinero to envision modified marriage and revised theatrical conventions, particularly their efforts to imagine dramatic closure, whether comic, tragic, or otherwise, without marriage at its center.

The play's first act consists of a house party reminiscent of Jones's and Wilde's Society comedies, featuring an assortment of gossiping upper-class guests. The gathering includes two young women whose matrimonial prospects excite general interest: naïve Scottish heiress Jean Dunbarton, newly engaged to prominent conservative politician Geoffrey Stonor, and the more worldly-wise and somewhat mysterious Vida Levering, who is initially described in the stage directions as *"the kind of whom men and women alike say, 'What's her story? Why doesn't she marry?'"* (*VW*, 33). Over the course of the play, the social and personal consequences of the two women's marriage choices are shown to be closely intertwined with wider political implications.

Jean views her engagement to Stonor both as romantic fulfillment and as a debut in political life. Much like her namesake in Robins's earlier play, she regards her fiancé as an ideal masculine hero, "the only man in the world worth marrying" (*VW*, 45).[8] Love, she declares, has transformed her intellectually as well as emotionally, stimulating her curiosity and political acumen: "Indeed, indeed, I can think of everything better than I ever did before. He has lit up everything for me—made everything vivider, more significant.... Oh, yes, I don't care about other things less but a thousand times more" (38). For his part, he speaks of her in Torvald Helmer-like terms as a "little girl," a "beautiful, tender, innocent child," a "poor little innocent," and an "absurd, ridiculous child" (*VW*, 84, 86, 87, 88). In marrying a well-known MP, Jean is taking a public, visible position. Her husband-to-be urges her to "take an interest in public affairs" and to "make nice little speeches with composure" (*VW*, 84, 68). Even as she eagerly anticipates her marriage, however, Jean is ambivalent toward the prominence of her position, and she attempts, to some degree, to keep her personal life separate from Geoffrey's public image. She is pleased at the prospect of having a *"real"* share" in his work, of being trusted to "counteract the pernicious influence of [his] opponent's glib wife" (*VW*, 47). Yet she also sees his public visibility as a threat to the intimacy of their courtship. She asks her relatives to conceal the engagement at least temporarily, having "her heart set upon having a few days with just her family in the secret, before the flood of congratulations breaks loose," a request that occasions several humorous conversational slips and much maneuvering to maintain the concealment (*VW*, 26). Through Jean's anxiety and desire for secrecy, Robins echoed earlier dramatic scenes in which Jones, Wilde, and Pinero had depicted upper-class social gatherings as critical sites of marriage on display, or couples seeking to avoid display.

Robins used the conventional scene of young love combined with the images of marriage performance anxiety, which earlier dramatists had made familiar in order to illustrate the "indirect influence" of well-to-do

Edwardian women. As a politician's bride, Jean looks forward to hosting social gatherings for her husband's adherents (her uncle teases her with "Jean! Already beginning to 'think in parties?'" [*VW*, 30]), discussing political issues with him, making speeches in his support, using her inherited wealth to gain him more political power, and reinforcing his image as a wholesome, respectable family man—all indirect and appropriately feminine methods of influencing the nation's political affairs, several of them methods by which Hedda had once thought to gratify her appetite for power in her short-lived scheme for getting Tesman into politics. These secondary political functions—confidant, adviser, political hostess, and occasional string-puller—allowed some wealthy women, like Jean and her older female relatives, considerable indirect power. Consequently, anti-suffragist leaders (many of whom came from this class) frequently held up feminine influence as a more-than-adequate substitute for the direct power of the vote. Esther Shkolnik, in studying prominent politicians' wives in late-Victorian and Edwardian England, suggests that some of these women were hostile or indifferent to women's suffrage because "[a]s conformists who accepted the mores of their time and were in turn accepted by Society, such women could actually influence the course of politics, however indirectly, to a far greater degree than could suffragists…who alienated a large percentage of the powers that were" (*Leading Ladies*, 10–11). Women such as Catherine Gladstone, Lady Salisbury, and Margot Asquith, Shkolnik argues, "saw in the women's movement a dangerous departure from the proper feminine role," as well as a potential threat to the power they themselves already wielded (*Leading Ladies*, 12–13). Woman's political role, according to these upper-class women, was closely aligned with her conjugal one, and with the traits of traditional femininity. The self-effacement, tact, and skill in domestic management which made a good wife were likewise the characteristics of a good political woman.

By the time Robins began to support suffrage actively, women's indirect political influence had become a divisive issue even among suffragists. While nonmilitant constitutionalist suffragists argued for peaceful persuasion as a means of gaining support for their cause in parliament, the more militant suffragettes insisted that this method had been tried since the time of John Stuart Mill without concrete results. Moreover, the idea of feminine persuasion, in many militants' minds, had an unsavory connection with sexual attraction, even with prostitution. Robins dramatized this debate on feminine influence in *Votes for Women!* with a skirmish between

Mrs. Freddy Tunbridge, a constitutionalist, and Vida Levering, who secretly sympathizes with the militants: when Mrs. Freddy maintains that "The only chance of our getting what we want is by *winning* over the men," Vida counters with, "'Winning over the men' has been the woman's way for centuries. Do you think the result should make us proud of our policy? Yes? Then go and walk in Piccadilly at midnight" (*VW*, 55). Women's reliance on indirect influence, Vida argues, has resulted in a society in which women's sole means of gaining power is sex appeal—the same power exerted by Nora Helmer as she manipulates her husband through dance, role-play, and masquerade—reducing all women to a state of virtual prostitution which can only be remedied by the more direct power a vote would entail.

Vida, for her part, attracts the romantic attentions of virtually all the unattached men in the play and the matchmaking interest of most of her married acquaintances. In their eyes, she is a romantic heroine whose love story is expected at any moment to begin, as Lord John Wynnstay, the country house host, emphasizes with his repeated refrain: "she's a *nice* creature; all she needs is to get some 'nice' fella to marry her" (*VW*, 32). Yet, as the audience hears in the first act, Vida's history is at odds with this image: ten years earlier, she became pregnant out of wedlock and was pressured by the child's father into having an abortion, after which they separated. Hence, in the eyes of the few who know, Vida is a "woman with a past," like Mrs. Tanqueray, Mrs. Dane, Mrs. Erlynne, and Mrs. Arbuthnot, who has with some success concealed her earlier transgression and reestablished herself as a respectable, marriageable woman.

Early in the play, Jean learns of Vida's past. Later, through a series of melodramatic plot devices—an unexpected meeting, a dropped handkerchief, the "*set, white face*" of the guilty man—she deduces that the erstwhile lover is her own fiancé, Geoffrey Stonor (*VW*, 79). She immediately envisions Vida's story as a standard seduction melodrama, asking Stonor, "Oh, *why* did you desert her?" (*VW*, 85). Promptly breaking her own engagement, she determines that Stonor should "right that old wrong" by marrying Vida (*VW*, 87). Stonor, like Wilde's Lord Illingworth, repudiates the role of designing villain, retorting on sensational accusations with prosaic facts: "If, woman like, you must recall the Past—I insist on your recalling it correctly" (*VW*, 98). The version of the story he presents, confronting Vida, is almost a reverse-gender melodrama with himself as victim and her as lying *femme fatale* who seeks to destroy both his happiness and Jean's: "I stood by you with a fidelity that was nothing short of Quixotic. . . .

[I]t was *you* who did the deserting.... Do you deny that you returned my letters unopened?...Do you deny that you refused to see me—and that, when I persisted, you vanished?" "I see you'd much rather punish me and see [Jean] revel in a morbid self-sacrifice" (*VW*, 97–98, 101). Yet he too, along with Jean, envisions marriage as the appropriate ending for Vida's story (though he would prefer it to be marriage with somebody else). Even after she has declined his own (extremely reluctant) proposal, he asks, "Why should you not find [happiness] still?" (*VW*, 104). The stage directions indicate that the line should be spoken "*significantly*," to suggest that he is hinting at her new admirer, suffrage sympathizer Allen Trent. This opinion is shared by Jean's aunt, Lady John Wynnstay, a tolerant and benevolent matron who knows of the past liaison between Stonor and Vida. Like Mrs. Erlynne's narrative, Vida's is to be a seduction melodrama with a modified ending: Vida too is to be rehabilitated from her "fallen" status with a respectable marriage.

Vida, however, rejects this recommendation as firmly as she has rebuffed attempts at flirtation and matchmaking throughout the play. All such simple solutions, she says, smack of "that old pretence...[t]hat to marry *at all costs* is every woman's dearest ambition till the grave closes over her" (*VW*, 92). Insofar as she has a grievance against Stonor, it is not for his failure to marry her, but for his insistence on her abortion. "You didn't know," she tells him, "that the ghost of a child that had never seen the light, the frail thing you meant to sweep aside and forget—have *swept* aside and forgotten—you didn't know it was strong enough to push you out of my life" (*VW*, 100). Yet her repudiation of marriage, either to Stonor or to anyone else, is not simply, as with Wilde's Mrs. Arbuthnot, the transfer of affection from a romantic bond to a maternal one, or the gratification of a personal grudge. Robins uses Vida's refusal to rebuke the self-absorbed sentimentality that melodramatic endings frequently ascribe to unmarried or unmarriageable women who are imagined as pining away or dying of broken hearts. Jean imagines her, Vida says, as a seduced, deserted, and heartbroken victim, and Vida allows her to think so because "Jean isn't old enough to be able to care as much about a principle as about a person" (*VW*, 93).

Vida, being more mature, has abandoned the melodramatic perspective and the privileging of persons over principles. When Lady John sympathetically observes that "The memory of a thing like that can never die," Vida contemptuously exclaims, "You don't seriously believe that a woman with anything else to think about, comes to the end of ten years still absorbed in a memory of that sort?" (*VW*, 92). When asked more minutely about her feelings for Stonor, she replies: "Geoffrey Stonor! For me he's simply one of the far back links in a chain of evidence. It's certain I think a hundred times of other women's present unhappiness, to once that I remember that old unhappiness of mine that's past. I think of the nail and chain makers of Cradley Heath. The sweated girls of the slums. I think of the army of ill-used women whose very existence I mustn't mention" (*VW*, 92). She has transferred her attention from her individual trouble to the troubles of women in general, and this has led her to dedicate her energies to women's suffrage, not as an end in itself, but as a starting point for reforming society on a gender-equal basis. Thus, she demands that Stonor "make amends" not by marrying her, but by using his political prominence as an MP and a probable future cabinet minister to support women's suffrage—endorsing it publicly and in writing, so that his promise cannot be easily retracted or ignored. She explains to Lady John: "The man who served one woman—God knows how many more—very ill, shall serve hundreds of thousands well. Geoffrey Stonor shall make it harder for his son, harder still for his grandson, to treat any woman as he treated me" (*VW*, 93). The plot culminates not with the death, exile, or marital rehabilitation of the seduced woman, nor in the (probably) restored engagement between Stonor and Jean, nor even in Vida's rejection of Stonor's proposal, but in the conversion of Vida, and through her, the conversions of Stonor and Jean (though all with different motives and different degrees of commitment) to the cause of women's rights. The question of marriage or non-marriage, which has absorbed the attention of audience and characters for much of the play, and for many plays before it, is rendered secondary, peripheral, almost incidental.

THE DRAMA OF THE PLATFORM

Vida's anti-melodramatic privileging of principles over persons is reinforced by the play's second act, in which the seduction narrative is thrown into the background and the scene is shifted from the Wynnstay House drawing room to a Trafalgar Square suffrage meeting. The entire act is dominated by speakers unconnected with Jean's and Vida's present and past romances, and who are seldom or never mentioned elsewhere in the play. The miscellaneous group of orators includes an unnamed middle-aged working-class woman who serves as a Poor Law Guardian, Mr. Pilcher, a working-class man and active member of the Labour party,

Ernestine Blunt, a young, single, middle-class woman, and Vida herself.[9] The group showcases the diversity of the movement's supporters and possibly pays homage to Robins's actual acquaintances and colleagues. Here, the play re-creates onstage an experience that, by Robins's account in *Way Stations*, was instrumental in her own conversion. The scene includes speeches based on transcripts of actual suffrage meetings, as well as a heckling onstage audience that, as in actual meetings, frequently drowns out the speakers' voices. The play's second-act meeting at once presents a collection of the suffrage campaign's most compelling arguments for playgoers who might have been unwilling to listen to them elsewhere and also creates a sort of immersive documentary spectacle, simulating the open-air Trafalgar Square experience inside the intimate Court Theatre space. The scene offers suffrage demonstration as a theatrical genre in its own right, itself a form of art and entertainment. The dramatically framed suffrage speeches justify the play's label as "dramatic tract"—the drama is made to serve propagandist ends, and at the same time, propaganda is given "dramatic" status.

With the abrupt shift of scene and character between the first act and the second, Robins signaled a contrast between the comfortably familiar Society play and the still developing suffrage propaganda or "tract" genre. The suave, lightly bantering drawing-room company is replaced by a jumbled collection of speakers and rowdy onlookers of a variety of classes, occupations, marital statuses, genders, ages, educational backgrounds, and speaking styles. Robins's concern for this unruly diversity is evident in the pains she took with the verisimilitude of the listeners' interruptions—where early drafts of the play simply indicate "*laughter and jeers*" and "*interruption*" at intervals, allowing the bystanders to ad-lib, later typescripts include penciled-in speeches such as "Go 'ome and darn yer old man's stockens!" and "The lydies! God bless 'em!" (*Votes for Women!* TS).[10] In staging the spectators, Granville-Barker (who may have contributed some of the "interruption" lines to the script) used seasoned Court Theatre actors rather than the inexperienced and disposable "extras" employed by many managers for such roles, and the carefully orchestrated ensemble playing won praise from reviewers. This democratic approach to playwriting and theatrical production offered an alternative to the star-based management system that had frustrated Robins early in her career.[11] Like other aspects of the play, the crowd scene drew comparisons with Ibsen's plays, particularly with the town hall meeting in *The Enemy of the People*. Penny Farfan suggests that Robins's multivocal crowd and diverse group of speakers may have been designed as a corrective to Ibsen's "problematically elitist philosophy of individualism," which Robins had criticized in her earlier writings. While Ibsen privileged the perspective of the "intellectual aristocrat" Dr. Stockmann in contrast with the wrongheaded "masses," Robins depicted all the speakers, with their varied backgrounds, as having unique insights, each contributing to the women's rights campaign ("From *Hedda Gabler* to *Votes for Women!*", 72).

As Jean and Stonor arrive among the spectators and Vida takes her place on the platform, the seduction narrative and the marriage plot compete with the democratic suffrage spectacle even as the speakers must literally compete with the crowd to be heard. The furtive endearments of the engaged couple are buried among the speakers' rhetoric and the crowd's shouts, and it is in the midst of Vida's speech that Jean's climactic realization occurs, as she recognizes her own fiancé as the guilty man. The suffrage meeting serves as a backdrop for Jean's discovery, and at the same time, the seduction narrative offers a frame or prologue for the speakers' discourses. In leaving the country house to make her first suffrage speech, Vida physically marks her departure from the Society drama, where she is regarded as a potential bride or as a reclaimable fallen woman, for a theatrical genre where her role does not depend on her sexual purity or other marital qualifications, but only on being a woman—or, even more generally, on being a human committed to "get[ting] the conditions of life made fairer" (*VW*, 79).

The two narrative strands merge as Vida, in her speech, recounts a recent infanticide case involving a Manchester working girl and her employer, the child's father—a seduction melodrama in outline. The familiar narrative of the outcast unwed mother and the father who goes scot-free mirrors Vida's own past with Stonor (as Jean infers on seeing Stonor's reaction). At the same time, within the context of Vida's speech, the story is used to demonstrate that women, like men, ought to be tried by "a jury of [their] peers" (*VW*, 78). This sentimental dramatic trope deployed for a political end highlights the function of the melodramatic plot within the play itself: Vida's seduction and Jean and Stonor's interrupted courtship serve not only as a frame for the more overtly polemic platform scene but also as an illustration of "the helplessness of women" (*VW*, 38). This mixing of genres and of issues was seen by some critics as a distraction from the suffrage discussion and a weakening of the play's persuasive effectiveness. *The Times*, for example, commented that Robins seemed unlikely to advance the suffrage project by "hanging it on to other questions of seduction, abortion, and infanticide" ("Court Theatre," 5). But to Robins, seduction, abortion, infanticide, and the vote were all parts of a larger issue. The standard seduction melodrama, with its preoccupation with women's humiliation, sexual danger, and economic dependence was, for Robins, a convenient showcase for the many evidences of the need for women's enfranchisement, and of the need for women to cooperate and support one another in order to pursue this goal. Vida herself ultimately acknowledges this as she relinquishes her role of melodramatic heroine and potential bride in order to affiliate herself with the suffrage cause and the platform drama.

THE USES OF FEMININE CHARM: BEAUTY AS PERFORMANCE

Vida's decision to remain single was unconventional in a dramatic heroine. Robins compounded this unexpectedness by repeatedly insisting on her elegance and graceful manners—traits that women were expected to cultivate to attract a husband. In the stage directions, she is described as "*an attractive, essentially feminine, and rather 'smart' woman of thirty-two, with a somewhat foreign grace*" (*VW*, 33). Vida is placed in deliberate opposition to earlier stage feminists such as Agnes in Arthur Wing Pinero's *The Notorious Mrs. Ebbsmith* (1895). Agnes, a would-be reformer originally played by Mrs. Patrick Campbell, wore a severe black dress which earned her the epithet of "dowdy demagogue" from the men in the play. When in mid-play she exchanged her plain costume for an elaborate, low-cut evening gown, the change signaled a surrender of her New Woman identity and an embrace of the feminine role of mistress to her lover, Lucas Cleeve. Even Shaw, though scornful of Pinero's oversimplified portrait of the female crusader, and though more sympathetic to the cause of women's rights, similarly emphasized the "plain and businesslike" clothes in his descriptions of New Woman characters in his early plays (*BH1*, 273). Tastes differ; what was "dowdy" in Pinero's eyes was "very becoming" in Shaw's (*TN1*, 64).[12] Yet, like other (usually male-authored) New Woman stage characters, Shaw's women generally presented feminism and feminine charm as mutually exclusive. Such portrayals, implicitly conflating femininity with sexual objectification, assumed that intellectual women would naturally despise the showy costumes and mannerisms traditionally used by women who adopted femininity as a theatrical role for men's entertainment.

Vida's "smart" and "attractive" appearance, like those of the play's other suffragist women, contrasts sharply with these earlier portrayals, and Robins repeatedly underscored the difference through the play's dialogue and descriptions. The caricatured stereotype of the mannish reformer is present mainly in the descriptions of male party guests in the first act, especially St. John Greatorex, a liberal MP who stereotypes political women as "the sort of woman who smells of India rubber. The typical English spinster" (*VW*, 34). Greatorex insists that the constitutionalist Mrs. Freddy Tunbridge is "too young and too happily married" to be interested in public affairs, while he discounts Vida's professed curiosity regarding militant meetings with "your frocks ain't serious enough" (*VW*, 34, 35). Robins's description of Ernestine Blunt, the youthful suffrage leader in Trafalgar Square, deflates the dowdy old-maid stereotype with a childlike image (her onlookers and even comrades refer to her not infrequently as "Little Blunt"). Ernestine is "*about twenty-four, but looks younger*," and has "*something amusing and attractive about her, as it were, against her will, and the more fetching for that*" (*VW*, 63). Vida's attractions draw not only Greatorex's flirtatious compliments, but the wistful romantic hopes of Richard Farnborough, a sycophantic political satellite of Stonor's, and Allen Trent, a supporter of the suffrage organization which Vida ultimately joins. Even Stonor, a very grudging suitor, admits, "You're one of the people the years have not taken from, but given more to.... You haven't lost your beauty" (*VW*, 104). In portraying her suffragist characters as feminine and graceful, Robins helped to counter detractors who caricatured feminists as mannish and abrasive spinsters. As Vida tells Greatorex, "I'm told it's an exploded notion that the Suffrage women are all dowdy and dull" (*VW*, 35).

Robins's appealing, feminine depictions of suffragists in her play reflected the policies of British suffrage societies. Fashionable dress for many militant suffrage leaders served as a political statement, an assertion that, contrary to their opponents' accusations, they did not wish to be men or to resemble or imitate men, but to exercise civil rights *as women*. Joel H. Kaplan and Sheila Stowell describe this dress policy as a demonstration of the "complementariness" of the different sexes, as well as "a living retort to the labels hung upon them by hostile witnesses" (*Theatre and Fashion*, 153). Renata Kobetts Miller, analyzing dress guidelines and press coverage from large demonstrations such as the 1911 Coronation Parade, suggests that the crux of the suffragists' dress strategy was "The self-conscious performance of femininity in the public world," which "dismantled the concept of the separation of spheres" (*The Victorian Actress*, 200). By cultivating an attractively feminine appearance, suffrage feminists both challenged and reassured those who felt threatened by their political activism. Vida's elegant dress and manners allow her to remain (like Robins herself) a welcome guest among upper-class anti-suffragist acquaintances even as her own political commitments become increasingly firm. Hence, she can offer a soft-spoken but shrewd dissent when the cause is ridiculed. Her beauty is also shown to endow her with persuasive powers. The *Times*, in reviewing the play, testified to this persuasive ability in its praise of Edith Wynne Matthison, who played the role, opining that the women's rights campaign "would make much more headway than it does if all its advocates were as fair to look upon, as agreeable to hear, and as beautifully dressed as Miss Wynne Matthison" ("Court Theatre," 5).

Yet this reviewer's remark, evidently intended as a compliment to the actress, reveals a tension inherent in the strategies of the suffrage movement. Suffrage feminists sought to win civil rights that would make them enfranchised participants in public life, no longer regarded simply as sex objects or potential wives. Yet some leaders feared that their practice of dressing fashionably might reinforce women's dependence on their manipulative sexual charms, or at least make them appear dependent to outsiders. Hostile journalists and cartoonists readily dramatized and exaggerated this suspicion: as the mannish spinster image ceased to ring true, another stereotype began to circulate, characterizing the suffragette as a frivolous woman who, while mouthing the phrases of liberty and women's rights, reserved her real interest for hats, dresses, and sweethearts. The *Times* review of *Votes for Women!*, even while complimenting Edith Wynne Matthison for the persuasive power of her face and costumes, pointed to those same looks in questioning the sincerity of Vida's insistence that she is not eager to marry. The reviewer asked slyly: "Why…does Miss Levering take such care to make the best of her good looks and pretty figure and wear such charming frocks? Is it to please other women?" ("Court Theatre," 5). If the purpose of feminine attraction was to secure a husband, then an attractive woman who remained single by choice was a perplexing figure. Farfan argues that Robins sought in *Votes for Women!* to challenge or propose meaningful alternatives to the patriarchal practices of playwriting and theatrical production, and that she ultimately failed in these goals because, "through her tactic of employing a 'womanly woman' to secure feminist points," she became complicit in "the very attitudes and practices that had been so oppressive and demeaning to her as a theatre artist"

("From *Hedda Gabler* to *Votes for Women!*," 73). Irving had years earlier insisted on "sweet feminine charm" as the chief qualification for an actress, and society at large seemingly shared this insistence, considering all women as virtual performers (*Both Sides of the Curtain*, 241). Women were deemed successful insofar as they resembled romantic heroines—that is, insofar as their physical charms enabled them to gain husbands and whatever other goals they pursued. Robins, Farfan alleges, helped to reinforce this tendency even as she sought to undermine it.

Robins was aware of the tensions within her project and of the difficulty of articulating a value for a woman's beauty other than the conventional marital and sexual values. Some of her frustration at this dilemma might be read in the play's closing dialogue, as Vida expresses her ambivalence to her own good looks: when Stonor assures her, "You haven't lost your beauty," she replies, "The gods saw it was so little effectual, it wasn't worth taking away" (*VW*, 104). In *The Convert*, her novel adaptation of the play, Robins discussed at greater length the uses and meanings of feminine charm from the feminist perspective. At one high Society gathering in which the topic of suffrage demonstrations is (as usual) roundly mocked and abused, one anti-suffragist lady jokingly suggests, "Now, if we got our maids to do those women's hair for them—if we lent them our French hats—ah, *then*...they'd convert you [male] creatures fast enough then." Vida responds, "What if it's the aim of the movement to get away from the need of just those little dodges?" Her interlocutor is baffled, and the narrator muses: "Miss Levering must have seen that she had been speaking in an unknown tongue. A world where beauty exists for beauty's sake—which is love's sake—and not for tricking money or power out of men, even the possibility of such a world is beyond the imagining of many" (*The Convert*, 137–138). Robins, along with Christabel Pankhurst, Cicely Hamilton, and others, was attempting to reimagine a feminine identity that would not be primarily defined by women's sexual or marital relations to men that would not present womanliness and sensuality as synonymous. In one sense, the smart costumes worn by Vida and others like her were indeed worn, as the *Times* reviewer facetiously remarked, "to please other women," to invite identification and camaraderie and to demonstrate, by gathering en masse in their best gowns, the possibility of women's clothes and figures as "beauty for beauty's sake." The responses to this new conception of femininity, both within Robins's dialogue and from reviewers, illustrate the momentous challenge to conventional thinking that this new definition represented.

The Suffrage Genre and the Marriage Plot: Social Movement as Theater

With its beautiful woman with a past who chooses political activism rather than marriage, exile, or a brokenhearted death, *Votes for Women!* is a seduction melodrama and Society play with an unorthodox ending, relegating central questions of marriage and singleness to side issues as larger questions of women's rights claim primary attention. At the same time, in combining drama with political propaganda and in bringing an actual Trafalgar Square meeting onstage in her "dramatic tract," Robins helped lay the foundation and set precedents for suffrage plays.

Robins was among the first dramatists to appreciate the connections between the stage and the suffrage movement, and the ways in which these links might be used for the benefit of theater and the women's cause. The more militant branches of the movement, in fact, as they were portrayed by both their adherents and detractors, contained many of the ingredients of mid-Victorian melodrama, from passionate speeches and self-sacrificing heroism to spectacles of window-breaking, explosions, and police fights to rival Boucicault's sensation scenes. The women who staged these demonstrations—particularly those who were arrested and imprisoned as a result—appropriated familiarly gendered theatrical roles, but often with unorthodox variations. Supporters described these women in masculine terms as heroes and warriors. Yet these warlike images were intermingled with traditionally feminine language of suffering victims who had mistakenly trusted in men's "chivalry" (a word Robins frequently repeated with ironic emphasis in her journalistic suffrage writings).

In *Votes for Women!* and in *The Convert*, Robins repeatedly highlights the theatricality of suffrage protests and of the suffragist identity in general by drawing comparisons between these demonstrations and specific theatrical genres and stock characters: one speaker declaims like "an overblown Adelphi heroine," another raises laughs like "the favourite comedian" (*The Convert*, 87, 100). Mrs. Freddy Tunbridge, venting her chagrin after a protest in the House of Commons, reports: "I've never been so moved in public. No tragedy, no great opera ever gripped an audience as the situation in the House did that night" (*VW*, 51). These similes are made more frequently in the novel version of the narrative than in the play (onstage, the theatrical resonances of the Trafalgar Square speakers may well have been self-evident). Robins most frequently placed these comparisons in the mouths of undecided, later-to-be-converted observers of the demonstrators—of Vida early in the novel, of Jean nearer the end—suggesting that the stagey techniques served a practical recruiting purpose: those who came for entertainment might stay to join.

Especially significant among the novel's theatrical similes is Jean's Ibsenesque impression of Ernestine Blunt at the final Trafalgar Square meeting, likening her to the free-spirited Hilda Wangel in *The Master Builder*, an embodiment of the irrepressible "Younger Generation," a character Robins herself had played more than a decade earlier. Ernestine is "Hilda, harnessed to a purpose" (*The Convert*, 253). The allusion signals, as Maroula Joannou has argued, both a "theatrical *homage*" to Robins's early mentor and "a radical break with Ibsen's dramaturgy" ("Hilda, Harnessed to a Purpose," 188).[13] Ibsen's women—Nora, Hedda, and Hilda among them—had rebelled against their assigned gender roles and disrupted comfortable assumptions about domesticity, but had found no constructive outlets for their energy and frustration, and so expended them through irritable chafing, solitary wandering, or destructive action. The suffragists, Robins implied, shared the discontent of Ibsen's heroines, but used it as fuel in their efforts to organize themselves and alter laws. Ibsen was similarly invoked by the suffragists in the 1911 Coronation Procession, an enormous demonstration involving more than 40,000 participants. As Robins noted with satisfaction, among the marchers appeared "Hedda Gabler, in the accomplished person of the Princess Bariatinsky on horseback" (*Way Stations*, 250).[14] The prominent inclusion of Hedda in the suffrage procession marked Ibsen's continued importance as literary inspiration to women's rights efforts. Yet, as Farfan has pointed out, to present Hedda as a figurehead in a feminist parade entailed a significant revision of the bored, spiteful, and ultimately suicidal woman created by Ibsen. The Hedda of the procession was "not the character that Ibsen depicted in his 1890 play but, rather, the character that they [the suffragists] themselves imagined Hedda would have been had she somehow existed outside Ibsen's play" ("From *Hedda Gabler* to *Votes for Women!*", 59). As Ibsen had rewritten and dismantled the conventions of domestic melodrama, the suffragist performers now rewrote Ibsen's drama, transforming his purposeless, isolated protagonist into an ardent activist, defined not by her unhappy marriage but by her zeal to reform stage and society and her solidarity with her fellow-reformers.

Many women of the theater recognized the inherent theatricality of the suffrage movement and the potential usefulness of theater as a publicity tool, as well as the contributions to the movement that actresses were especially qualified to make. In 1908, 400 actresses and former actresses, Robins among them, formed the AFL, an organization whose members gave speeches, held workshops to train novice orators, and wrote and produced an extensive repertoire of propaganda plays. Edith Wynne Matthison, the Vida of *Votes for Women!*, also joined, as did three other women from the play's cast. In encouraging women to write plays and offering venues for having those plays performed, the AFL offered agency to women who, like Robins in her pre-Ibsen years, had been accustomed to the role of "leading lady in leading strings" (*Theatre and Friendship*, 53). AFL members also embraced the possibility of using their public performance skills for a wider social good, a cause beyond individual livelihood, popularity, or even artistic achievement, gaining dignity for a profession that in the past had often been condemned as frivolous and even immoral. As Miller has noted, the AFL's use of drama to pursue shared political goals encouraged a spirit of community among women who had long been accustomed to competition both in the marriage market and in the professional theaters dominated by male actor-managers (*The Victorian Actress*, 197). Robins, in her early observations of suffrage speakers, praised the "civilising, ennobling" effect of using public speaking skills for "a great impersonal object" rather than in theatrical productions "innocent of political significance." Whereas in non-political drama "the actor's necessary preoccupation with the things of the imagination may divorce him from the larger realities of life," the reform speakers' enthusiasm for their cause endowed them with "high earnestness" and "forgetfulness of themselves" (*Way Stations*, 39–40). The immediate possibility of enfranchisement within the theater in pursuit of the more distant goal of political franchise probably accounts, at least in large part, for the success of suffrage leaders in recruiting theatrical women to their cause.

The AFL Play Department, headed by Australian-born actress Inez Bensusan, commissioned, staged, and published numerous plays about suffrage and other social and political issues affecting women. These plays served both as propaganda and as fundraisers for the AFL and other suffrage organizations. Other organizations, in particular, Edith Craig's Pioneer Players, later took part in the AFL's projects of supporting women's rights through drama and producing plays by and for women. Though these plays varied widely in their tone and form—some serious, some comic, some in realistic settings, some in the form of pageant or allegory—many came to follow a formula loosely modeled on Robins's *Votes for Women!*. Like Robins's play, many suffrage dramas were structured around the conversion (or in some cases, the non-conversion) of a hostile or undecided person to the suffrage cause. Evelyn Glover's *Miss Appleyard's Awakening* and *A Chat with Mrs. Chicky* and Cicely Hamilton and Christopher St. John's *How the Vote was Won* are a few examples. This dramatic structure allowed a convenient format for listing pro-suffrage arguments and for refuting or ridiculing anti-suffrage claims (though few writers went to the length of re-creating an entire series of Trafalgar Square speeches, as Robins did in her second act).

These later plays also frequently emphasized bonds between women as friends, comrades, and fellow-workers, much as the action of *Votes for Women!* is largely determined by Jean's growing admiration and sympathy for Vida. This female camaraderie is stressed in Beatrice Harraden's *Lady Geraldine's Speech* and Margaret Wynne Nevinson's *In the Workhouse*, both of which are centered on communities of women who rely on one another for advice and moral support. In many cases, though not always, these two ideas—female loyalties and dedication to the suffrage campaign, or one of the two—were explicitly presented as alternatives to heterosexual marriage or romance. In Bessie Hatton's *Before Sunrise*, for example, the protagonist's self-reliant, politically conscious best friend urges her to leave her restrictive family and her disagreeable (and possibly syphilitic) suitor to form a household together, offering what is, in effect, a female marriage proposal. This emphasis on platonic, romantic, and quasi-marital bonds between women mirrored the reality of some suffrage dramatists' lives (Edith Craig's partnership with Christopher St. John is one prominent example). It also foregrounded and valorized the female partnerships which, as Sharon Marcus has documented in *Between Women*, had been widely acknowledged and accepted in nineteenth-century social life as "variation[s] on legal marriage," and which had sometimes served as catalysts for marriage reform and other feminist causes (*Between Women*, 203).[15] Yet this de-centering of heterosexual marriage, and of men in general, from women's narratives could be distorted and used as a weapon by opponents. Katharine Cockin reports that "The anti-suffragists demonised the suffragettes as a threat to heterosexuality" (*Women and Theatre*, 129). This "threat" need not be explicitly that of transgressive sexuality—opposing propaganda frequently targeted celibate women, labeling them as "unsexed," as embittered spinsters and man-haters whose political agitation was a thin mask for personal disappointment, or as lazy and frivolous housewives who simply sought to escape their domestic responsibilities. Yet it may not be a coincidence that the years of militant suffrage activity overlapped with the early twentieth-century period during which lesbian sexuality was being defined and classified as deviant.

Despite these stigmas, suffragists' emphasis on female community and on celibacy in support of a cause also helped to reinforce the religious iconography of female martyrs, saints, and nuns—images integral to suffrage propaganda. Such religious representation was used when, in some plays, women were shown as married to The Cause. The suffrage campaign was represented as an all-encompassing commitment equivalent to marriage in its exclusiveness and its power to define a person's primary identity. As Cockin has shown, this religious iconography was especially prominent in militant propaganda: "The suffragists' appropriation of religious discourse, with its emphasis on martyrdom, sacrifice and comradeship, endorsed an oppositional political position, lending it authority by the allusion to a religious precedent" (*Women and Theatre*, 127). Suffrage activists readily pointed out that many of these religious heroines had been attacked in their own time for failure to adhere to normative femininity— Joan of Arc was a frequently cited figure in WSPU literature.[16] In *Votes for Women!*, Vida likens the persecution of militants to witch-hunts of the Middle Ages: "'Mad.' 'Unsexed.' Those are the words of today. In the Middle Ages men cried out 'Witch!' and burnt her—the woman who served no man's bed or board" (*VW*, 101). The newly converted Jean, in Vida's vision, may be "the new Joan of Arc" (*VW*, 101). The likening of suffrage activism to religious conversion and sainthood was reinforced by suffrage speakers' reminders that the label of "Christian," like that of "Suffragette," had been first coined as a taunt before being proudly claimed and appropriated by the derided group themselves.[17]

More broadly, Robins and other suffrage dramatists presented political activism as a possible means of satisfying women's desire for work or vocation outside the domestic sphere—a desire that had been widely discussed in nineteenth-century writings on marriage and women's rights. Talia Schaffer, in her study of the marriage plot in Victorian fiction, argues that "Victorian novels often passionately insisted on women's 'calling' to exercise their talents, improve their society, and engage in meaningful occupation.... However, Victorian novels did not often imagine a plot in which those women could succeed" (*Romance's Rival*, 207). She suggests that women's efforts at non-domestic work carried a stigma akin to that of sexual transgression: "Middle-class women often regarded their desire for work (like sex) to be a source of shame—the work itself had to be hidden from strangers, done at odd hours.... Female vocationalism had its perversities, its forbidden pleasures associated with queer individuals (perhaps we should call them vocational inverts)" (*Romance's Rival*, 213). Schaffer's reading of women's work as transgression offers a useful way to think of some of the marriage performance dramas discussed earlier in this study, with the would-be feminist reformers such as Elaine Shrimpton and Agnes Ebbsmith, who are mocked or condemned by Jones and Pinero. And Nora Helmer, long before leaving the doll's house, has secretly been working as a copyist to pay her debt to Krogstad (a practice that, interestingly, she never reveals to Torvald, even in the final reckoning scene). She confides to Mrs. Linden: "[I]t was splendid to work in that way and earn money. I almost felt as if I was a man" (*DH*, 22). Suffrage dramas such as *Votes for Women!* attempt to resolve the long-standing tension between idealized domesticity and censured vocational desire by bringing vocation proudly to the foreground, inviting women to partake openly of a once-forbidden pleasure.

This is not to say that suffragist writers and speakers regarded marriage and political activism as invariably antagonistic—indeed, some speakers valorized and repurposed the language of domesticity to depict women's civic participation as a logical extension of their social contributions as wives, mothers, and homemakers, allowing women to serve as men's partners and helpers in government as they did in the home. Women's votes and civic participation, it was argued, would ultimately benefit the domestic sphere by using women's domestic expertise to alter economic policies that were harmful to families and children. One of the Trafalgar Square speakers in Robins's play, the working-class woman who is a Poor Law Guardian, makes such an argument, insisting that politics is "just 'ousekeepin' on a big scyle," and that the country's political problems result from men's attempts to "do the national 'ousekeepin' without the women" (*VW*, 60). Some suffrage plays stressed the need for better understanding between men and women and for cooperation between the sexes—this was an especially common theme in male-authored suffrage drama, such as Graham Moffat's *The Maid and the Magistrate* and Henry Arncliffe-Sennett's *An Englishwoman's Home*. In the latter, for example, Arncliffe-Sennett offers a mock-heroic and, nonetheless, rather touching depiction of a bachelor lodger minding the house while his landlady attends a suffrage meeting, performing the courageous feat of picking up a crying baby for the first time. Such scenes comically suggested that men and women might both gain from working together in domestic management as well as in government policymaking.

In rejecting or revising the plot devices of domestic melodrama, social comedy, and Ibsenite play of ideas, Robins and other suffragist writers after her developed another set of dramatic devices and conventions. Where marriage (or failed marriage or a decision against marrying) had once supplied the endpoint of the drama, the suffrage drama's trajectory was most frequently shaped by a conversion narrative, by the protagonist's movement toward (or occasionally, refusal to move toward) involvement in the suffrage cause, or, more generally, toward an awakened knowledge of women's situation in society. Marriage or romantic desire might or might not be featured among the secondary factors that facilitate or impede the plot's main action, along with the woman's interactions with other women. And whereas secondary characters in earlier plays had been absorbed in watching and interpreting the protagonists' marriages, now suffrage activism was made the object of observation by the onstage audiences and those in the auditorium.

Conclusion

In *A Doll's House*, Ibsen presented marriage and theatrical performance as closely linked, mutually dependent issues, each shaping and shaped by a common set of assumptions about sexuality, gender roles, morality, and narrative trajectory. As Nora dismantled these assumptions one by one, she profoundly altered both her marriage and the play, ultimately leaving both unfinished and unresolved. Ibsen's later plays, such as *Hedda Gabler*, though they did not link marriage and theater in such literal ways, continued to dwell on the problems of traditional marriage and to challenge audiences' assumptions about what a play ought to be, altering conventional character types and subverting the tidy closure of the well-made play. His plays, especially his characterization of Hedda, critiqued the ideal of the "womanly woman," the woman defined exclusively as wife and mother, sex object and caregiver, suggesting that in some cases this "natural" character might be little more than a dramatic role adopted of necessity and cynically played.

Dramatists writing in late-Victorian England recognized the double challenge which Ibsen's plays posed to marriage and to theater, and answered in varying ways, whether they welcomed Ibsen's influence or resisted it. Wilde, Pinero, and Jones, in considering theatrical marriage, focused attention on the acquaintances and neighbors who served as spectators. Their plays emphasized social performances such as dinner parties, dances, and formal calls as sites of marital tension and infused these events with echoes of familiar scenes from such theatrical genres as burlesque, domestic comedy, and seduction melodrama. In *Candida*, *Getting Married*, and other plays, Shaw adopted and adapted Ibsen's vision of marriage as theater, suggesting marital play-acting to be a characteristic masculine activity as well as a feminine one, and echoing Ibsen's insistence on the need for discussion at the center of marriage and theater alike. For each dramatist, the use of social and theatrical performance genres enabled a re-examination of the moral and aesthetic assumptions on which those genres were based—in particular, their plays questioned the linking of marriage with "happy ending" and exclusion from marriage as "unhappy," and degrees of sexual experience or inexperience that were held to qualify or disqualify men and (especially) women as marriage partners—ideas that had generally been accepted without challenge in plays earlier in the century. Even dramatists who came to fairly conservative conclusions on these subjects, such as Pinero and Jones, to some degree questioned the inevitability and naturalness of those conclusions—conventional morality, they suggested, like conventional dramatic structure, might be a matter less of universal rightness than of audience demand, "the eyes of the world."

Robins was initially drawn to Ibsen's plays for the opportunities they offered to her and to other women as actresses, as managers, and as spectators seeing their lives and circumstances credibly reflected onstage. She took part in the debate over the New Drama first as a performer and manager, later as a writer, with *Alan's Wife* and later with *Votes for Women!*, creating strong and varied theatrical roles for women both inside and outside marriage. In this process, she borrowed and repurposed conventions and character types from the "old-fashioned" genres that had earlier been critiqued and revised by Ibsen, Pinero, and others. She also innovated on the newer genres they had developed and introduced, such as the Society drama and the discussion play—genres which by the first decade of the twentieth century, had become familiar and, in some eyes, old-hat theatrical templates.

Like *A Doll's House*, *Candida*, and other works associated with New Drama, *Alan's Wife* faced critical accusations of being "not a play" or "not art"—of transgressing the boundaries of drama so far as to be outside them. Later, with *Votes for Women!*, Robins herself disavowed the claim to playwriting, titling her work not a "play" but a "dramatic tract." In labeling the piece a "tract" and claiming a purpose apart from simple art or entertainment, Robins further stretched definitions of art and theater: if a "tract" had a didactic agenda and was not "art for art's sake," might it still be "art"? If not, then was it necessarily lower or less worthwhile than works that could claim artistic status?

At the same time, Robins attempted in *Votes for Women!* to address the question that had been implicit in Ibsen's plays and many responses to them: if marriage isn't to be the central structuring device in drama, then what should be? Robins proposed suffrage and women's rights activism as one possible answer to this question—an answer that appears to have appealed to other women who, as actresses and writers, sought the theatrical responsibility and agency that Robins had found in performing and producing Ibsen's plays. In abandoning the marriage-centered dramatic conventions that earlier New Drama works had explored and grappled with, Robins and other suffrage dramatists developed another set of conventions. The suffrage dramatists also explored innovative possibilities for what plays could be about and what functions they could serve, seeking to make the theater a mirror of life as they saw it and as they wished to see it. If the earlier dramas reflected the social hierarchy and gender roles of Victorian society both in their plot and characters and in their process of production, Robins's productions of Ibsen and later productions by the AFL presented small-scale pictures of a more democratic creative process, requiring cooperation among women and between women and men.

Notes

1. Despite the glowing tone of Robins's published writings about Wilde, Kerry Powell has argued, based on Robins's diaries, letters, and unpublished writings, that the early mentor-pupil relationship between Wilde and Robins would later become more complicated, with Robins increasingly taking an admonitory role in urging Wilde to use his influence and literary skills to support "the Theatre of the Future" (*Women and Victorian Theatre*, 149).
2. For details on the translation, copyright, and persons involved, see Joanne E. Gates, "Elizabeth Robins and the 1891 Production of Hedda Gabler," *Modern Drama* 28, no. 4 (1985): 611–19.
3. The baby's physical deformities are not described in detail in the play, but in Ameen's original story, he is born with no legs and only one arm.
4. This resemblance to Hardy's novel led several critics to suspect him of being the play's anonymous author. Hardy, for his part, was evidently concerned that he might be accused of plagiarizing the baptism scene from

Ameen's *Befriad*, for he took considerable pains to demonstrate that the resemblance was accidental: *Befriad* had been published in *Ur Dagens Kronika*, a Swedish magazine, in January 1891, five months before the baptism episode of *Tess* appeared in *The Fortnightly Review*, but, Hardy explained, he had submitted this section of his novel to Tillotson and Sons in September 1889, though he had subsequently withdrawn it (Thomas Hardy, "Letter to the Westminster Gazette," 55).

5. Bell had previously authored several less controversial plays which had been published or produced under her name, in two of which (*A Joint Household* and *Karin*) Robins had performed.
6. Kingston, though she eventually became an active supporter of the suffrage campaign, appears to have been hesitant to produce a play with so controversial a topic so early in her managerial career (John, *Elizabeth Robins: Staging a Life*, 147).
7. Winkiel primarily refers to *The Convert*, Robins's novel adaptation of *Votes for Women!*, but much of her analysis could be usefully applied to the play as well.
8. In earlier drafts of the play, the character is called "Beatrice." The change to "Jean" underscores her identification with Joan of Arc, to whom she is compared late in the play, but may also serve to associate her with Robins's earlier controversial protagonist in *Alan's Wife*.
9. Angela John, Sheila Stowell, and Maroula Joannou have all suggested possible real-life counterparts for the speakers: the working woman has been identified with Mrs. Baldock (John 145) and Hannah Mitchell (Stowell 28), Pilcher with Labour MP Keir Hardie (Joannou 191), and Ernestine with Christabel Pankhurst (Stowell 29) and Teresa Billington-Greig (John 145).
10. Bernard F. Dukore notes that Shaw began to experiment with writing "interruption" dialogue for his crowd scene around this same time, notably for Johnston Forbes-Robertson's 1906 New York production of *Caesar and Cleopatra* ("Bernard Shaw: The Director as Dramatist," 136–67).
11. Jan McDonald points out that Granville-Barker, throughout his term of management at the Court Theatre, was a committed opponent of the star system (*The "New Drama" 1900–1914*, 17–18).
12. Shaw's verdict on Mrs. Ebbsmith's revealing evening gown, by contrast, was "a horrifying confection apparently made of Japanese bronze wallpaper," "appallingly ugly," and "cut rather lower in the pectoral region than I expected" (*TN1*, 64).
13. Joannou also points out that 1906, the year in which Robins wrote *Votes for Women*, was also the year of Ibsen's death, and suggests that his death might have "concentrated the thoughts of Ibsenites on the cultural significance of his legacy to the stage" ("Hilda, Harnessed to a Purpose," 188).

14. "Princess Bariatinsky" was the pseudonym of actress Lydia Yavorskaia, who had starred in a Russian language production of *Hedda Gabler* at His Majesty's Theatre in July 1909.
15. Marcus suggests that female marriages may have served as models for reformers who sought to shape more flexible and egalitarian heterosexual marriage laws.
16. Shaw, in turn, more than once alluded to the suffrage activists a decade later in his preface to *Saint Joan*.
17. Robins, in early drafts of *Votes for Women*, invoked this analogy by naming her central character "Christian Levering," though, as Angela John explains, she eventually changed the name to "Vida" in response to Mrs. Pankhurst's concerns that the character's sexually transgressive backstory might reflect scandal on her daughter Christabel (*Elizabeth Robins: Staging a Life*, 145).

REFERENCES

Archer, William. "Introduction." In *Alan's Wife: A Dramatic Study in Three Scenes*, edited by Elizabeth Robins and Florence Bell. London: Henry, 1893.

Arncliffe-Sennett, Henry. *An Englishwoman's Home*. In *Literature of the Women's Suffrage Campaign in England*, edited by Carolyn Christensen Nelson, 233–45. Peterborough: Broadview, 2004.

"At the Play." *Hearth and Home*, May 11, 1893.

Cockin, Katharine. *Women and Theatre in the Age of Suffrage: The Pioneer Players, 1911–1925*. London: Palgrave Macmillan, 2001.

"Court Theatre." *The Times*, April 10, 1907.

Dukore, Bernard F. "Bernard Shaw: The Director as Dramatist." *SHAW: The Journal of Bernard Shaw Studies* 36, no. 2 (2015): 136–67.

Farfan, Penny. "From *Hedda Gabler* to *Votes for Women!*: Elizabeth Robins's Early Feminist Critique of Ibsen." *Theatre Journal* 48, no. 1 (1996): 59–78.

"Feathers from the Wings." *Moonshine*, May 13, 1893.

Gates, Joanne E. "Elizabeth Robins and the 1891 Production of Hedda Gabler." *Modern Drama* 28, no. 4 (1985): 611–19.

Glover, Evelyn. *A Chat with Mrs. Chicky*. In *Literature of the Women's Suffrage Campaign in England*, edited by Carolyn Christensen Nelson, 265–76. Peterborough: Broadview, 2004a.

———. *Miss Appleyard's Awakening*. In *Literature of the Women's Suffrage Campaign in England*, edited by Carolyn Christensen Nelson, 277–87. Peterborough: Broadview, 2004b.

Grein, J. T. "Introduction." In *Alan's Wife: A Dramatic Study in Three Scenes*, edited by Elizabeth Robins and Florence Bell, v–viii. London: Henry, 1893.

Hamilton, Cicely, and Christopher St. John. "How the Vote Was Won." In *Literature of the Women's Suffrage Campaign in England*, edited by Carolyn Christensen Nelson, 184–200. Peterborough: Broadview, 2004.
Hardy, Thomas. "Letter to the Westminster Gazette, 9 May 1893." In *Alan's Wife: A Dramatic Study in Three Scenes*, by Elizabeth Robins and Florence Bell and edited by J. T. Grein, 55. London: Henry, 1893.
Hatton, Bessie. *Before Sunrise*. In *Literature of the Women's Suffrage Campaign in England*, edited by Carolyn Christensen Nelson, 209–20. Peterborough: Broadview, 2004.
Ibsen, Henrik. *A Doll's House*. Translated by William Archer. London: T. Fisher Unwin, 1889.
Joannou, Maroula. "'Hilda, Harnessed to a Purpose': Elizabeth Robins, Ibsen, and the Vote." *Comparative Drama* 44, no. 2 (2010): 172–200.
John, Angela V. *Elizabeth Robins: Staging a Life 1862–1952*. New York: Routledge, 1995.
Kaplan, Joel H., and Sheila Stowell. *Theatre and Fashion: Oscar Wilde to the Suffragettes*. Cambridge: Cambridge University Press, 1994.
Marcus, Sharon. *Between Women: Friendship, Desire, and Marriage in Victorian England*. Princeton: Princeton University Press, 2007.
McDonald, Jan. *The "New Drama" 1900–1914*. London: Macmillan, 1986.
Miller, Renata Kobetts. *The Victorian Actress in the Novel and on the Stage*. Edinburgh: Edinburgh University Press, 2018.
Moffat, Graham. *The Maid and the Magistrate*. In *Literature of the Women's Suffrage Campaign in England*, edited by Carolyn Christensen Nelson, 256–64. Peterborough: Broadview, 2004.
"Our London Letter." *Derby Daily Telegraph*, May 1, 1893.
Pinero, Arthur Wing. *The Social Plays of Arthur Wing Pinero*. Edited by Clayton Hamilton. 4 vols. New York: Dutton, 1917.
Powell, Kerry. *Women and Victorian Theatre*. Cambridge: Cambridge University Press, 1997.
Robins, Elizabeth. *Ancilla's Share: An Indictment of Sex Antagonism*. Westport, CT: Hyperion, 1976.
———. *Both Sides of the Curtain*. London: Heinemann, 1940.
———. *Ibsen and the Actress*. New York: Haskell House, 1973.
———. *The Convert*. London: Women's Press, 1980.
———. *Theatre and Friendship: Some Henry James Letters*. New York: Putnam's Sons, 1932.
———. "Votes for Women!" TS. New York, 1907. Fales Library.
———. "Votes for Women!: A Dramatic Tract in Three Acts." In *Votes for Women and Other Plays*, edited by Susan Croft, 21–106. Twickenham, UK: Aurora Metro, 2009.
———. *Way Stations*. London: Hodder & Stoughton, 1913.

Robins, Elizabeth, and Florence Bell. *Alan's Wife: A Dramatic Study in Three Scenes.* Edited by J. T. Grein. London: Henry, 1893.

Schaffer, Talia. *Romance's Rival: Familiar Marriage in Victorian Fiction.* Oxford: Oxford University Press, 2016.

Scott, Clement. "Hedda Gabler." In *Ibsen: The Critical Heritage*, edited by Michael Egan, 225–28. London: Routledge, 1972.

———. *Our Theatres in the Nineties.* 3 vols. London: Constable, 1932.

———. "Preface." In *The Theatrical "World" of 1894*, edited by William Archer, xi–xxx. London: Walter Scott, 1895.

———. *The Bodley Head Bernard Shaw: Collected Plays with Their Prefaces.* Edited by Dan H. Laurence. 7 vols. London: The Bodley Head, 1970.

Shkolnik, Esther Simon. *Leading Ladies: A Study of Eight Late Victorian and Edwardian Political Wives.* New York: Garland, 1987.

Stowell, Sheila. *A Stage of Their Own: Feminist Playwrights in the Suffrage Era.* Ann Arbor: University of Michigan Press, 1992.

"Terry's Theatre." *The Morning Post*, May 1, 1893.

"To-Day's London Letter." *Edinburgh Evening News*, May 1, 1893.

Winkiel, Laura A. "A Suffrage Burlesque: Modernist Performance in Elizabeth Robins's The Convert." *MFS Modern Fiction Studies* 40, no. 3 (2004): 570–94.

Index[1]

A

Achurch, Janet, 4, 26, 42n2, 42n3, 93, 147, 158n9, 164, 166
Actresses' Franchise League (AFL), 17, 124, 174, 188, 194
Adelphi Theatre, 92
Alexander, George, 15, 51, 52, 59, 86, 92, 93, 99, 104–106
Anti-theatricality, 10, 11
Archer, William, 4, 21, 22, 24, 25, 27, 31, 34, 35, 41, 42n2, 50, 51, 65, 68, 72, 73, 81–83, 90, 94, 95, 103, 108, 113, 115, 117, 157n6, 166, 170, 171
Arncliffe-Sennett, Henry, 191
An Englishwoman's Home, 191
Ashwell, Lena, 124, 167
Austin, J. L., 9, 73

B

Beerbohm Tree, Herbert, 47, 52, 70, 128n2, 163
Bell, Florence, 168–171, 173, 195n5
Alan's Wife, 168, 170, 171, 193, 195n8
Bernhardt, Sarah, 46
Besant, Walter, 14, 23, 39–41
"The Doll's House—And After," 39
Boucicault, Dion, 3, 4, 70, 107, 143, 186
The Colleen Bawn, 3
The Octoroon, 69, 107, 143
Brookfield, Charles H. E., 49, 50, 52, 53, 56, 57
The Poet and the Puppets, 49, 50, 53, 56, 57
Burlesque, 49, 53, 56, 95–97, 99, 101n5, 193
Butler, Judith, 8, 22, 42n1

---

[1] Note: Page numbers followed by 'n' refer to notes.

C

Caird, Mona, 5, 10, 100
Campbell, Stella (Mrs. Patrick), 4, 92–94, 106, 108, 124, 182
Charrington, Charles, 4, 42n2, 144, 157–158n7
Cobbe, Frances Power, 3
Contagious Diseases Act, 3
Court Theatre, 180, 182, 184, 195n11
Custody of Infants Act, 3

D

Dickens, Charles, 3, 99
  Our Mutual Friend, 9, 89
Divorce, 34, 90, 99, 112, 115, 147–152, 188
Du Maurier, George, 25, 46, 137
Dumas, Alexandre, 2, 4, 42n4, 49, 85
  La Dame Aux Camélias, 2

E

Eliot, George, 3, 12
  Middlemarch, 9

G

Garrick Theatre, 98
Gilbert, W. S., 4, 45, 133, 137–140, 146, 157n3, 157n6
  Patience, 45, 46, 53, 137, 138, 140, 157n3
  The Sorcerer, 133
Glover, Evelyn, 189
  A Chat with Mrs. Chicky, 189
  Miss Appleyard's Awakening, 189
Glover, J. M., 49, 50, 53
  The Poet and the Puppets, 49, 50, 53, 56, 57
Granville-Barker, Harley, 21, 174, 180, 195n11

Grein, J. T., 4, 50, 82, 124, 125, 127, 168, 170, 171, 174
Grundy, Sydney, 39, 40, 42n3
  The New Woman, 39
Guthrie, Thomas Anstey, 14, 23
  Mr. Punch's Pocket Ibsen, 38

H

Hamilton, Cicely, 119, 172, 185, 189
  How the Vote was Won, 189
  Just to Get Married, 119
Hardy, Edward John, 9, 10, 76n4
  How to be Happy Though Married, 9
Hardy, Thomas, 74, 169, 171, 194–195n4
  Tess of the D'Urbervilles, 56
Hare, John, 49, 98, 99
Hatton, Bessie, 172, 189
  Before Sunrise, 189
Headlam, Stewart Duckworth, 134
Herman, Henry, 14, 23, 30, 31, 35, 36, 41, 103
  Breaking a Butterfly, 30, 31, 35, 103, 115

I

Ibsen, Henrik, 1, 2, 5, 6, 8, 9, 12–17, 21–42, 42n4, 43n6, 50, 51, 59, 60, 82–85, 93, 94, 98, 99, 103, 110, 115, 117, 124, 128, 131–133, 144, 146, 147, 156, 161–174, 180, 181, 187, 192–194, 195n13
  A Doll's House, 1, 2, 5, 7, 14–17, 21–23, 26, 29–33, 36, 39–41, 47, 68, 71, 82, 84, 101n3, 103, 112, 115, 127, 144, 146, 148, 156, 157n7, 161, 164, 165, 169, 170, 174, 193
  Ghosts, 5, 29, 124, 133, 169

Hedda Gabler, 5, 161, 163–171, 174, 192, 196n14
Little Eyolf, 94
Rosmersholm, 42n6, 133
Independent Theatre Society, 124, 168

J
James, Henry, 12, 18n2, 90, 173
Guy Domville, 18n2
Jones, Henry Arthur, 2, 4–6, 10, 12, 14–16, 23, 30, 31, 35, 36, 39–42, 51, 52, 75, 90, 103–128, 128n1, 133, 140, 141, 143, 147, 156, 163, 174, 175, 191–193
Breaking a Butterfly, 30, 31, 35, 103, 115
The Case of Rebellious Susan, 6, 15, 39, 110, 111, 113, 116, 117, 121
The Foundations of a National Drama, 104
The Liars, 12, 105, 110, 122, 128n1
The Masqueraders, 12, 15, 16, 93, 105–107, 110, 111, 140, 141, 143
Michael and his Lost Angel, 115, 133
Mrs. Dane's Defence, 110, 112, 116, 122–125, 127
The Renascence of the English Drama, 103, 104, 114, 115, 120
The Tempter, 115, 116
Joyce, James, 12

K
Kingston, Gertrude, 118, 119, 128–129n4, 167, 173, 195n6

M
Married Women's Property Act, 3, 4
Martineau, Harriet, 33
Marx, Eleanor, 14, 23, 36–38, 41
"A Doll's House Repaired," 36, 37
Matrimonial Causes Act, 3, 150
Melodrama, 8, 14–17, 22, 23, 26, 32, 33, 38, 40, 41, 48, 49, 54, 59, 68, 75, 84, 91–95, 99, 107, 115, 116, 148, 149, 174, 177, 178, 181, 182, 186, 187, 192, 193
Meredith, George, 3, 82, 90, 99
Modern Love, 9, 90
Metadrama, 7, 8
Metatheater/Metatheatre, 7, 22, 68
Mill, John Stuart, 3, 33, 176
Moffat, Graham, 191
The Maid and the Magistrate, 191
Moore, Mary, 117, 121, 125, 127, 129n5

N
Nevinson, Margaret Wynne, 189
In the Workhouse, 189
Novelty Theatre, 21, 30, 42n2, 164

P
Palmer, T. A., 61
Stage adaptation of *East Lynne*, 61
Pinero, Arthur Wing, 2, 4, 5, 10, 14–16, 39, 40, 51, 52, 81–100, 101n1, 101n2, 103–105, 112, 117, 128n4, 147, 156, 163, 164, 174, 175, 182, 191–193
The Benefit of the Doubt, 90, 91
The Gay Lord Quex, 99
His House in Order, 86
Mid-Channel, 86, 99
The Notorious Mrs. Ebbsmith, 39, 94, 101n1, 117, 182

Pinero, Arthur Wing (*cont.*)
  The Profligate, 98, 164
  The Second Mrs. Tanqueray, 15, 81–85, 87, 90, 91, 95, 99, 105, 117
Problem play, 15, 32, 82–84, 116

R
Robertson, Graham, 92, 94
Robertson, Tom, 2–4, 30
  Caste, 3
  Ours, 2
  School, 2
Robins, Elizabeth, 2, 4–6, 12, 14, 16–18, 21, 22, 24, 93, 110, 128n2, 161–194, 194n1, 194n2, 195n5, 195n7, 195n8, 195n13, 196n17
  Alan's Wife, 168, 170, 171, 193, 195n8
  Ancilla's Share, 164
  The Convert, 185–187, 195n7
  Ibsen and the Actress, 21, 22, 161, 162, 164–168
  Theatre and Friendship, 188
  Votes for Women!, 16, 17, 162, 173, 174, 176, 180, 181, 184–191, 193, 194, 195n7, 195n13, 196n17
  Way Stations, 162, 172, 173, 180, 187, 188

S
Scott, Clement, 167, 168
Sedgwick, Eve, 9, 22, 27, 62
Shaw, Bernard, 1, 2, 4–6, 10–14, 16, 18n2, 23, 28, 31, 32, 35, 36, 39–42, 50, 51, 57, 70, 82, 83, 91, 94, 101n1, 101n4, 104, 105, 107–110, 115, 118, 124, 128, 128n3, 128n4, 131–157, 157n1, 157n4, 157n6, 157n7, 158n10, 163, 166, 170, 174, 182, 193, 195n10, 195n12, 196n16
  "Acting, by One who does Not Believe in It," 11, 134
  Candida, 16, 43n6, 84, 131–135, 140, 141, 147, 148, 151, 152, 154, 156, 157, 157n6, 170, 193
  The Devil's Disciple, 16
  Getting Married, 16, 148, 150, 151, 153–156, 193
  Man and Superman, 16, 154
  The Philanderer, 40, 110
  The Quintessence of Ibsenism, 1, 5, 32, 51, 148
  "Still After the Doll's House," 39, 40, 131
  "The Theatre of the Future," 147, 194n1
  Mrs. Warren's Profession, 5, 12, 153
  You Never Can Tell, 70, 91
St. James's Theatre, 15, 18n2, 45, 49, 52, 55, 81, 92, 93, 105, 128
Suffrage drama, 161–194

T
Taylor, Tom
  Still Waters Run Deep, 3, 59, 139
  Victims, 3, 59, 139
Terry, Ellen, 4, 108, 147, 166
Terry's Theatre, 168, 170, 171
Thackeray, William Makepeace, 12
Theatricality, 7, 8, 10–12, 27, 40, 41, 46–48, 60, 62, 63, 75, 186, 187
Trollope, Anthony, 3

W

Walkley, Arthur Bingham, 3, 4, 6, 24, 51, 157n6
Wilde, Constance Lloyd, 45
Wilde, Oscar, 2, 4, 10, 12–16, 43n6, 45–76, 76n4, 76n5, 83–85, 89, 99, 104, 105, 110, 112, 128n1, 163, 174, 175, 177, 178, 192, 194n1
  "The Decay of Lying," 50, 51, 104
  De Profundis, 12, 47
  An Ideal Husband, 43n6, 46, 51, 57
  The Importance of Being Earnest, 45, 47, 110
  Lady Windermere's Fan, 15, 48, 49, 51–55, 64, 65, 74, 76n4, 81
  The Picture of Dorian Gray, 70
  Salomé, 46
  A Woman of No Importance, 15, 47, 48, 56, 64–66, 68, 70, 72–74
Wollstonecraft, Mary, 33
Women Writers' Suffrage League (WWSL), 172, 174
Wood, Ellen, 2, 42n3, 59
  East Lynne, 2, 3, 42n3, 59–61, 76n5
Wyndham, Charles, 6, 105, 110–112, 119–124, 126, 128, 128n2, 129n5

Z

Zangwill, Israel, 23, 36–38, 41
  "A Doll's House Repaired," 36, 37